OECD Public Governance Reviews

Towards a New Partnership with Citizens

JORDAN'S DECENTRALISATION REFORM

OECD
BETTER POLICIES FOR BETTER LIVES

Please cite this publication as:
OECD (2017), *Towards a New Partnership with Citizens: Jordan's Decentralisation Reform*, OECD Public Governance Reviews, OECD Publishing, Paris.
http://dx.doi.org/10.1787/9789264275461-en

ISBN 978-92-64-27545-4 (print)
ISBN 978-92-64-27546-1 (PDF)

Series: OECD Public Governance Reviews
ISSN 2219-0406 (print)
ISSN 2219-0414 (online)

Photo credits: Cover design by Mohamad Sabra; © Maksim Kabakou – Fotolia.com; © Peshkova/Shutterstock.com; © gagarych/Shutterstock.com; © SJ Travel Photo and Video/Shutterstock.com; © Sergey Nivens/Shutterstock.com.

Corrigenda to OECD publications may be found on line at: *www.oecd.org/about/publishing/corrigenda.htm*.

Foreword

As part of its efforts to promote better public governance and state modernisation, Jordan has embarked on an ambitious decentralisation reform agenda to address the social and economic challenges rooted in its highly centralised political and administrative system. Two laws approved in 2015, one focusing on governorates and one on municipalities, provide the key foundations of this process. Together, these laws create elected governorate and local councils that are designed to foster a bottom-up approach to national planning and socio-economic development.

The decentralisation reform is aligned with the objectives of the country's ten-year vision, "Jordan 2025", as well as the "Executive Development Programme 2016-18". It also coincides with the approval of Jordan's third National Action Plan (2016-18) for the Open Government Partnership (OGP), which is the country's most ambitious, comprehensive, and concrete attempt to date to promote the implementation of the principles of open government (i.e. transparency, accountability and citizen participation) in its public administration. Taken together, these initiatives provide an integrated policy framework for the country's long term commitment to continue to move forward with its efforts to improve good governance and to strengthen its democratic institutions at central and local levels.

This report focuses on how the principles and practices of open government are integrated in and supported by Jordan's decentralisation reforms (namely, the creation of elected bodies at the subnational level and the transfer of powers from central government to lower levels) and administrative deconcentration initiatives (where central government offices are relocated to the subnational level while leadership remains centralised). In fact, promoting the role of citizens, non-governmental stakeholders and civil society across all levels of government is at the heart of this process. For the first time, elections of the governorate and local councils – the major institutional change introduced by the new legal framework – will take place in August 2017. Accordingly, the reforms have raised public expectations that citizens' needs, particularly those of vulnerable groups, will be better represented, ultimately resulting in increasing levels of transparency and accountability.

However, the new policy and legal frameworks do not yet seem to provide for a major transfer of competencies and resources to subnational levels of government and do not yet fully define the vertical and horizontal relationships between them and with the central administration. This situation presents the government with the dual challenge of simultaneously managing the high expectations among citizens and civil society organisations (CSOs) regarding their new roles and relationships with different government levels, while continuing the process of clarifying what kind of decentralisation will be implemented in Jordan and of designing the related institutional, legal and policy requirements.

Building on OECD principles, as well as good practices from OECD member countries and countries from the MENA region, this report highlights the need for Jordan to develop a roadmap on how the reform policy objectives will be achieved in order to facilitate the centre of government's ability to support and monitor their implementation. The report also recommends that the government better specifies roles and responsibilities for the reform implementation across ministries and government levels and communicate them to public officials and citizens. Additionally, the report stresses the importance of building the capacity of local offices, including of the members of elected councils, to allow them to successfully fulfil their new roles, including – in particular – the new competences they will have in the areas of strategic planning and citizen engagement. Finally, the report points to the need to better foster a culture of open and participatory government across the different levels of the administration and in the population by disseminating the tenets of open government as well as providing adequate training, financial resources and, most importantly, concrete opportunities for stakeholder consultation and engagement.

This report was prepared in the framework of OECD's broader engagement to strengthen good governance, open and inclusive policy-making in Jordan. Notably, as a founding member of the MENA-OECD Governance Programme, Jordan has been working closely with the OECD to reform its public sector in line with OECD best practices. This includes OECD support for an inclusive formulation and implementation of the country's OGP Action Plan, the participation of women in parliament and policy-making, and of youth in public life.

Acknowledgements

The OECD Secretariat wishes to express its gratitude to all those who made this report possible, starting with the Jordanian government, which has been fully committed and has mobilised all relevant stakeholders, and Jordanian Civil Society Organisations for sharing their insights and enthusiasm. In particular, the OECD would like to thank H.E. Fakhoury Minister of National Development Planning and his team for their continuous support, among them, Zeina Tukan, Secretary General and Nasser Al Zubi from the International Cooperation Department as well as Hatem Habahbeh and Luna Obaidat. The Review team also wishes to thank the different participants in the interviews and seminars that took place during the fact-finding missions, in particular members of the Decentralisation Committee. They represent a wide variety of both governmental and non-governmental institutions, and the insights gathered during these events were helpful in improving the understanding of the local context and recommending courses of action that reflect the local context and priorities. The OECD is also grateful for their help in organising the missions of OECD staff and experts and facilitating data collection.

The OECD would also like to extend its gratitude to the following public officials who acted as peer reviewers: Jean-Louis Rocheron (Deputy Finance Director, Region Nouvelle-Aquitaine, France) and Enrique Orduña Prada (Director of the Office of Territorial Administration Claims, Council of Transparency and Good Governance, Spain.). Special thanks to Dr. Amer Bani Amer, General Director and Daniel Amareen, Senior Monitoring & Evaluation Officer at Al-Hayat Center for Civil Society Development for providing logistic and administrative support to the project as well as for the substantial contributions to the report. A number of international experts made substantive contributions; in particular Jonathan Morice (France) and Hamdi Qubeilat (Jordan).

This Strategic Assessment was prepared by the Public Governance Directorate of the OECD, headed by Rolf Alter. It is part of the series of the OECD Public Governance Reviews developed by the Governance Reviews and Partnerships Division, under the responsibility of Martin Forst. The Strategic Assessment of Jordan was elaborated under the strategic direction of Alessandro Bellantoni, senior policy analyst and co-ordinator of the Open Government Programme, who provided extensive comments on all chapters and harmonised the narrative. The process of drafting was co-ordinated by Paqui Santonja. The Report was written by Moritz Ader (Chapters 1 and 4) and Paqui Santonja (Chapters 2 and 3). The report received valuable comments from Miriam Allam, head of MENA Governance Programme. Editorial work and quality control were provided by Elizabeth Zachary and Ciara Muller, who prepared the manuscript for publication. Administrative support was provided by Michelle Ortiz.

The Strategic Assessment was funded by the G7 Deauville Partnership MENA Transition Fund project.

Table of contents

Acronyms and abbreviations 11

Executive summary 13

Assessment and recommendations 17

Chapter 1. Contextualising decentralisation reform and open government in Jordan 31

- Introduction 32
- A new momentum for democratic reform 32
- Achieving economic resilience and a more balanced development 33
- A young, diverse and dispersed population 36
- The political and administrative context: Jordan's government system 37
- Notes 46
- References 49

Chapter 2. The role of the centre of government in driving decentralisation reform in Jordan 53

- Decentralisation and governance in Jordan 54
- Centre of government in Jordan 75
- The role of Parliament 85
- Assessment and recommendations 86
- Notes 91
- References 93

Chapter 3. Enablers for an effective and efficient public service delivery at the local level in Jordan: Overview of good practice 97

- The framework for service delivery at the subnational level: The key role of Local Development Units 98
- The Fiscal Dimension 105
- Strategic planning 110
- Promoting inter-institutional dialogue 116
- Building local capacities and human resource management at the subnational level 126
- Assessment and recommendations 132
- Reinforcing institutional arrangements to deliver effective decentralised governance 133
- Notes 136
- References 137

Chapter 4. Openness and participation in Jordan: The expected impact of decentralisation reform 141

- Improve the state of play for open government in Jordan 144

Leverage decentralisation reform to foster open government and genuine citizen participation at the local level 163
Assessment and recommendations 175
Notes 181
References 183

Annex A. The French experience of decentralisation 189

Annex B. The Spanish decentralisation model 216

Figures

Figure 1.1. Poverty rates by governorate (2014 and 2025 target) 34
Figure 1.2. Economic activity among young men and women aged 15-24 (2014) 36
Figure 1.3. Organisational structure of public entities in Jordan 40
Figure 1.4. Key pillars of Jordan 2025 45
Figure 2.1. Jordan population density per governorate 55
Figure 2.2. New governorate structure 69
Figure 2.3. Organisational chart of the municipality and local councils under the 2015 ML 73
Figure 2.4. Institutional arrangements at the governorate and municipal level 75
Figure 2.5. Centre of government's main responsibilities 77
Figure 2.6. Core priorities for Government in Vision 2025 79
Figure 2.7. Centre of government for decentralisation reform in Jordan 83
Figure 3.1. Local Development Units at the governorate level 101
Figure 3.2. Proposed structure of the local development unit in the governorates 101
Figure 3.3. Institutional set-up of MLDUs - The example of Ajloun 103
Figure 3.4. Institutional arrangements in the new decentralisation framework 104
Figure 3.5. Subnational government expenditure as a percentage of GDP and total public expenditure in OECD countries, 2014 105
Figure 3.6. Institutional mechanism of consultation: Governorate development plans 111
Figure 3.7. Employment in government (general government) by level of government (2005) 127
Figure 3.8. The distribution of civil service employees by governorates, 2014 130
Figure 4.1. Gender gap in local councils in Jordan (2014) 167

Tables

Table 2.1. Challenges at the governorate level: GINI, unemployment and poverty in 2014 56
Table 2.2. Number of subnational governments in the OECD in 2015, with figures on Jordan 57
Table 2.3. Institutional organisation in the OECD, and number of subnational layers 58
Table 2.4. Regionalisation trends in OECD countries 66
Table 2.5. Decentralisation priorities in Jordan 2025 80
Table 2.6. Key performance indicators on Decentralisation reform in Jordan 2025 81
Table 3.1. Expenditure of Jordanian local governments 106
Table 3.2. Central government transfers to municipalities in 2010 (in millions JD) 106
Table 3.3. Loans granted to municipalities by CVDB (by governorates) in 2010 107

Table 3.4. Budget allocation of governorates ... 109
Table 3.5. Employment systems in OECD countries ... 128
Table 3.6. Number of civil servants distributed by governorate ... 129
Table 4.1. Tools and mechanisms used to implement the open government agenda in Jordan, selected Middle East and North Africa (MENA) countries and the OECD ... 147
Table 4.2. OECD countries: Breadth of central government freedom of information laws (2010) ... 152
Table B.1. List of municipalities with large populations ... 231

Boxes

Box 2.1. Subnational government structure in OECD countries ... 57
Box 2.2. Territorial organisations in selected MENA Countries/Territories ... 59
Box 2.3. Theoretic approach to decentralisation ... 60
Box 2.4. Decentralisation trends in MENA countries: Morocco and Tunisia ... 64
Box 2.5. Role of the “Préfet” in France ... 67
Box 2.6. “Putting people first - Action programme for effective and local government”: Irish reform of local government ... 71
Box 2.7. Remaining barriers to women’s participation in representative bodies in Jordan ... 73
Box 2.8. CoG: Observations and trends in 2014, vision, leadership and innovation ... 78
Box 2.9. The strategic role of the CoG in the implementation process: The case of Spain ... 84
Box 2.10. Allocation of responsibilities to the lower tiers of government: France, Germany and Poland ... 87
Box 3.1. Strategies for local service delivery in the United Kingdom ... 99
Box 3.2. The Spanish Technical Assistance Service for municipalities ... 104
Box 3.3. Strategic planning at regional and local levels ... 112
Box 3.4. Turkey's new national regional development agency model ... 114
Box 3.5. TANMIA strategic toolkit ... 116
Box 3.6. The seven gaps in multi-level governance ... 117
Box 3.7. Main mechanisms for vertical and horizontal co-ordination in OECD countries ... 120
Box 3.8. OECD Recommendation on Co-ordinating Public Investments across Levels of Government ... 122
Box 3.9. Integrating lower levels of government in consultation procedures: The cases of Spain, Sweden and Switzerland ... 123
Box 3.10. Inter-municipal co-operation: France and the intercommunalité ... 124
Box 3.11. Jordan Valley Authority ... 126
Box 3.12. Maison de l'élu - Morocco ... 130
Box 3.13. Local government officials with a national qualification: Spain ... 131
Box 3.14. Civil service recruitment at subnational levels of government in France ... 131
Box 4.1. Potential benefits of open government ... 143
Box 4.2. Jordan’s third National Action Plan for the Open Government Partnership ... 146
Box 4.3. Open government at the local level in Colombia’s second OGP Action Plan ... 147
Box 4.4. How to institutionalise non-governmental organisation (NGO) participation in the open government agenda: The example of Tunisia ... 148

Box 4.5. Selection of open government achievements prior to Jordan's OGP membership (2012) ... 149
Box 4.6. Guidance on consultation: The case of the United Kingdom ... 159
Box 4.7. Creating a forum for open dialogue at the local level: The example of "Diwanieh" ... 162
Box 4.8. Youth in the open government agenda in Tunisia ... 162
Box 4.9. Factors shaping turnout in local elections: The example of New Zealand ... 166
Box 4.10. Latin America's local citizen councils ... 169
Box 4.11. Opening municipalities in the province of Biscay in Spain ... 170
Box 4.12. Engaging citizens at the local level in the national planning and development process ... 171
Box 4.13. Participatory planning as a performance catalyst in the north of Morocco ... 171
Box 4.14. Participatory budgeting at the local level: Experiences from Sfax (Tunisia) and Paris (France) ... 173

Acronyms and abbreviations

GoJ	Government of Jordan
MoMA	Ministry of Municipal Affairs
MoPIC	Ministry of Planning and International Cooperation
MoF	Ministry of Finance
MoH	Ministry of Health
MoI	Ministry of Interior
MoPPA	Ministry of Political and Parliamentary Affairs
MoPSD	Ministry of Public Sector Development
LCDCs	Local Community Development Committees (Ireland)
LDUs	Local Development Units
GLDUs	Governorate Local Development Units
MLDUs	Municipal Local Development Units
ML	2015 Municipalities Law
DL	2015 Decentralisation Law
JSC	Joint Service Council
HRM	Human Resources Management
CSO(s)	Civil society organisation(s)
CoG	Centre of Government
OGP	Open Government Partnership
GDP	Gross Domestic Product
JOB	Jordanian Ombudsman Bureau
JACC	Jordan Integrity and Anti-Corruption Commission
GAM	Greater Amman Municipality
AECID	Agencia Española de Cooperación Internacional para el Desarrollo (Spanish Agency for International Development Cooperation)
ASEZA	Aqaba Special Economic Zone Authority
ATI	Access to Information
CoG	Centre of Government
CORA	Commission for the Reform of the Public Administration (Spain)
CVDB	Cities and Villages Development Bank
CSB	Civil Service Bureau
DCLG	Department for Communities and Local Government (United Kingdom)
EDP	Executive Development Programme

FedDev	Ontario Federal Economic Development Agency for Southern Ontario (Canada)
FOI	Freedom of Information
GIS	Geographic Information Systems
GNI	Gross National Income
GONGOs	Government Non-Governmental Organisations
GDD	Governorates Development Programmes
HRM	Human Resource Management
ICTs / IT	Information and Communication Technologies / Information Technology
IRM	Independent Reporting Mechanism
JHCP	Jordan Health Communication Partnership
JIPA	Institute of Public Administration
KPIs	Key Performance Indicators
LOB	Legislative and Opinion Bureau
MENA	Middle East and North Africa
MWI	Ministry of Water and Irrigation
NGOs	Non-Governmental Organisations
OPSI	OECD Observatory of Public Sector Innovation
RDA	Regional Development Agency
RGPP	General Revue of Public Policies (France)
RONGOs	Royal Non-Governmental Organisations
SALAR	Swedish Association of Local Authorities and Regions
SMEs	Small and medium-sized enterprises
SNGs	Subnational governments?
SNTV	Single Non-Transferable Vote
UN	United Nations
UNDP	United Nations Development Programme
UNESCO	United Nations Educational, Scientific and Cultural Organization
UNHCR	United Nations High Commissioner for Refugees
UNICEF	United Nations International Children's Fund
USAID	United States Agency for International Development
WINN	Western Innovation Initiative (Canada)

Executive summary

The 2015 Decentralisation Law (DL) and Municipality Law (ML) mark a milestone in Jordan's democratic development and ongoing effort to improve public governance. In line with the objectives of "Jordan 2025", the country's strategic vision, the laws represent an unprecedented effort to place citizens and their needs at the heart of policymaking and service delivery.

Jordan is a unitary state with a high degree of political, administrative and financial centralisation. In such a centralised system, planning can become detached from citizens' needs. Jordanian authorities are therefore seeking to overcome this centralisation while at the same time addressing rising levels of dissatisfaction with government performance. The 2015 DL and ML form key elements of this reform effort, which has since been complemented by the creation of Jordan's third National Action Plan for the Open Government Partnership (OGP) in early 2017. Notably, this reform process is being rolled out amid complex economic and security challenges – aggravated by the conflicts in Syria and Iraq and the refugee crisis – that have put increasing pressures on economic resources and public services.

The creation of elected governorate and local councils has induced high expectations that public service delivery will be more responsive to the needs of local communities. Importantly, however, the new legal framework does not include a major transfer of powers to subnational levels of government. In fact, it sustains a largely concentrated system of day-to-day service delivery while providing for a more active (yet still undefined) role for local non-governmental stakeholders in the development process.

There is thus a need to manage the expectations among civil society organisations (CSOs) and citizens regarding their role, as well as to provide additional information on the tools and mechanisms available to them and to the newly elected public officials in the governorate and local councils.

A clear roadmap for implementing the new legal framework

The focus of the 2015 DL and ML leaves important issues, such as mandates, competencies and procedures, to be developed through the drafting of subsequent by-laws. For instance, the relationships between the elected councils themselves and between the elected councils and other government levels are not yet fully defined. In some cases, lines of accountability are blurred.

An implementation roadmap setting out short-, medium- and long-term objectives would ensure more coherent implementation of both laws and relevant by-laws for key actors, such as the members of the inter-ministerial committee that steers the decentralisation reform. In particular, a more integrated approach could align the activities of the Ministry of Interior, Ministry of Municipal Affairs and the Ministry of Planning and International Co-operation. Although the reform does not push for greater financial decentralisation, the role of the Ministry of Finance in rolling out the reform could be strengthened to ensure that subnational expenditure information is included in development planning, as well as to strengthen fiscal and budgeting capacity at all levels.

Clear responsibilities need to be assigned to each entity across all levels of government for both day-to-day service delivery and in the national development process. The roadmap could outline the tools and systems needed (e.g. data management) to facilitate communication and co-ordination. Through training and dissemination campaigns, roles and procedures should be communicated among public officials, CSOs and citizens to ensure a common understanding of the reform's implications. In an effort to strengthen transparency, the government could submit an annual progress report on the reform's implementation to Parliament.

A bottom-up approach to identifying service needs and policy priorities

Shifting from a highly centralised to a more locally-driven process of identifying needs and policy priorities is challenging. The report therefore identifies four factors that could support the effective operation of the new system and increase public support for the reform process.

First, local development units at the governorate and municipal level should be supported in their efforts to promote local needs by increasing their human and financial capacities, identifying common operational procedures and reinforcing the interaction with each other and with other subnational entities. Second, governorates could establish specific offices to improve strategic planning and ensure that the inputs from the municipalities are integrated in the governorate and national development plans. Third, capacity building and training should be provided for the members of elected councils to ensure they have the skills to fulfil their new responsibilities, as well as the ability to work with CSOs and citizens. Finally, the creation of co-ordination bodies, such as a council of governorates and associations of municipalities, could facilitate the exchange of information and experience and, over time, institutionalise collaboration across and within levels of government.

Fostering a culture of open, participatory, transparent and accountable governance across all levels of government

Jordan's open government agenda, within and beyond its OGP Action Plan, would benefit from more input from subnational stakeholders (both public officials and representatives of CSOs). A thorough review of legislative, institutional and procedural obstacles is needed, as well as efforts to promote better production and access to public sector information and data, the definition of guidelines for public officials on strengthening citizen participation, and the development of new mechanisms to foster a culture of monitoring and evaluation of participatory initiatives.

Creating momentum for reform among public officials, CSOs, and citizens

The creation of elected subnational councils is an important step toward strengthening local democracy. Nonetheless, the predominance of the central level in addressing the day-to-day demands of citizens and in providing funding for subnational levels may slow the rise of a more decentralised governance culture.

The mandates of the elected councils and sub-bodies tasked with representing citizens' interests should be clarified and adequate resources provided. Initiatives to support vulnerable members of society, such as women and youth, could encourage their participation as candidates and voters in local elections. Initiatives that promote inclusion and diversity, such as e-participation tools and citizen advisory councils, should also be developed to facilitate citizen participation. Furthermore, direct engagement activities, such as petitions and participatory budgeting schemes, can complement representative and deliberative approaches.

Assessment and recommendations

Located at the intersection of three continents and within the Middle East region between the Gulf and the Levant, the Hashemite Kingdom of Jordan is highly exposed to the political, economic and security turmoil which has shaken the region over the past decades. Recently, the influx of the second largest number of refugees per capita from the war-torn areas in Syria and Iraq has added unprecedented pressures on fiscal capacities, economic opportunities and the government's capacities to deliver quality public services.

Despite these difficult conditions, Jordan has embarked on an ambitious reform process to address the shortcomings of a highly centralised political, administrative and financial system in favour of a new paradigm that political development "should start at the grassroots level, then move up to decision-making centres, and not vice-versa" (King Abdullah II, 2005).

By passing the Decentralisation Law and Municipality Law in late 2015, Jordan has initiated a process to strengthen local governance with a view to redefining the role of CSOs, citizens and other non-governmental stakeholders at subnational level (e.g. governorates, municipalities, districts) in the national development process. Most notably, the creation of elected councils at the governorate and local level which introduces new layers of government has raised high expectations among government officials and CSOs to result in a more active stance of local communities in identifying local development needs and priorities. These efforts resonate with the objectives of Jordan's broader democratization reform and its membership in the Open Government Partnership (OGP). In early 2017, Jordan approved its third National Action Plan for the OGP after joining the Partnership as the first Arab country in 2011.

However, as the new legal framework does not suggest a major transfer of political, administrative nor fiscal competencies to lower tiers of government, the assessment also emphasises the need for a national dialogue on the future architecture of the state. A clarification of mandates and accountability mechanisms for all actors in the new and complex multi-level governance framework will be critical to foster new partnerships with citizens, allocate development benefits more equally across the Kingdom and improving overall government performance.

At the request of the Government of Jordan, this Strategic Assessment provides an analysis of the ongoing decentralisation reform covering the following three key public governance themes which were, in close collaboration with the Government of Jordan, identified as priorities in the context of the Transition Fund project "*Supporting Jordan's ongoing decentralization efforts by promoting good governance and open government policies and practices with a focus on municipalities*":

- Enhancing the role of the Centre of Government in driving decentralisation reform in Jordan.
- Enabling effective public service delivery at the local level.

- Openness and participation in Jordan: The expected impact of decentralisation reform.

The assessment and recommendations provide an overview of the main findings and recommendations based on OECD principles and standards as well as good practices and lessons learned from both OECD member and non-member countries. It aims at supporting the efforts of the Government of Jordan in tackling key barriers to the ongoing reform process and towards a successful implementation of the decentralisation and open government agenda.

The role of the centre of government in driving decentralisation reform in Jordan

The Decentralisation Law and Municipality Law adopted in 2015 reflect the commitment of the Government of Jordan to move towards a culture of popular participation at the subnational layers of government and local democracy. However, for King Abdullah II's vision of a political development process that starts at the grassroots level, and moves up to higher decision-making centres to fully materialise, a number of key challenges needs to be addressed.

Importantly, the Government of Jordan has a strong political commitment to pursuing decentralisation reform that allows central/local dynamics to evolve, and that takes into consideration the potential instability of the political framework. Jordan is at the first stage of a long path towards decentralisation. The official discourse on decentralisation needs to take into consideration the political, financial and administrative components that such a reform requires. The introduction of the democratic component by including elections at the governorate and local level is an important step that will also bring responsibilities and duties to the Jordanian public administration. The establishment and consolidation of local democratic administrations will also require a profound change in the administrative, working and regulatory culture between government and constituencies.

Sustaining high-level political support is key to ensuring the success of the reform. Nevertheless, the donor attention paid to supporting the decentralisation reform speaks to the political commitment to carry it out. The fact that the leading body is in the Centre of Government also illustrates political support from the top level, and grants authority to request the participation of line ministries and agencies.

Given the importance of making the decentralisation reform happen, and to ensure a long-lasting reform, the government could consider the following recommendations:

The need of clarifying roles, competences and the relevance of the implementation process of the decentralisation reform:

- **Clarify roles and responsibilities at the national, governorate and local level.** This could include a clearer identification of services to be provided by each level of government, the line ministries' role, and the opinion of governorates and local governments that share competencies. This would be complemented by a comprehensive list of competency distributions across the different levels. Organisational charts would be published on line in the websites of each administration.

- **Publish guides and materials on the Decentralisation and Municipalities Laws,** their implications and effects at the national, governorate and local level with a focus on the forthcoming elections at the governorate and local level. These guides will be an important working tool for public servants and employees at the national, governorate and local level, and will ensure a common understanding of the implications and expected outcomes of the reform.
- **Promote a general and comprehensive debate on the new role of governorates, and in particular of the governor, Governorate Council and the Executive Council, especially before the 2017 elections.** Clarify the relationship between governors and the Executive Council (and line ministries in Amman), as well their co-ordination role with municipalities.
- Once the new elected bodies take up their duties, **council members will need support to understand the dynamics of each administration and how to contribute to them**. Government of Jordan will need to concentrate on reinforcing the capacities of the members of the newly elected bodies to ensure that the citizens' expectations on their role and functions will be appropriately met.
- **A follow-up committee should be created to bring updated and evidence-based information to the Cabinet on a regular basis**. Such a committee will also help promote a more integrated approach between the MoI and MoMA to ensure that a "subnational dimension" is fully integrated on the implementation strategy and the road map.

A stronger and more co-ordinated centre of government (CoG)

- **Consolidate and reinforce the role of Jordan's centre of government on implementing the decentralisation reform,** that the Cabinet Office, MoI and MoMA, MoPIC and MoPPA will play a key role.
- **Strengthen and reinforce co-operation and co-ordination among the CoG institutions implicated in the decentralisation reform as well as with the rest of the public administration**. Crucially, this could contribute to overcoming the existing silo-based approach to service delivery at the local level (as outlined in Chapter 3), while ensuring that policy and spending are better linked and potential overlap and duplication reduced. The GoJ must also ensure effective communication and co-ordination between CoG institutions and collectively with line ministries and citizens by developing a clear communication strategy towards citizens to explain the decentralisation reform through seminars and a dissemination campaign across the country. Some initiatives such as the national dialogue launched by the Ministry of Political and Parliamentary Affairs together with the Jordan NGOs coalition is an initiative that could be replicated even prior to the elections.
- In so doing, **the Decentralisation Committee needs to follow an implementation road map agreed and approved by the Council of Ministers that includes a set of short, medium and long-term objectives**, as well as expected outputs and outcomes. These outputs and outcomes should include performance indicators and could be published and disseminated regularly.

- **Develop a centralised monitoring mechanism** to evaluate and make adjustments during and after the implementation of the decentralisation programme.
- **Strengthen capacity to implement decentralisation reform in the structures within the CoG by reinforcing the human and financial resources of the MoI, MoMA and MoSPD** so that they can work closely with governorates and municipalities on designing and implementing decentralisation strategic policy and assessing and monitoring progress, and feed this information into governorate programmes.
- **Reinforce the working relationships between the MoI and MoMA so that all are working to achieve the same strategic decentralisation objectives and to mainstream decentralisation within Jordan 2025**. These ministries could work with MoPIC, which is responsible for integrating all strands of national development strategy, including decentralisation and regional development, inclusive growth, and public administration reform at the subnational levels into the Biannual Development Programme (currently 2016-2018).
- **Parliament should play a greater role in the follow-up of the implementation of the reform**. The Government of Jordan (through the Ministry of Political and Parliamentary Affairs) could consider submitting annual decentralisation reports to the Parliament by developing performance indicators on decentralisation and their impact against the objectives of the reform.

Enablers for an effective and efficient public service delivery at the local level in Jordan

Jordan has developed an ambitious discourse on decentralisation that does not seem to be fully aligned with the current arrangements on the ground. Several challenges inhibit Jordan's ability to ensure policymaking and service delivery at the local level from a bottom-up perspective, including: a mismatch between municipal and governorates' fiscal capacities and allocation of competences; fragmentation and low levels of co-ordination and co-operation both vertically among levels of government and horizontally within the two subnational levels.

For the decentralisation reform to be effective and for subnational governments to be able to deliver public services, Jordan needs to strengthen existing structures and institutional co-ordination mechanisms to ensure effective and efficient administrative management. In this sense, the decentralisation reform is at a delicate stage. On the one hand, newly elected bodies maybe with no previous experience on local politics will start working while, on the other hand, the administrative machinery to support decentralisation needs to be reinforced to comply with the new competences and achieve the established objectives. Decentralisation reform is much more than an objective in itself as it is a mean to get services and policies more adapted to citizens' and businesses 'needs and should be gradually implemented and adapted to the country's reality.[*]

Successful implementation of the reform also requires clear leadership, a roadmap and a regular follow-up and monitoring performance of the expected outcomes from the central level. In so doing, Jordan needs to reinforce a multi-sectoral and multi-stakeholder dialogue approach where the central government not only the leading ministries MoI and

[*] http://unpan1.un.org/intradoc/groups/public/documents/un/unpan006230.pdf.

MoMA but also line ministries on the ground- co-ordinate with the governorate and the municipal levels so that a constructive dialogue can take place between key stakeholders

In this context, the local development units at the governorate and municipal levels can become key actors. Nevertheless, all of the actors involved in decentralisation, including communities, local governments, the central governments and international donors, should make an effort to learn from experiences to date. The Jordanian central government needs to be aware of the importance of seizing the "momentum" that is conducive to good governance and that supports lower levels of government and civil society as they move forward with the reform. At the same time, governorates and municipalities need to realise that they can take important actions autonomously to improve local governance. While subnational level of government do not have to stand by until the centre moves forward, they nevertheless need to ensure they work with an accurately represent, communities. Donors also need to be aware that decentralisation is a long-term process and requires a great deal of national consensus building. All actors should recognise that they must work together in creative and mutually supportive ways to make local governments more effective.

To address these issues, the Government of Jordan could consider the following recommendations:

Reinforcing institutional arrangements to deliver effective decentralised governance

The framework for service delivery: Local Development Units

- **Local Development Units, in municipalities and governorates, should be enhanced by more clearly delineating their roles and activities**. In addition to their development and data collection role, they have the potential to play a horizontal co-ordination function as the interface between the technical administration and the elected institutions both in Governorates and Municipalities. This would go hand in hand with a direct line of co-operation between LDUs in municipalities and governorates.

- **Promote a closer relationship between MoI and MoMA on decentralisation matters**. Better communication from the top could then easier be reflected across levels of government. A first step could be to establish common administrative procedures and a common system for data collection for LDUs at the governorate and municipal levels (such a focus could include shared IT tools, etc.).

- **Consider reinforcing capacity in the administrative unit(s) supporting the governor** to enable functions to be carried out effectively in governorates, and reinforce interface capacity within governorates to engage effectively with local and central administrations.

- **Ensure that governorates and municipalities can contribute substantially to national strategy setting and implementation through effective multi-level governance.**

- **Implement an outcomes-based performance monitoring system for decentralisation and subnational management and administration**. This system should be aligned with an integrated centre of government (CoG) monitoring and evaluation system. Budgetary programmes should be aligned at the three levels of government.

An ambitious reform with scarce new resources at the governorate and municipal level

- **Adapt and strengthen the financial arrangement of governorates according to their new competencies**. It will be essential to build up expertise to deal with budgeting and financial responsibilities, taking into consideration the governorate's situation regarding: population, area, poverty, geographical situation, and other vital indicators. Hiring professional staff and capacity building should also be considered.
- **Governorates could promote and give support to the creation of Joint Council Services** for once needs are identified.
- **Strengthen the working relationship on decentralisation with the MoF to ensure that performance budgeting is implemented at the subnational level**, and that subnational expenditure performance information is fed back into biannual development programme planning.
- Over time, **consider creating a specific unit within the governorate that is dedicated to strategic planning.** This unit could count on MoPIC's expertise (and could even include public officials from MoPIC) with operational responsibility to work with governorate and local governments to implement decentralisation in each governorate. This could include managing intergovernmental arrangements (such as contracts, see below) to deliver co-ordinated fiscal resources to subnational governments, and helping to monitor expenditure performance against the achievement of results for regional development, regional disparity reduction and improved outcomes for people in each governorate. The cases of Morocco or Turkey with regional development agencies could serve as inspiration for Jordan.
- **Mandate the MoF and MoMA to strengthen municipal government fiscal capacity and administrative capacity for fiscal management and collecting local taxes.** Local governments could also raise citizens' awareness for paying taxes on time so as to deliver better basic public services.
- **Improve municipal budgeting and accounting processes.**
- **Promote accountability through improved management of municipal financial information.**

Strategic planning

- **Strengthen the partnership between the municipal and district councils, the private sector and international donors in order to enhance the role of municipal and district councils in approving and implementing development projects in local communities.** Municipal and district councils should have a key role in the partnership by providing the appropriate environment to stimulate investment, especially regarding the simplification of procedures and the provision of appropriate infrastructure.
- **MoPIC could play a greater role in providing support to Governorates and in particular to the GLDUs in the Executive Development Programme 2016-2018** and implementation of governorate strategic plan. Specific training and capacity-building could also be addressed.

- Once the strategic unit within the GLDUs created, **MoPIC could second qualified staff at the governorate level that would support the strategic unit within the GLDUs.**

Promoting Inter-institutional dialogue

- **Institutionalise mechanisms for the inter-governmental co-ordination** of the decentralisation process by implementing a more flexible and adapted structure and ensuring that it is fully supported by centre of government structures and line ministries. This could include:
  - Effective **interministerial co-ordination**. National ministers responsible for key policies will need to work together more effectively. There is a large variation in economic conditions and governance capability across the country, and a need to better integrate national policies at the regional level. Vertical co-ordination occurs within a complex governance system. The national government therefore needs to co-ordinate more effectively and in a way that accounts for the diversity and differences in capability across the governorates.
  - Establish **a co-ordination council between governorates** to share experiences, information and tackle challenges. This would also allow governorates to share experiences on decentralisation implementation and strategic planning, together with the designing and implementing of a basic single framework for subnational management that is linked to performance-based management. This co-ordination council could be composed of the CoG at the central level and representatives of each governorate (political, governor and a technical manager).
- **Ensure that the leading role given to governorates in strategic planning through a bottom-up approach effectively integrates the lowest levels of the administration,** as well as civil society and the private sector.
- **Municipalities, and in particular mayors, could also gather in a national association** to promote the role of municipalities in strengthening decentralisation reform and local development.

Capacity building and human resource management at the subnational level

- **Identify the specific needs of civil servants at the governorate and local level in the context of the decentralisation reform**, and provide capacity building and training at the subnational level to ensure a well-prepared, competent and efficient civil service.
- **Develop and extend the national Law on Civil Service Reform** and the tasks attributed to the Civil Service Bureau to the governorate and municipal levels.
- **All levels of government should be encouraged to define and plan for the types of workers they will need in order to carry out new responsibilities.** Training should contribute to the formation of new working relationships. In addition to building local capacity, training can be a tool for creating personal networks among various levels of government, regions, or types of government workers. One recommendation, for example, might be to train career civil

servants and local politicians together to insure that they better understand what is expected of them and what they can expect from each other.

- **Create a network of community agents to provide local government with capacity building especially to the LDUs.** A national federation/association of municipalities (once created) may also be involved to connect local experiences and identify good policy practices across municipalities. Councils should involve citizens and non-governmental organisations in the identification of key local assets and economic drivers, which should be taken into account in local development strategies.
- **Greater flexibility in managing the workforce at the local level is required.** Subnational governments need to develop competency-management systems so that they can ensure they have a well-selected, trained and evaluated public workforce.
- This regime should be co-ordinated by key ministries such the Civil Service Bureau (together with the Ministry of the Public Sector), MoI and MoMA.

Openness and participation in Jordan: The expected impact of decentralisation reform

The validation of the 2015 Decentralisation Law and Municipality Law is a significant step towards reinforcing local governance, and holds the potential of moving forward the open government agenda at the level of governorates, municipalities and districts. With the approval of bylaws regulating the election and function of the governorate councils, work on training programmes for local public officials, and awareness raising activities at the governorate level, the Government of Jordan has initiated a series of urgent measures to translate the new legal framework into practice ahead of the local elections in August 2017.

This chapter discusses the links between the current decentralisation reform process, the open government agenda and the broader democratisation agenda in Jordan. It illustrates the mutual reinforcement mechanisms that exist between the three agendas, which culminate in the King's vision that "political development should start at the grassroots level, then move up to decision-making centres". The current reform holds great potential to encourage the emergence of a "culture of governance based on innovative and sustainable policies and practices inspired by the principles of transparency, accountability, and participation that fosters democracy and inclusive growth" at the local level. With the creation of elected councils at the governorate and local level, there is a momentum for a coalition of local public officials and civil society actors to foster representative, deliberative and direct forms of citizen participation. The involvement of local CSOs, citizens and other non-governmental stakeholders in identifying service needs and policy priorities, and the monitoring of government performance, can increase transparency and accountability mechanisms, which have, so far, suffered from severe shortcomings.

However, it must also be noted that many of the detailed procedures and chains of responsibility are still to be defined. Despite a generally positive attitude towards the objectives of the reform process among CSOs and most government officials, some scepticism prevails as to whether the government is indeed serious in allowing for a bottom-up process to planning and development and new forms of citizen participation.

For instance, criticism focuses on the limited attention that has been devoted to increasing popular awareness and grassroots support during the reform process. For some CSOs, the government's orchestrated approach is perceived as a tool to stimulate "defensive democratisation" (i.e. concessionary democratic reforms to pre-empt more fundamental challenges to the status quo), which is unlikely to vitalise greater citizen participation, transparency and accountability (Identity Center, n.d.).

This chapter points to two critical determinants for the success of the reform. First, it stresses the need to improve the overall context for open and participatory government across the different layers of government (e.g. access to information framework, a review of decisions affecting the freedom of the media and expression, and the operational freedom of civil society). It reflects that a vibrant civil society is critical for increasing popular awareness and grassroots support for the reform, and, as soon as the local councils begin their work, holding representatives to account. Second, the Chapter highlights the need to establish effective tools and mechanisms to strengthen representative, deliberative and direct forms of citizen engagement at subnational level.

In his recent visit to the Ministry of Interior, the Prime Minister stressed the urgency of raising awareness for the law and the future function of the governorate council. The Prime Minister suggested the prospect of organising debates in the governorates regarding the preparation of the state budget to experiment with the interaction between the councils and central government (Watnjo, 2016). Led by the Ministry of Political and Parliamentary Affairs, a national dialogue to raise awareness for the decentralisation reform was initiated in December 2016, featuring meetings with local authorities and community members in each governorate. The sustainability of these initiatives will be critical for ensuring that the current reform process will be understood as a unique opportunity for citizens to shape development in their region. According to the Ministry of the Interior, the Inter-Ministerial Committee in charge of the reform is currently preparing capacity building programmes for different target groups (e.g. youth, CSOs, private sector).

In pursuing the objective of improving the state-of-play for open government in Jordan, and to lever the decentralisation reform to increase popular participation, transparency and accountability at the subnational level, the Government of Jordan could consider the following recommendations:

Turning commitments into results: The process towards a culture of open and inclusive governance

Jordan's membership of the Open Government Partnership

- **Consider formulating a single national open government strategy** to overcome fragmented initiatives and foster a whole-of-government approach across the different levels of government. The strategy should build on a national vision for how open government can contribute to broader policy objectives, such as those identified in Jordan 2025. The evidence for such a strategy should be gathered through a collective process starting at the community level (e.g. local elected councils), before being consolidated in the municipalities and governorates and ultimately at central level. Parliament, civil society, the private sector, independent state institutions, media and academics should be involved in a clear and transparent procedure.

- **Upgrade the role of the parliament and the subnational level in the national open government agenda** by organising large-scale training programmes for parliamentarians and local authorities, in particular for the elected representatives in local, municipality and governorate councils and relevant directorates in the LDUs. Local authorities could become involved in the National Commission, which is tasked with elaborating the country's National Action Plan for the OGP.
- **Foster a culture of monitoring and evaluation to increase transparency and accountability**. The creation of an independent reporting mechanism as part of the membership of the OGP to assess the progress in delivering on open government commitments should be encouraged to increase public scrutiny.

Access to information

- **Consider revising laws and regulations that may impede the public's access to information** (Protection of the State's Secrets and Documents Law No. 50, 1971) in line with the objective of the 3rd National Action Plan for the OGP to "strengthen the legislative framework governing access to information."
- **Consider amending the Law of Access to Information to extend its scope to the subnational level**. Access to reliable government data and information is a precondition for local media, CSOs and independent state institutions to exercise effective scrutiny over the performance of state institutions at the subnational level in delivering public services and spending decisions.
- **Define clear criteria as to what information is considered "classified", "secret" or "protected by other legislation"** to provide guidance for public officials and increase legal certainty for citizens and businesses. Periodic reviews by an independent agency, which could be discussed by Parliament, could provide information on the use of the right in practice, indicate potential violations and support the creation of a community of practice.
- **Organise an awareness campaign targeting public officials, Parliament, the media, civil society and citizens** with a view to explaining the critical importance that access to reliable information plays in achieving broader policy objectives (e.g. increasing the access to and quality of public services).

Freedom of the media and freedom of expression

- **Conduct a review of recent regulations and decisions affecting the freedom of media and freedom of expression** in line with the commitment stressed in the Third National Action Plan for the OGP to "strengthen the framework governing the freedom of the media". Independent investigations and reporting by journalists present important pillars for long-term stability and democratic development in Jordan. The criteria for imposing media bans or restrictions on news content should be clarified and disseminated widely to increase transparency and legal certainty for journalists, CSOs and citizens.
- **Foster the emergence of independent local media outlets** (e.g. radio programmes, newspapers, online) to stimulate a culture of debate and dialogue at the community level and to increase the diversity of available information channels. Diverse sources of traditional and new media can play a significant role

in promoting active citizenship and increasing the level of transparency among existing and future power holders in the governorates and municipalities.

- **Foster a genuine culture of monitoring and evaluation among all levels of government, as well as governmental and non-governmental bodies**, to ensure that scarce resources are allocated for their intended purpose. In this respect, the role of the legislative and main oversight agencies should be redefined and upgraded with a view to addressing overlapping responsibilities (e.g. co-ordinate work plans, avoid parallel investigations and duplications, and encourage a culture of sharing information among the Anti-Corruption Commission, the National Audit Bureau and the Ombudsman Office) and the lack of capacity.
- **Increase transparency in the allocation of grants by members of parliament at the subnational level**. For instance, a dedicated database could be created following the example of France (http://data.senat.fr/dotation-daction-parlementaire/) to be able to trace back the grants suggested by members of parliament for parliamentary action, beneficiaries and the resources allocated.
- **Strengthen decentralised control mechanisms by seeking partnerships with independent local media and CSOs and** educating citizens against the hazards of corruption.

Budget transparency

- **Establish a formal mechanism through which CSOs and citizens can participate in the budget process**, in particular at local level, to tailor the allocation of public expenditure to their needs and priorities. Experiments with participatory budgeting schemes at the subnational level (e.g. Ministry of Municipal Affairs and three pilot municipalities) could be replicated on a bigger scale to foster a sense of participatory policy making in practice, in particular among the disengaged and vulnerable groups in society.

Legal status and operational freedom of civil society

- **Request that the Registration Management Council justifies the rejection of an application** by a written statement. This requirement would increase the transparency of the application procedure and increase legal certainty among CSOs to operate legally.
- **Organise a national consultation process about the potential amendments of the 2008 Law No. 51 on Society** to increase awareness among civil society organisations and ensure that all relevant stakeholders can highlight their concerns. Moreover, these amendments should be reconsidered in light of the critical role that CSOs, particularly at municipal and district level, play in providing services to neglected groups in society.

2016 Election Law

- **Raise awareness among citizens about the work of Parliament to increase public interest and scrutiny over its activities**.
- **Organise a nationwide awareness campaign to inform citizens about the impact of the bylaws related to the election of the governorate** (e.g. Governorate Councils Districting Bylaw) **and local councils,** in collaboration

with local stakeholders from media and civil society to encourage all segments of society, including vulnerable groups, to participate in the 2017 local elections Specific activities should be organised to raise awareness among youth and other groups in society with a lower interest in voting. Initiatives such as *Naseej* (fabric), which brought together 130 young people from different governorates to enhance youth participation in the 2016 parliamentary elections, illustrate that promising citizen-driven initiative have been underway in this regard.

Open government in practice: Enhancing current practices across the different levels of government

- **Formalise citizen consultation to overcome ad hoc approaches and open up participation across the different levels of government to new groups and close the feedback loop.**
- **Review the channels and tools used by government entities to inform the public about consultation and engagement opportunities.** Provide clear indications on who will deal with citizen feedback, and create social media accounts while continuing to use traditional mass media. Awareness for existing manuals (e.g. "Participatory Approach to Strategic Planning in the Public Sector") should be increased so that they become a reference document public officials.
- **Create mechanisms and institutions to make vulnerable segments of society a partner in the open government agenda and the national development process.** That almost 70% of the population in Jordan is younger than 30 years of age suggests that engaging youth in public life and policy making should be a priority for the government. The examples of Finland and Tunisia illustrate that the OGP National Action Plan can feature youth-related commitments and may, due to the cross-sectorial scope and ambition of the plan and the international scrutiny provided by the OGP, act as an effective lever to turn commitments into actual practice.
- **Reinforce existing mechanisms to collect citizen feedback on the performance of public service delivery and quality**, such as the Central Government Complaints System and the citizen satisfaction survey conducted by the King Abdullah II Centre of Excellence. Support new initiatives, such as the development of an individual Customer Service Charter for each government institution (Ministry of Public Sector Development). More regular use of surveys could help close the feedback loop, which would increase transparency and ultimately the quality of public services. For this purpose, all relevant information from surveys or consultation activities should be made public.

Leverage the decentralisation reform to foster open government and genuine citizen participation at the local level

- **Increase popular awareness and grassroots support for the ongoing decentralisation reform** in line with the current efforts undertaken through the national dialogue (Ministry of Political and Parliamentary Affairs). The role of the Network of Civil Society Organisations for Open Government at the Local Level in Jordan could be upgraded so that its members act as the link between government and other local CSOs in raising awareness for the reform and its practical implications for local governance and CSO activity.

- **Apply a context-sensitive approach to fostering a culture of open and participatory government at the local level.** Based on a strategic assessment of the available open government capacities and the maturity of open government practices in the governorates, municipalities and districts, a guide could be created to support local authorities and non-governmental stakeholders to implement open government principles and practices, with a view to fostering inclusion and diversity.
- **Build up effective capacities and tools for use by the directorates responsible for liaising with CSOs and citizens** inside the LDUs and among the elected members of the governorate and local councils. Local public officials, both elected and appointed, should have access to training in order to implement a participatory approach to assessing local needs in collaboration with CSOs and citizens. Existing institutions, such as the National Institute for Training, could produce training modules that link engagement practices to the broader objective of reinforcing mechanisms for greater openness, transparency and accountability.

Towards a culture of open and democratic local governance in Jordan: Living diverse forms of democracy

The 2017 local elections: A test for representative democracy

- **Foster the equal participation of women in local decision making** through mentoring programmes that link female candidates and women holding office. Such activities could encourage female candidates to run for local or governorate councils, and would ultimately result in more balanced participation of women in local councils.
- **Support initiatives to enhance youth participation in local elections and create institutional mechanisms** through which they can play a constructive role in the identification of needs and priorities in their community. The organisation of school parliaments and similar initiatives can raise awareness of the importance of local elections in Jordan's democratisation process. Existing infrastructure, such as local youth councils, could be modernised and used more effectively to empower them to apply open government principles and democracy in practice.

Consultation, active participation and evaluation beyond election day

- **Foster a culture of civic engagement, volunteering and political participation at the local level** by including a civics component in the school curriculum to teach children about the rights and responsibilities of each citizen, as suggested by Jordan 2025.
- **Formalise the participation of non-governmental stakeholders** (e.g. CSOs, citizens, private sector, academia) **in determining development priorities**. Depending on the available capacities and characteristics in each municipality (size, geography, demography, etc.), the most appropriate approach may vary between more and less institutionalised forms (e.g. advisory committees for CSOs or specific groups in society vs. survey) and the reliance on traditional (e.g. gatherings with local authorities) and more innovative forms (e.g. online surveys,

use of social media). Neither a one-fits-all solution for each municipality, nor a narrow focus on one particular approach, is likely to encourage non-governmental stakeholders to participate in the national planning and development process.

- **Create a website and social media presence for each municipality and use digital technologies more systematically to inform the local community about its work and opportunities for engagement.** The online presence could feature the organisation chart, a complaint mechanism to allow for a direct response from local authorities, the minutes of meetings from the gatherings of the municipal and district councils, access to relevant administrative documents, and other useful information. The creation of a joint online presence of all municipalities could be considered to encourage the flow of information and good practice across administrative boundaries.
- **Encourage innovative engagement practices at the municipal and governorate level** by establishing a category in the National Honours Program, the creation of which is foreseen by Jordan 2025, to reward Jordanians for their contribution to Jordanian society, for outstanding partnership approaches between CSOs or citizens and local government.

New partnerships between local authorities and community members

- **Replicate experiments with participatory budgeting schemes** to involve a larger number of citizens in the allocation of a share of the municipality or district budget. Citizens should be involved from the beginning of the process (e.g. identification of projects) to create the necessary buy-in and interest.

Chapter 1.

Contextualising decentralisation reform and open government in Jordan

This chapter sets out the historical, political and administrative system in which Jordan's decentralisation reform process is taking place. It places the approval of the 2015 Decentralisation Law and Municipality in the broader context of the democratisation process over the last decade and discusses the objective of the reform with a view to the economic (e.g. achieving economic resilience and a more balanced development across the country) and social (e.g. a young, diverse and dispersed population) realities. By referring to King Abdullah II's vision of a political development process that starts at the grassroots level and key provisions in Jordan 2025, the Chapter carves out the leitmotif of the reform that is to improve economic conditions, deliver quality public services and encourage local economic development driven by a new culture of popular participation at the subnational levels of government.

Introduction

The Hashemite Kingdom of Jordan is located at the intersection of three continents, and is within the Middle East region, between the Gulf and the Levant. With a land mass of 89 320 km², Jordan is comparable in size to OECD countries such as Portugal and Hungary[1].

Despite the political turmoil in the region, Jordan has benefited from a stable political climate that is backed by strong financial and technical support from the international community, and its membership in regional (e.g. Arab League, Arab Fund for Economic and Social Development, Organisation of Islamic Cooperation) and international alliances (e.g. United Nations, International Monetary Fund, European Bank for Reconstruction and Development, Union for the Mediterranean, European Neighbourhood Policy). However, the war in Syria and Jordan's proximity to the Iraqi border (Jordan shares a 375 km border with Syria and 181 km with Iraq) have resulted in a large influx of refugees, which has challenged the government to ensure the provision of basic public services to the second biggest number of refugees per capita in the world (UNHCR, 2015). The Kingdom is scarce in natural resources and heavily relies on foreign loans and aid. Fears of terrorist extremism have risen due to occasional attacks in the border regions and the city of Karak in 2016.

In this context, stability and security considerations compete with the ongoing political, institutional and economic reform. The strong dependency of the Jordanian economy on foreign resources calls for diversification and stimulation to create new job opportunities, in particular at the level of the governorates and municipalities with high poverty rates. Since even before the "Arab Spring", Jordan has tried to face the complex challenge of reconciling traditional power structures with increasing demands from citizens for more open, inclusive and participatory policy making, and equal opportunities for all segments of society, including women and youth, in all spheres of life.

A new momentum for democratic reform

Jordan has come a long way in implementing democratic reforms since its recognition as an independent sovereign state in 1946 and the full withdrawal of British troops in 1957, despite recurrent backlashes. Home to Palestinian refugees from the 1948 Arab-Israeli fighting and the Six-Day War in 1967, Iraqi refugees since the war in 2003 and now Syrians, Jordan has been heavily affected by the consequences of the detrimental political events in a region that has seen short periods of peace and stability and continues to be shaped by major conflicts.

Since 1946, the political landscape in Jordan has seen alternating periods of political liberalisation reforms and moments when the freedom and opportunities available to political parties and organised interests have been cut back. The 1950s witnessed a proliferation of political parties, women's and students' organisations and charities, which culminated in a liberal Constitution in 1953 and the first Political Parties Law in 1955 under King Talal. However, with the dissolution of the parliament in 1956, and a coup attempt in 1957, political parties were banned until 1992, when a new Political Parties Law was approved. Martial law, which had existed since the Six-Day War in 1967, was lifted in 1991 in the midst of a new wave of political liberalisation (Hamid, 2016). The "one-vote" electoral law, introduced in 1993, encouraged voting in line with tribal affiliations and resulted in the boycott of parliamentary elections by several parties, in particular the Muslim Brotherhood. This organisation continued to exist as a charitable organisation throughout the ban, which allowed it to expand its civil society networks and garner grassroots support (Identity Center, 2014). Following the death of King Hussein in 1999, his eldest son, Crown Prince King Abdullah II bin al-Hussein, succeeded to the throne. In June 2003, the first parliamentary elections were held under the new King. The first local elections since 1999 were held in July 2007, and parliamentary elections were held in the same year, which saw the withdrawal of the main opposition party, the Islamic Action Front (the political arm of the Muslim Brotherhood) over concerns about the integrity of procedures. This was replicated during parliamentary elections in November 2010 and January 2013, despite a new electoral law in 2010.

Although the last decade of political life in Jordan is characterised by a short lifespan of governments and parliaments, Jordan has achieved some remarkable results. In 2011, Jordan became the first Arab country to join the Open Government Partnership (OGP), which coincided with the "Arab Spring" that swept throughout countries in the Middle East and North Africa (MENA) including Jordan where people engaged in large-scale street protests, especially in Amman. As a response to this, between 2011 and 2012, four different governments were tasked by the King to carry out political reforms. The gradual approach to drive political reform forward resulted in a series of constitutional amendments (e.g. creation of the Independent Election Commission and a Constitutional Court) and parliamentary elections held under a new Law on Political Parties and Election Law, which were approved in 2015 and 2016 respectively.[2] The objective of the reform process was underpinned by King Abdullah's third discussion paper in 2013, in which he stressed that the "transition to parliamentary government will deepen through "successive parliamentary cycles" (King Abdullah II, 02 March 2013).

The approval of the 2015 Decentralisation Law and Municipality Law comes at a time of increasing momentum for democratic reform. In his Speech from the Throne to parliament on 15 November 2015, the King declared that the new legal framework shall act "as a cornerstone for broadening the role and responsibilities of local administrations in our governorates. These laws are also crucial for deepening citizens' participation and empowering them to contribute towards identifying their priorities, in addition to formulating a future vision for their areas' development plans and distributing developmental gains more equally and effectively (King Abdullah II, 15 November 2015)."[3]

Achieving economic resilience and a more balanced development

Since 2012, Jordan has been classified by the World Bank as an "upper-middle income" country due to steady growth rates of between 4% and 8% during the years 2000s. Following the onset of the global financial and economic crisis, the first half of the years 2010s has seen significantly lower levels of growth, averaging around 2.6% between 2010 and 2015 according to data from the World Bank.[4] This is due to, among other aspects, a decline in remittances and foreign grants and increasing oil and commodity prices amidst the economic slowdown in Europe and Gulf Council countries. Over the 2010-2015 period, GDP per capita declined by 0.6% on average, while it increased by 1.4% in the MENA region.[5] Although the country has suffered a drop in tourism and the collapse of trade with Iraq and Syria, the announcement of investments in large-scale infrastructure projects (e.g. the Red-Dead Sea Canal and the national rail network) has raised hopes that economic resilience could be enhanced.

Despite its strategic location at the intersection of Europe, Africa and Asia, Jordan's economy suffers from structural challenges. For instance, in light of weak private sector activity, the OECD SME Policy Index recommends Jordan to improve the regulatory framework to support entrepreneurship and SME development, in particular in non-energy-intensive and high-technology sectors, and continue efforts aimed at building a knowledge economy (OECD, 2014a). On a similar note, to spur private sector development, the World Economic Forum refers to the need to remove bureaucratic obstacles, strengthen investor protection and improve access to credit and the tax system (World Economic Forum, 2014). Moreover, Jordan is extremely scarce of water, energy and arable land. With the third lowest water resources in the world, only around 3% of arable land, and energy (97%) and food (81%) consumption that is largely satisfied by imports, the economy is vulnerable to external shocks, in particular to the fluctuations in international commodity prices. The situation is exacerbated by increasing consumption needs due to the influx of large numbers of refugees fleeing the war-torn areas in Syria and Iraq. In the water sector, OECD analysis has pointed to the uncertainty surrounding the institutional and legislative framework for water and private sector participation as a major impediment to private sector activity (OECD, 2014b).

In 2010, 14% of the population was considered poor according to national poverty lines affecting both the rural (16.8%) and urban (13.9%) populations.[6] According to Jordan 2025 (Inform, 2015a), the country's ten-year national strategy, poverty remains a national challenge and is more pronounced the further a governorate is located from Amman, which stresses the urgency that disparities between governorates must be reduced.

Figure 1.1. Poverty rates by governorate (2014 and 2025 target)

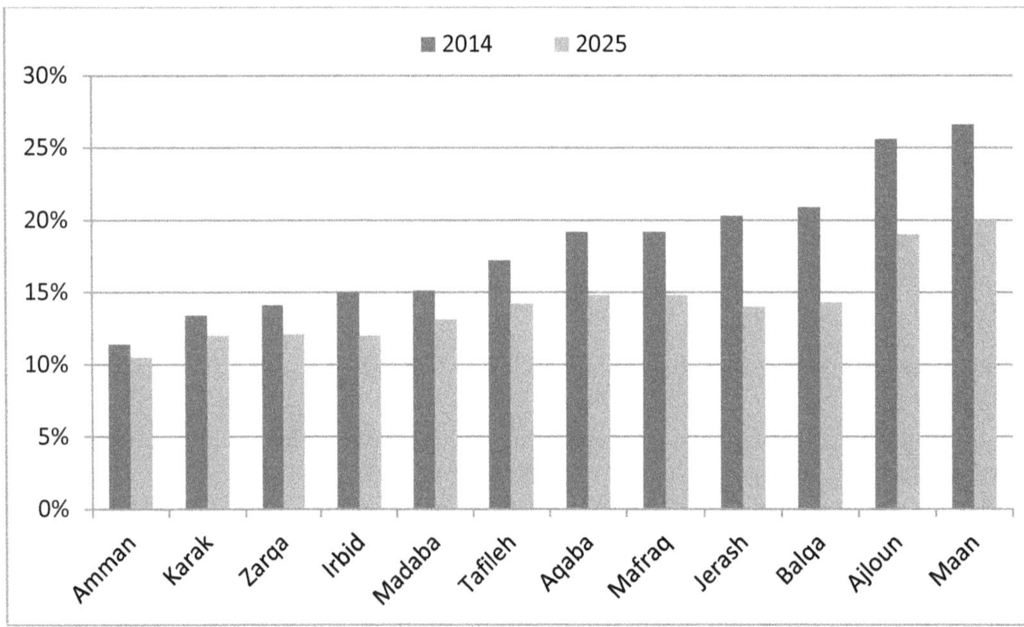

Source: OECD's own work based on data in Inform (2015a), *Jordan 2025*, Ministry of Planning and International Cooperation, Amman, http://inform.gov.jo/en-us/By-Date/Report-Details/ArticleId/247/Jordan-2025.

The Executive Development Programme 2016-18 acknowledges the large variations in local economic development between regions and governorates, especially between the governorate centres, Badia[7] and rural areas (Government of Jordan, 2016). It highlights that regular and up-to-date evidence on development is lacking, and there is little research on local investment opportunities, as well as limited capabilities of and co-ordination among bodies working in local development. The reduction of the development disparities between the governorates is an explicit objective of the decentralisation reform.

The considerable disparities in economic weight across the territory go along with a challenging macroeconomic environment. The twin deficit of a negative fiscal (-3.6% of GDP in 2015) and current account balance (-9.0% of GDP in 2015)[8] has put a major strain on the economy and restricts the policy options available to the government. The chronic trade deficit is acknowledged to be "one of the most important challenges facing [Jordan's] national financial position" in Jordan 2025 (Inform, 2015a).

The challenging macroeconomic conditions are mirrored by weak private sector activity, unemployment levels and low economic participation rates among all groups in society. In 2014, only 67% of men were economically active compared to 75% in the MENA region and 77% in the group of upper middle-income countries.[9] The job challenge is somewhat more acute for women, as Jordan displays one of the lowest female labour force participation in the world (16% compared to 22% in MENA countries and 57% in upper middle income countries).[10] As in many MENA countries, young job seekers, especially well-educated graduates, are disproportionally affected by the lack of economic opportunities as well as limited opportunities to shape (labour market) policy outcomes in their favour as noted by the OECD report "Youth in the MENA region: How to bring them in" (2016). According to data from the Department of Statistics, the unemployment rate for young men (15-24) in 2014 was 39% in the Aqaba Governorate, for young women in the Mafraq Governorate it was around 79%.[11] The absence of economic opportunities translates into low levels of economic inclusion (see Figure 1.2). The lack of job prospects has led many Jordanians to seek employment opportunities elsewhere, in particular in Saudi Arabia, the United Arab Emirates and Kuwait (Inform, 2015a).

Figure 1.2. Economic activity among young men and women aged 15-24 (2014)

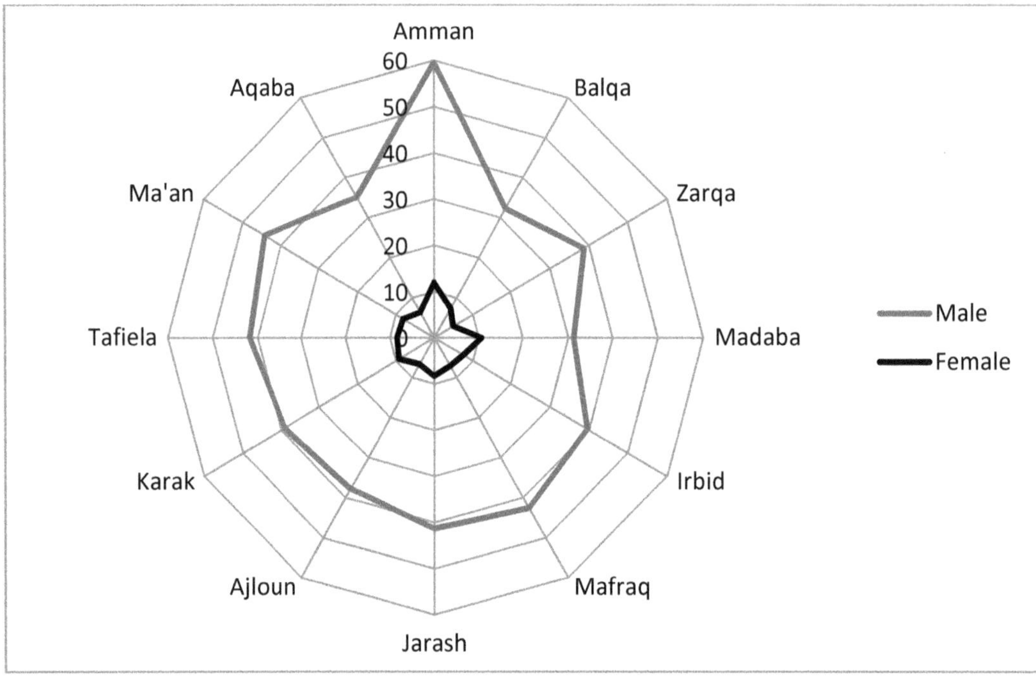

Source: OECD's own work based on: Department of Statistics (2014), *Jordanian Woman Indicators, Gender Perspective 2014*, http://www.dos.gov.jo/dos_home_e/main/population/gender/wom_index2.htm.

A young, diverse and dispersed population

According to the 2015 Census, conducted by the Department of Statistics, the population stood at 9.5 million, including 6.6 million Jordanians and 2.9 non-Jordanian residents.[12] Among the non-Jordanian residents, most come from Syria (1.26 million residents of which around 655 000 were registered refugees with the United Nations Refugee Agency [UNHCR] in January 2017),[13] Egypt (636 000), and residents from the Palestinian Authority without a national ID (634 000). Iraqi nationals account for 131 000 residents (of which 61 000 were registered refugees with the UNHCR in December 2016).[14] Jordan hosts the second largest number of refugees in relation to its national population in the world, only surpassed by Lebanon (UNHCR, 2015). This has contributed to increasing consumption needs of water, land, energy and infrastructure, and hence pressure on the access to basic education, health and other services, in particular in the northern governorates of Irbid and Al Mafraq that border Syria, and the adjacent governorates of Zarqa and Amman which host large refugee communities.[15]

The Human Development Index positions Jordan at 86 out of 188 countries and territories (UNDP, 2015b). On the three dimensions of human development measured by the Index (long and healthy life, access to knowledge, decent standard of living), Jordan has significantly improved over the last decades. For instance, between 1980s and 2014, life expectancy at birth increased by 7.8 years, mean years of schooling increased by 6.8 years and Jordan's Gross National Income (GNI) per capita increased by about 24.1% (UNDP, 2015a).

With a median age of 22.5 years in 2015, Jordan's population is one of the youngest in the world, even when compared to other countries in the MENA region, and even more so when compared to Latin America and the Caribbean (29.2), Northern America (38.3) and Europe (41.7) (United Nations, Department of Economic and Social Affairs, Population Division, 2015). Although Jordan has one of the highest educational attainments in the Arab world, the Arab Human Development Report 2016 notes that more than 55% believe that their economic prospects will decrease in the future. Support for gender equality and civic engagement in this age group are among the lowest in the Arab world. In light of the objective of the decentralisation reform, this age composition requires the Government of Jordan to provide adequate tools and mechanisms through which all age groups, including young men and women, can participate in the development process.

Moreover, the population is distributed very unevenly across the Jordanian territory. The major governorates of Amman (4 million), Irbid (1.77 million) and Zarqa (1.36 million) together host around 75% of the population, while the remaining nine governorates account for only 25% (The Jordan Times, 2016). According to the perception of government and civil society representatives from the impoverished areas in the south and other remote areas, government attention has focused on the major governorates, in particular Amman, at the expense of addressing the specific demands of less-populated regions.[16] Living outside the centre of government attention has therefore had detrimental implications for the accessibility of public services.

In line with the global trend, urbanisation has progressed rapidly in Jordan. In 2015, the share of the rural population among the total population was 16%, down from 33% in 1985. Urbanisation has advanced somewhat slower in Middle East and North African countries in which the share of the rural population decreased from 47% to 36% over the same period.[17] The growing urban population in Jordan has caused new challenges for managing scarce resources (e.g. water), addressing environmental degradation and discussing changing socio-cultural conditions.

The political and administrative context: Jordan's government system

Strong powers vested in the King and a limited policy-making role for the parliament

Jordan is a monarchy with a parliamentary system recognised in the Constitution adopted in 1952. It mandates the separation of the executive, legislative, and judicial branches of government, with the King holding extensive legislative and executive prerogatives (Hashemite Kingdom of Jordan Constitutional Court, n.d.).

The Throne of the Hashemite Kingdom is hereditary to the dynasty of King Abdullah Ibn Al-Hussein, who is a 41st generation direct descendant of the Prophet Muhammad and passes in a direct line from the throne holder to his eldest son. The King, whose prerogatives are anchored in Article 28-40 of the Constitution, is the Head of State and the Supreme Commander of the Land, Naval and Air Forces, while being immune from any liability and responsibility (Article 30 of the Constitution). The King appoints the Prime Minister and the Ministers and may dismiss them. He appoints the members of the Senate and its Speaker and may, due to an amendment to the Constitution in 1974, dissolve the Senate or relieve any Senator of membership. The powers vested in the King are exercised by Royal Decree, which needs to be countersigned by the Prime Minister and the Ministers concerned. He ratifies and promulgates the laws, and directs their enactment as may be necessary for their implementation. In his relation to the parliament, the King is entitled to issue orders to hold elections and may dissolve the Chamber of Deputies.

The prerogatives of the government are outlined in the Articles 41-61 of the Constitution. The Council of Ministers is entrusted with the responsibility of administering all affairs of the State, internal and external, unless specified otherwise by the Constitution or by any other legislation to any other person or body (Article 45). Every Minister is responsible for the conduct of all matters pertaining to his Ministry (Article 47). The current government was sworn in on 28 September 2016 and is composed of 29 ministers, 27 of which are male (7% of Ministers are women compared to an OECD average of 29% in 2015) (OECD, 2015). In a government reshuffle in January 2017, five ministers were replaced. Unlike in most OECD countries, the cabinet in Jordan is not formed on a party basis (e.g. mandate to form a cabinet is given to the party or coalition of parties that obtained the most votes), instead it is appointed by the King.[18] However, the Council of Ministers is collectively responsible before the Chamber of Deputies in respect of the public policy of the state, and each Minister holds individual responsibility for his or her portfolio. The Chamber of Deputies can force the Council of Ministers or an individual Minister to resign through a motion of no confidence. In practice, however, parliamentarians loyal to the government and the King of East Bank and rural origin tend to dominate the parliament over urban, Palestinian-Jordanians and supporters of the Muslim Brotherhood. According to Freedom House, the dominance of parliamentary representatives loyal to the government and the Royal Court has been sustained by previous electoral laws and the practice of gerrymandering (Freedom House, 2016).

Jordan has adopted a bi-cameral parliamentary system in which the National Assembly consists of a Senate whose members are appointed from among former high-level political figures from the government, parliament, judiciary or retired military, and a House of Representatives whose members (130) are elected in general direct elections for a term of four years. Both Houses have the right of legislative initiative, provided that the draft law is proposed by at least ten Senators or Deputies (see Articles 62-96 of the Constitution), however, the Chamber of Deputies cannot enact laws without the assent of the appointed Senate. According to the Government of Jordan, the decentralisation reform will help to upgrade the role parliament plays in shaping the policy agenda in Jordan. In the current system, parliamentarians are frequently approached by citizens or (interest) groups from local constituencies hence limiting its function as policy makers or, collectively, as an effective oversight body of government action (Jamal Shakir Al-Khateeb, 2010). The tribal affiliations of most parliamentarians, many of which rely on the support of their tribe in running for parliamentary elections, risk favouring narrow interests over the general interest. In this context, ensuring inclusive stakeholder consultation and engagement along the policy cycle is of particular concern.

The government, including the Prime Minister, is responsible before the Chamber of Deputies both collectively and individually in respect of the affairs of each Ministry (Article 51, Constitution). The Integrity Plan 2012 defines three main oversight agencies with an independent legal status: the Audit Bureau, the Anti-Corruption Commission and the Ombudsman Bureau. Together with a number of other (state) institutions, they are tasked with regulating different sectors of the integrity framework (Inform, 2012). The Audit Bureau exercises independent administrative oversight of state revenues and expenditures of governmental ministries, departments and agencies, public institutions, municipal boards, boards for corporate services and the Greater Municipality of Amman and corporations with a government share of more than 50%.[19] For each fiscal year, an annual report is prepared and presented to parliament. Since 2006, the Jordan Integrity and Anti-Corruption Commission (JACC) has been tasked with investigating corruption, undertaking measures to prevent corruption, and educating the public against corruption hazards with a view to increasing citizens' trust in government institutions and consolidating the values of justice, integrity and ensuring equal opportunities. JACC publishes an annual report on its website.[20] The Jordanian Ombudsman Bureau (JOB) examines complaints from individuals relating to any decree, procedure, practice or any act of refusal by public administration, and publishes an annual report.[21] In 2006, as part of wider modernisation efforts, the Ministry of Public Sector Development developed a Code of Conduct to establish ethical standards, rules and basic principles for public offices and officials. A review of its implementation conducted by the OECD in 2010 identified six priorities to strengthen its implementation such as appointing an administration body and clarifying the legal basis and enforcement procedures (OECD, 2010).

Although the institutional setting is similar to control frameworks in most OECD countries, a 2013 OECD assessment concludes that in the Jordanian cases, it suffers from a lack of co-ordination between and within the institutions, and a lack of clarity regarding individual mandate and jurisdiction (OECD, 2013). Another challenge for accountability and social cohesion identified by Jordan 2025 is that "wasta"[22] "is deeply anchored in the Jordanian and other societies in the region and is supposed to frequently occur in the interaction with government officials and the way in which economic and social issues and conflicts are dealt with (e.g. renewal of documents, hiring decisions) (Inform, 2015a)." According to a survey conducted by Transparency International in 2016, 75% believe that corruption rose in the 12 months prior to the survey, and 61% feel that the government is doing badly in fighting corruption (Transparency International, 2016a). However, in the same perception-based survey, Jordan scores the lowest bribery rates for public service use among nine Arab countries, while, due to perceived increasing requests for bribes and petty corruption, Jordan lost twelve places compared to the previous year in the 2016 edition of Transparency International's Corruption Perceptions Index (57th of 178 countries) (Transparency International, 2016b).

According to the Constitution, the Judicial Power is autonomous and independent (Article 97: judges are subject to no authority other than that of the law in the exercise of their judicial functions; and Article 101: courts are open to all and free from any interference). The legal system is based on a combination of principles of civil law and Shari'a law. The court system is divided into religious courts (sub-divided into Shari'a courts and tribunals for non-Muslim religious communities), and civil courts that exercise jurisdiction over all persons in all civil and criminal matters. The King appoints the Court of Cassation's chief justice, whereas the other judges are nominated by the Judicial Council, an 11-member judicial policy-making body whose members are approved by the King. Special courts, appointed by the Court of Cassation, decide in case a dispute arises between two religious courts or between religious and civil courts (ACRLI, 2004).

Figure 1.3. Organisational structure of public entities in Jordan

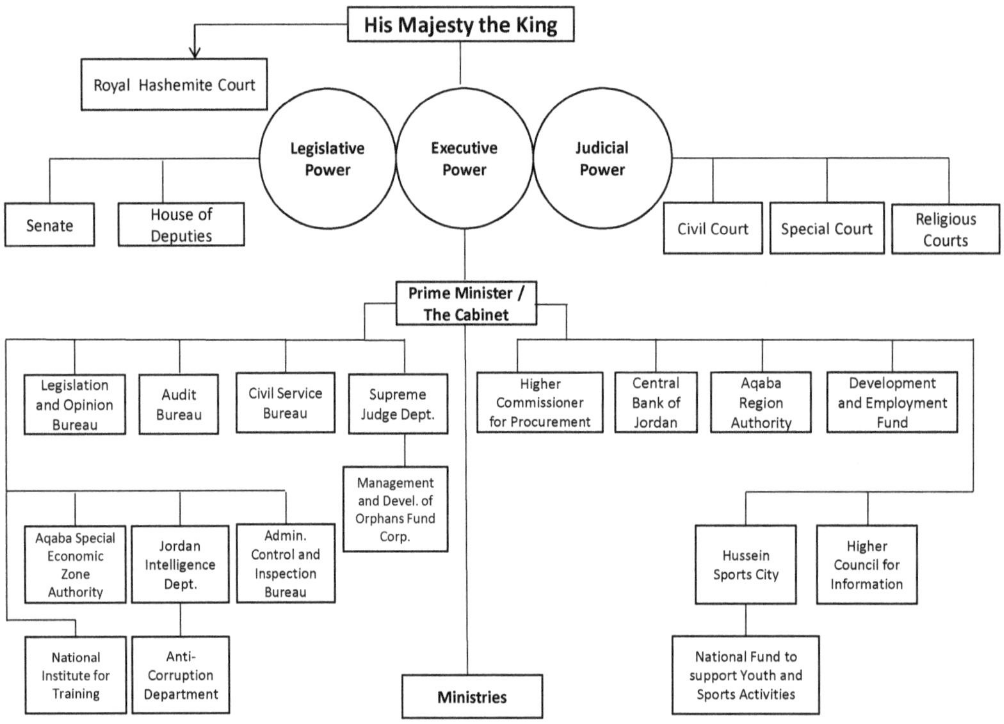

Source: Information provided by the Government of Jordan (2017).

Individual freedoms and rights granted by the Constitution

The revision of the traditional approach of centralised policy making towards a bottom-up process is the key objective in the reforms Jordan has been leading in the last decade. The new approach relies on local civil society organisations (CSOs) and citizens and their active participation in the identification of service needs and policy priorities. To fulfil their new role, citizens need to understand the implications of the new legal framework and must rely on (democratic) rights and freedoms without any undue interference.

The Constitution guarantees the rights and duties of the citizens of Jordan in Articles 5-23, including equality before the law and freedom of religion (Article 6), personal freedoms (Article 7), freedom of speech and press (Article 15), freedom of association and political parties (Article 16), and the right to elect parliamentary representatives (Article 67). The Constitution stresses that municipal and local council affairs shall be administered by municipal or local councils in accordance with special laws (Article 121). These are basic rights, but indispensable for creating a culture of more open and participatory governance at the local level. Article 6 (ii) holds that the government is requested to ensure equal opportunities to all Jordanians, and emphasises the principles of inclusiveness and fairness that should guide decision makers. With a view to the integrity of official appointments to government offices and government-attached institutions, or any municipal office, the Constitution promulgates that hiring decisions should be made on the basis of merit and qualifications (Article 22). The limits to the rights granted by the Constitution concern the freedom of the press and publications, as limited censorship on newspapers, publications, books and broadcasts affecting public safety and national defence can be imposed in the event of the declaration of martial law or a state of emergency.

While the recent constitutional amendments from 4 May 2016 did not affect any of the rights and duties outlined above, the changes have further concentrated power in the King at the expense of the Council of Ministers. In particular, they grant the King the sole power, without any countersignature by the Prime Minister or Ministers concerned, to appoint key figures in the political apparatus, for instance the Crown Prince, the Regent, the Senate Speaker and members, the Chairman and members of the Constitutional Court, the Chief Justice, the commander of the army, and the heads of Intelligence and the Gendarmerie. There has also been criticism about the short timeframe of a process that did not provide sufficient opportunity for the public to voice their opinions on the amendments (Obeidat, 2016).

Administrative organisation and challenges: The rationale for reform

Jordan is a highly centralised state. The centralisation of political power and administrative organisation dates back to the 1920s, when Transjordan was under the control of the British mandate (Ababsa, 2013).

Local governance has operated on two complementary administrative levels: governorates and municipalities. The Kingdom is organised into 12 governorates (Ajlun, Aqaba, Balqa, Al-Kark, Mafraq, Amman, Tafilah, Zarqa, Irbid, Jarash, Ma'an, and Madaba), each headed by a governor who is appointed by the King through the Minister of the Interior. The governor and related bodies, who act as the executive organ for carrying out cabinet decisions at the local level, are essentially an extension of central government and are supervised by the Ministry of the Interior. The municipal system is composed of 100 municipalities and breaks down into four sub-categories, which reflect their different size: governorate centres (11 plus Greater Amman Municipality, GAM), district centres (with a population of over 15 000), caza centres (with a population of between 5 000 and 15 000) and a fourth category for all other municipalities (Ababsa, 2013). Mayors and municipal councils are directly elected and supervised by the Ministry of Municipality Affairs, except for the mayor of GAM who is appointed by the King. GAM and the Aqaba Special Economic Zone are managed independently, under the Prime Minister.

Under the multi-level governance system[23] that existed in Jordan before the 2015 reform, municipalities lacked the authority to formulate policy and identify service needs autonomously. The central level has kept a firm grip on the allocation of budgets to the lower administrative layers, moreover, the municipal level traditionally suffers from a lack of resources and self-generated revenues, which leaves many indebted with the Cities and Villages Development Bank, or dependent on grants from donors and the central government (see Chapter 2). The limited role for governorates and municipalities in local development has resulted in a lack of opportunities for local communities – local CSOs, citizens and other non-governmental stakeholders – to shape the national planning and development process.[24] With little space provided for participation in the assessment of needs and definition of priorities, public satisfaction levels have declined over the past decade across all major areas of service delivery, which is impacting the daily life of

Jordanians, according to Jordan 2025. The detachment of planning from the service needs on the ground, exacerbated by the lack of a culture of monitoring and performance evaluation, has resulted in increasing dissatisfaction with local government performance (Al-Qds Center for Political Studies, 2016).

The challenge of reducing the gap between the planning and delivery of services, as well as centralised policy making and public participation, coexists with the need to increase overall government performance. Jordan's public sector is one of the largest in the world, and suffers from overemployment. According to Jordan 2025, the civil service accounts for 20% of GDP. Moreover, public sector salaries and pension obligations account for 27% of annual government expenditure, which restricts the fiscal space for public investments. The decentralisation reform can increase the performance of the government, provided that it eliminates unnecessary double structures and improves co-ordination across and within the different levels of government. At the same time, the reform adds new institutions – elected councils at governorate and local level – with additional resource needs (see Chapter 2). It will be critical for the new administrative system to operate efficiently and effectively in order not to worsen the already difficult situation of the public sector and, very importantly, because its performance will shape citizens' perception and trust in the new public officials and institutions.

In 2002, the number of municipalities was consolidated through mergers down from 328 municipalities to the present system of 100 municipalities. The municipal law adopted in 2007 reintroduced the elections of the mayor and the municipal council (except for GAM), which was replaced by state-appointed local committees in 2002. In 2006, the King established a high-level committee, which proposed to divide the territory into a Northern, Middle and Southern region, each with a regional parliament formed by elected local representatives. However, the plans were dropped over concerns that such a reform could undermine the state's future unity (Identity Center, n.d.).

The 2015 Decentralisation Law and Municipality Law, which lay out the King's vision of a political development process that starts at the grassroots level, are expected to make a significant contribution to the democratisation agenda in Jordan. The reform acknowledges that political development in Jordan should strengthen bottom-up approaches through which CSOs, citizens and other non-governmental stakeholders shall participate in the assessment of service needs and the identification of policy priorities, rather than being "passive" recipients of political decisions made in Amman. The ideological roots of the reform go back to 2005 when King Abdullah II announced his plans to widen the public's role in decision making in his Address to the Nation, stressing that: "[a]s political development is the gateway to the full participation of all segments of the grassroots and civil society institutions in the various aspects of the development process, I assert here that political development should start at the grassroots level, then move up to decision-making centres, and not vice-versa" (King Abdullah II, 26 January 2005).

The 2015 laws: A new legal framework for decentralisation and/or citizen engagement

As will be further explained in Chapter 2, decentralisation is a gradual process by nature and describes a transfer of public functions from higher tiers to lower tiers of governance. Decentralisation reform can take the form of a transfer of civil servants and public functions to lower layers (administrative), the devolution of fiscal resources and the power to generate revenues (fiscal), the devolution of decision-making powers (political), or, as in most cases, a combination thereof.

The key feature introduced by the 2015 Decentralisation Law (DL) and Municipality Law (ML) is the creation of elected councils at the governorate level that shall enjoy financial and administrative independence (Art. 6 DL) and at the local (sub-municipal) level (Art. 3 ML). Upon the recommendation of the Minister of the Interior, a maximum of 15% of the members of the governorate council can be appointed, provided that at least one in three is a woman (Article 3 DL); all members of the local councils are elected by popular vote. For the creation of local councils, a decree by the Minister of Municipality Affairs is required, who also determines the boundaries of the local councils and the number of its elected members (at least five). Under the new legal framework, the municipality shall be managed by a municipal council composed of a chairman, the heads of local councils, and a number of members of local councils who won the highest number of votes, except for Aqaba Special Economic Zone Authority (ASEZA) and Petra Tourism Developmental Authority (Article 3 ML) which are designated special economic zones managed under the Prime Minister's Office. In essence, where local councils are created, the so far directly elected municipal councils are transformed into indirectly elected bodies. The Minister may, with the approval of the Cabinet, appoint two additional members to each Municipal Council who enjoy the same rights of elected members (Article 69 ML). The Greater Municipality of Amman is an exception as 25% of the council members and the Mayor are appointed.

It is to be stressed that, while an important step in the democratisation of public life in the country, the two laws do not result in a significant transfer of responsibilities from the Amman to the governorates or municipalities, or in the devolution of fiscal resources to them (see Chapter 2). In fact, the functions of the elected governorate council, as identified in Article 8 of the DL, suggest that they will mainly act as consulting bodies. For instance, they will be tasked with approving the draft strategic and executive plans of the governorate, its budget and the development and service projects referred by the Executive Council.[25] Moreover, they will discuss reports on the implementation of plans, projects, and programmes to be implemented by the (deconcentrated) directorates. The elected members are further invited to propose the establishment of investment projects, develop recommendations to improve the performance of government departments and public institutions inside the governorate, and to propose solutions to ensure better service delivery.

Similarly, in line with the King's vision of a grassroots approach to the national development process, the elected local councils are tasked with proposing development projects and contributing to the preparation of strategic and development plans of the municipalities based on the identification of needs in co-operation with civil society organisations (Article 6 ML). Their work is then submitted to the municipal council. The local councils shall fulfil various tasks in identifying the location of public sites (e.g. public and vocational schools; places of worship; course of water, electricity and gas distribution network; public hospitals and health facilities), and exercising monitoring and control functions (e.g. public markets, roads maintenance, street cleaning, lightening, public transport stops, restaurants, cafes and other public amusements).

The creation of the elected governorate and local councils as foreseen by the DL and ML has created strong expectations among civil society and the private sector that public participation in policymaking and service delivery processes will increase, as well as their transparency and accountability. In his Designation Letter to the Prime Minister in

September 2016, the King stressed that "enhancing people's participation in the development-related decision making process [...] contributes to the development and capacity building of governorates, ensuring fairer distribution of development gains".[26] However, given the lack of a major transfer of actual competencies and powers to the subnational layers of government, the label "decentralisation reform" may be misleading. The engagement narrative provided by the Royal Court and the government may more adequately reflect the main intention of the reform, that is, to strengthen public participation and scrutiny in the national planning and development process.

At the same time, the two laws do not specify how a bottom-up approach is expected to be implemented in practical terms. As discussed in Chapter 4, so far, the creation of local councils reduces the distance of citizens to their elected representatives, which may result in a better representation of local citizens' needs and better tailored public service delivery that responds to the individual needs of local communities. What remains to be defined, however, is the future interaction between the local councils and CSOs and citizens in the identification of service needs and policy priorities, and the chain of command across the different layers of government (local, municipal, governorate, central) to ensure that citizens' considerations are reflected in the final version of the development plan.

There is hence a need to reconcile the expectations among CSOs and citizens and the actual role, tools and mechanisms available to them and to the newly elected public officials in the governorate and local councils, possibly ahead of the first local elections under the new legal framework. The reform process offers a unique momentum to empower civil society and citizens and hence foster democratic principles and a culture of openness, transparency, accountability and inclusiveness at the community level. In this sense, the reform could contribute to improving government performance and moving forward the broader open government and democratisation agenda based on a new impetus from the local level.

The first local elections under the new legal framework are expected to take place in August 2017, which ties the government to a tight schedule to accurately disseminate the content of the DL and ML and for the finalisation of the relevant by-laws.

Jordan 2025: Placing citizens at the heart of the development process

Jordan 2025, the country's long-term national vision, features more than 400 policies or procedures that "should be implemented through a participatory approach between the government, business sector and civil society" (Inform, 2015a). The King's letter from 29 March 2014, which precedes the Vision, stresses that the economic blueprint should be based, among others, on the principle of enhancing local governance and implementing decentralisation, and be rolled out in a way that ensures a "just distribution of developmental dividends by giving priority to governorates' development programmes." Jordan 2025 stresses the need to "improve the welfare of citizens and the basic services provided to them, and to create a balanced society where opportunities are available to all and the gap between governorates is bridged."

As shown in Figure 1.4, and in line with the objective of the 2015 Decentralisation Law and Municipality Law, Jordan 2025 places citizens at the centre of the development process.

Figure 1.4. Key pillars of Jordan 2025

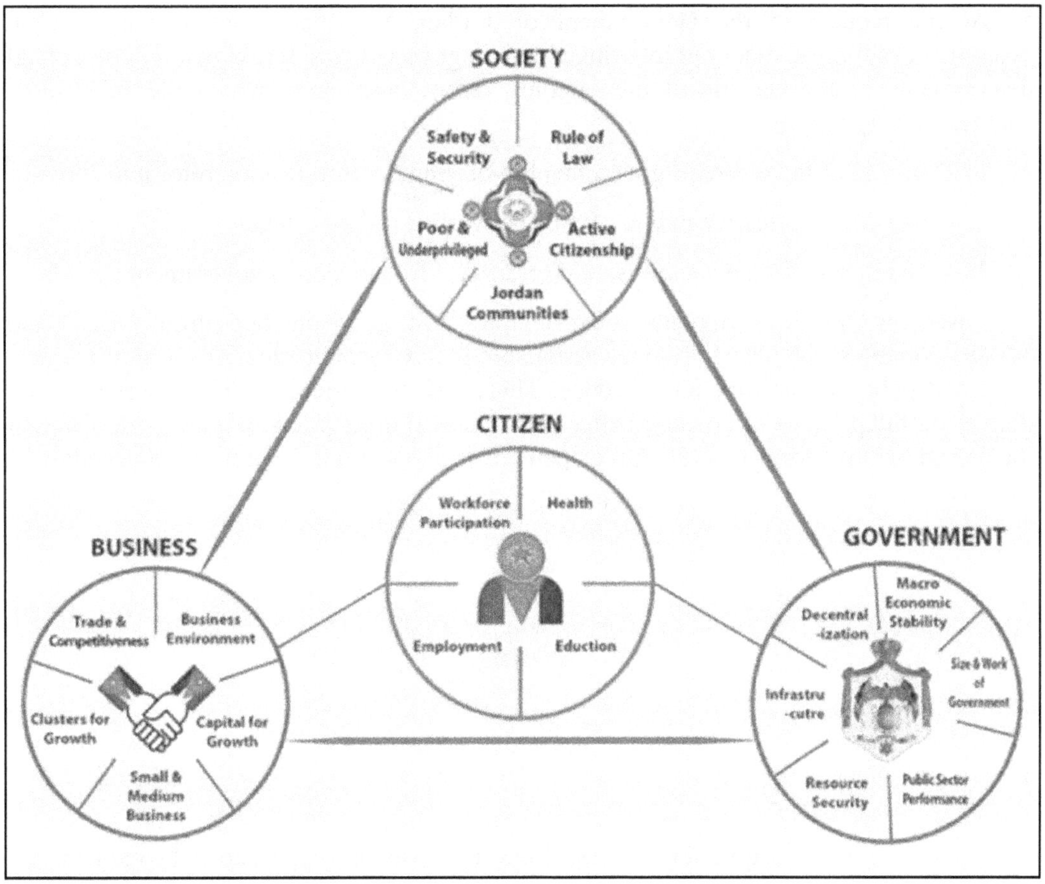

Source: Inform (2015b), *Jordan 2025 - A National Vision and Strategy, Part 1*, http://inform.gov.jo/Portals/0/Report%20PDFs/0.%20General/jo2025part1.pdf.

The Strategy acknowledges that active civic engagement and political participation are indispensable for a democratic culture at the local level to emerge. Moreover, by explicitly seeking to advance the principles of participation, transparency and accountability, Jordan 2025 strongly supports Jordan's open government agenda. This is further reinforced by parallel efforts to foster the fair representation of citizens (2016 Electoral Law, which largely presents a return to the 1989 election law) and the creation of political parties (Law of Political Parties of 2015, No 39) (Independent Election Commission), with a view to cutting back on the influence of the tribal affiliations that have tended to dominate political, social and economic life in Jordan until the present day.

Structure of the strategic assessment

At the request of the Government of Jordan, this report provides a strategic assessment of three distinct but interlinked public governance areas, which will be critical determinants of the success of the ongoing reform and along which the subsequent chapters are organised:

1. The role of the centre of government in driving decentralisation reform in Jordan.
2. Enablers for effective public service delivery at the local level.
3. The impact of the decentralisation reform on Jordan's open government agenda.

Based on OECD instruments and principles, and good practices from OECD and MENA countries, the report provides actionable policy recommendations to turn the new legal and policy framework into practice. There will be a focus on how the reform can deliver on the promise to create a better performance of government across the different levels and to move forward in Jordan's open government and democratisation agenda.

Notes

1. http://data.worldbank.org/indicator/ag.srf.totl.k2?contextual=similar&locations=jo&view=chart.
2. The 2015 Political Parties Law facilitated the creation of new parties by reducing the threshold of members required for registration from 500 to 150 and shifted the authority to license and supervise parties from the Ministry of Interior to the Ministry of Political and Parliamentary Affairs. The law abolished the foundation of parties based on religion, ethnicity, race, or gender.
3. https://kingabdullah.jo/en/news/king-inaugurates-17th-parliament-third-ordinary-session.
4. http://data.worldbank.org/indicator/ny.gdp.mktp.kd.zg?end=2015&locations=jo&start=2000.
5. http://data.worldbank.org/indicator/ny.gdp.pcap.kd.zg?end=2015&locations=jo-zq&start=2008.
6. http://data.worldbank.org/indicator/SI.POV.RUHC?locations=JO (rural), http://data.worldbank.org/indicator/SI.POV.URHC?locations=JO (urban).
7. The Jordan Badia constitutes 80% of the Hashemite Kingdom of Jordan and comprises the predominantly arid and semi-arid and less populated areas of the Kingdom. The Jordan Badia is divided into the Northern Badia, the Middle Badia and Southern Badia. The Badia is home to Bedouin livestock breeders, many of whom live a nomadic lifestyle (The Hashemite Fund for Development of Jordan Badia, www.badiafund.gov.jo/en/node/310).
8. http://pubdocs.worldbank.org/en/738781475460665083/Jordan-MEM-Fall-2016-ENG.pdf.
9. http://data.worldbank.org/indicator/SL.TLF.CACT.MA.ZS?locations=JO-ZQ-XT.

10. http://data.worldbank.org/indicator/SL.TLF.CACT.FE.ZS?locations=JO-ZQ-XT.

11. Department of Statistics, Jordanian Woman Indicators, Gender Perspective 2014, www.dos.gov.jo/dos_home_e/main/population/gender/wom_index2.htm.

12. Data from the World Bank estimates that the population in Jordan was 7.6 million in 2015 (http://data.worldbank.org/indicator/SP.POP.TOTL?end=2015&locations=JO&start=1960).

13. The discrepancy between the official numbers of Syrian refugees disseminated by the UNHCR and by the Government of Jordan can be explained by the fact that there are, de facto, two groups: first, foreign workers and business owners with a residence and work permits living in Jordan before the outbreak of the war in 2011; and second, the actual refugees from the ongoing war (Bertelsmann, July 2016, Facts on the European Dimension of Displacement and Asylum: Jordan, www.bertelsmann-stiftung.de/fileadmin/files/BSt/Publikationen/GrauePublikationen/EZ_Factsheet_Jordan_07_16_ENG.pdf).

14. http://census.dos.gov.jo/; http://data.unhcr.org/syrianrefugees/download.php?id=12630.

15. http://data.unhcr.org/syrianrefugees/country.php?id=107.

16. Answers received during two fact-finding missions conducted by the OECD in May and July 2017 and meetings with the Network of Civil Society Organisations for Open Government at the Local Level in Jordan.

17. http://data.worldbank.org/indicator/SP.RUR.TOTL.ZS?end=2015&locations=JO-ZQ&start=1985&view=chart.

18. The only exception dates back to 1956 when King Hussein asked the party leader of the party who won the majority of votes to form a cabinet. The coalition cabinet only lasted for six months before it was dismissed by the King and political parties were dissolved and banned until the early 1990s (Obeidat, 2016, Jordan's 2016 constitutional amendments: A return to absolute monarchy? www.constitutionnet.org/news/jordans-2016-constitutional-amendments-return-absolute-monarchy).

19. www.audit-bureau.gov.jo/en.

20. www.jiacc.gov.jo/en-us/knowledgebase/reportsandstatistics/reports/annualreports.aspx.

21. www.ombudsman.org.jo/.

22. The term *wasta* stems from the Arabic root for "middle" or "medium" and describes the phenomenon of using "connections" to find job, government services or other favours to circumvent bureaucracy or bypass the system as a whole. The effects of *wasta* may be both positive (e.g. lower transaction costs, reduce the problem of asymmetric information) or negative (e.g. individuals are placed or promoted to positions beyond their technical, educational or professional capacities and capabilities), and is a phenomenon that exists through similar concepts in other cultures and regions of the world (Ramady, 2016).

23. OECD work on multi-level governance addresses both vertical and horizontal dimensions. The "vertical" dimension refers to the linkages between higher and lower levels of government, including their institutional, financial, and informational aspects. The "horizontal" dimension refers to co-operation arrangements between

regions or between municipalities (www.oecd.org/regional/regional-policy/multi-levelgovernance.htm).

24. In various discussions with public officials and civil society representatives, the lack of a decentralised chain of decision making was also deplored with regard to the internal operations of ministries and other public institutions, in particular when it came to routine procedures and instructions that had to be sent up the chain of command instead of being delegated to middle-level managers.

25. The Executive Council is chaired by the Governor and is composed of the Directors of the (deconcentrated) Executive Directorates and Service Administrations in the Governorate, the Deputy Governor and provincial heads, two District Administrators, and the Governor's Assistant for Development Affairs. If any, Directors of development and industrial zones in the Governorate are also part of the Executive Council and so may, by a maximum of three municipal executive directors in the governorate, be nominated by the Minister of Municipal Affairs. Special additional conditions apply in the governorate of Aqaba and Ma'an (Article 4).

26. It must be noted that the analysis presented in this report builds on the available evidence in December 2016. Given that the reform process is advancing in parallel, and that many of the concrete procedures are yet to be defined, the assessment and recommendations reflect the progress achieved to this point.

References

Ababsa M. (2013), *Atlas of Jordan. History, Territories and Society*. Atlas al Urdunn. Al-tarikh, al-ardh, al-mujtama`, Beyrouth, Presses de l'Ifpo, p. 485, http://books.openedition.org/Ifpo/4560.

ACRLI (2004), *National Report on the State of the Judiciary in Hashemite Kingdom of Jordan*, Arab Center for the Development of the Rule of Law and Integrity, www.arabruleoflaw.org/Files/128085773006703750_Jordan_CountryProfiles.pdf.

Al-Qds Center for Political Studies (2016), QCPS Workshop Calls for Enhancing Women's Role in Municipal Councils, www.alqudscenter.org/home/english/news-article/2234#.wkw-yg8rkul.

Bertelsmann Stiftung (2016), Facts on the European Dimension of Displacement and Asylum: Jordan, July, www.bertelsmann-stiftung.de/en/publications/publication/did/facts-on-the-european-dimension-of-displacement-and-asylum-jordan/.

Department of Statistics (2015), Census, http://census.dos.gov.jo/ (Arabic).

Department of Statistics (2014), *Jordanian Woman Indicators, Gender Perspective 2014*, www.dos.gov.jo/dos_home_e/main/population/gender/wom_index2.htm.

Freedom House (2016), *Jordan, Freedom in the World 2016*, Freedom House, Washington DC, https://freedomhouse.org/report/freedom-world/2016/jordan.

Government of Jordan (2016), Executive Development Program 2016-18, www.mop.gov.jo/Pages/viewpage.aspx?pageID=103.

Hamid, S. (2016), *Political party development before and after the Arab Spring*, www.brookings.edu/wp-content/uploads/2016/06/Beyond-the-Arab-Spring.pdf.

Hashemite Kingdom of Jordan - Constitutional Court (n.d.), The Constitution of Jordan, http://cco.gov.jo/Portals/0/constitution_en.pdf.

Hashemite Kingdom of Jordan - Integrity and Anti-Corruption Commission (n.d.), Annual reports, www.jacc.gov.jo/enus/knowledgebase/reportsandstatistics/reports/annualreports.aspx.

Identity Center (2014), *Map of Political Parties and Movements in Jordan 2013/14*, Identity Centre, Amman, http://identity-center.org/sites/default/files/map%20of%20political%20parties%20and%20movements%20in%20jordan%20english.pdf.

Identity Center (n.d.), *Policy Paper: Building grassroots participation for decentralization*, www.identity-center.org/sites/default/files/identity%20center%20policy%20paper%20-%20decentralization_0.pdf.

Independent Election Commission (2016), Law on the Election of the House of Representatives, No (6) of 2016, www.iec.jo/sites/default/files/2ParliamentaryElectionLawMay2016EN.docx%20%281%29_0.pdf.

Independent Election Commission (2015a), Law on Municipalities 2015, Law No 41 of 2015, www.iec.jo/sites/default/files/2015%20Municipalities%20Law%20EN.pdf.

Independent Election Commission (2015b), Law on Decentralisation 2015, Law No 49 of 2015, www.iec.jo/sites/default/files/2015%20Decentralisation%20Law%20EN.pdf.

Independent Election Commission (2015c), Law of Political Parties of 2015 (No 39), https://iec.jo/sites/default/files/7%20Political%20Parties%20Law%202015%20EN%20(1)_0.pdf.

Inform (2015a), *Jordan 2025*, Ministry of Planning and International Cooperation, Amman, http://inform.gov.jo/en-us/By-Date/Report-Details/ArticleId/247/Jordan-2025.

Inform (2015b*), Jordan 2025 - A National Vision and Strategy, Part 1*, http://inform.gov.jo/Portals/0/Report%20PDFs/0.%20General/jo2025part1.pdf.

Inform (2012), 2012 National Integrity Charter and Action Plan, Ministry of Planning and International Cooperation, Amman, http://inform.gov.jo/Portals/0/Report%20PDFs/7.%20Role%20&%20Performance%20of%20Government/iii.%20National%20Integrity%20Systems/2012%20National%20Integrity%20Charter%20and%20Action%20Plan.pdf.

Jamal Shakir Al-Khateeb (2010), “Decentralisation and Enhancing the Local Governance”, Minutes of the workshops organised by Al-Badeel Center for Studies and Research, www.albadeeljordan.org/pdf/decentralizatin2010.pdf.

King Abdullah II (2015), King inaugurates 17th Parliament third ordinary session, 15 November, https://kingabdullah.jo/en/news/king-inaugurates-17th-parliament-third-ordinary-session.

King Abdullah II (2013), Each Playing Our Part in a New Democracy, Third Discussion Paper, 02 March, https://kingabdullah.jo/en/discussion-papers/each-playing-our-part-new-democracy.

King Abdullah II (2005), Address by His Majesty King Abdullah II To the Nation Announcing the Decentralisation Plan, 26 January, https://kingabdullah.jo/en/speeches/nation-announcing-decentralisation-plan.

Obeidat, S. (2016), *Jordan's 2016 constitutional amendments: A return to absolute monarchy?*, Constitutionnet, Stockholm, www.constitutionnet.org/news/jordans-2016-constitutional-amendments-return-absolute-monarchy.

OECD (2016), Youth in the MENA Region: How to Bring Them In, OECD Publishing, Paris, http://dx.doi.org/10.1787/9789264265721-en.

OECD (2015), "Women in politics", in *Government at a Glance 2015*, OECD Publishing, Paris, http://dx.doi.org/10.1787/gov_glance-2015-24-en.

OECD (2014a), "Jordan", in SME Policy Index: The Mediterranean Middle East and North Africa 2014: Implementation of the Small Business Act for Europe, OECD Publishing, Paris, http://dx.doi.org/10.1787/9789264218413-22-en.

OECD (2014b), Water Governance in Jordan: Overcoming the Challenges to Private Sector Participation, OECD Publishing, Paris, http://dx.doi.org/10.1787/9789264213753-en.

OECD (2013), *OECD Investment Policy Reviews: Jordan 2013*, OECD Publishing, Paris, http://dx.doi.org/10.1787/9789264202276-en.

OECD (2010), Implementing a Code of Conduct for the Public Sector in Jordan, OECD Joint Learning Study, www.oecd.org/gov/ethics/45916428.pdf.

OECD (n.d.), Multi-level Governance and Public Finance, www.oecd.org/regional/regional-policy/multi-levelgovernance.htm.

Ramady, Mohamed A. (Ed.) (2016), The Political Economy of Wasta: Use and Abuse of Social Capital Network.

The Hashemite Fund for Development of Jordan Badia (2017), www.badiafund.gov.jo/en/node/310 (accessed 8 February 2017).

The Jordanian Ombudsman Bureau, www.ombudsman.org.jo/.

The Jordan Times (2016), Population stands at around 9.5 million, including 2.9 million guests, www.jordantimes.com/news/local/population-stands-around-95-million-including-29-million-guests (accessed 8 February 2017).

Transparency International (2016a), *People and Corruption: Middle East and North Africa Survey 2016*, Transparency International, Berlin, https://issuu.com/transparencyinternational/docs/2016_gcb_mena_en?e=2496456/35314511.

Transparency International (2016b), *Corruption Perceptions Index*, Transparency International, Berlin, https://issuu.com/transparencyinternational/docs/2016_cpireport_en?e=2496456/43483458.

UNDP (2016), Arab Human Development Report 2016, www.arab-hdr.org/reports/2016/english/ahdr2016en.pdf.

UNDP (2015a), *Briefing note for countries on the 2015 Human Development Report, Jordan*, United Nations Development Programme, New York, http://hdr.undp.org/sites/all/themes/hdr_theme/country-notes/JOR.pdf.

UNDP (2015b), Human Development Index and its components, http://hdr.undp.org/en/composite/HDI.

UNHCR (2017), Syria Regional Refugee Response, Inter-agency Information Sharing Portal, United Nations Refugee Agency, Geneva, http://data.unhcr.org/syrianrefugees/country.php?id=107 (accessed 15 April 2017).

UNHCR (2016), Registered Iraqis in Jordan, United Nations Refugee Agency, Geneva, http://data.unhcr.org~/syrianrefugees/download.php?id=12630.

UNHCR (2015), *Global Trends - Forced Displacement in 2015*, United Nations Refugee Agency, Geneva, http://www.unhcr.org/576408cd7.pdf.

United Nations, (2015), World Population Prospects: The 2015 Revision, custom data acquired via website, Department of Economic and Social Affairs, Population Division.

World Bank (2017a), Surface area (sq. km), Jordan, http://data.worldbank.org/indicator/ag.srf.totl.k2?contextual=similar&locations=jo&view=chart (accessed 15 April 2017).

World Bank (2017b), GDP growth (annual %), Jordan, 2000-2015, http://data.worldbank.org/indicator/ny.gdp.mktp.kd.zg?end=2015&locations=jo&start=2000.

World Bank (2017c), GDP per capita growth (annual %), Jordan and Middle East & North Africa, 2008 to 2015, http://data.worldbank.org/indicator/ny.gdp.pcap.kd.zg?end=2015&locations=jo-zq&start=2008.

World Bank (2017d), Rural poverty headcount ratio at national poverty lines (% of rural population), Jordan, http://data.worldbank.org/indicator/si.pov.ruhc?locations=jo.

World Bank (2017e), Urban poverty headcount ratio at national poverty lines (% of urban population), Jordan, http://data.worldbank.org/indicator/si.pov.urhc?locations=jo.

World Bank (2017f), Labor force participation rate, male (% of male population ages 15+) (modelled ILO estimate), Jordan and Middle East & North Africa & Upper middle income, http://data.worldbank.org/indicator/sl.tlf.cact.ma.zs?locations=jo-zq-xt.

World Bank (2017g), Labor force participation rate, female (% of female population ages 15+) (modelled ILO estimate), Jordan and Middle East & North Africa & Upper middle income, http://data.worldbank.org/indicator/sl.tlf.cact.fe.zs?locations=jo-zq-xt.

World Bank (2017h), Population, total, Jordan, 1960-2015, http://data.worldbank.org/indicator/sp.pop.totl?end=2015&locations=jo&start=1960.

World Bank (2017i), Rural population (% of total population), Jordan, 1985-2015, http://data.worldbank.org/indicator/sp.rur.totl.zs?end=2015&locations=jo&start=1985&view=chart.

World Bank (2016), Jordan's Economic Outlook - October 2016, http://pubdocs.worldbank.org/en/738781475460665083/jordan-mem-fall-2016-eng.pdf.

World Economic Forum (2014), *Global Competitiveness Index 2014-2015*, World Economic Forum, Cologny, http://www3.weforum.org/docs/WEF_GlobalCompetitivenessReport_2014-15.pdf.

Chapter 2.

The role of the centre of government in driving decentralisation reform in Jordan

This chapter analyses the current architecture of the state with a focus on the interplay between the central level, governorates and municipalities examining the autonomy of subnational bodies, accountability mechanisms and the challenges faced by government institutions across all levels of government to effectively deliver on their mandates. It raises the (yet unanswered) question whether the creation of elected councils at governorate and local level will eventually go along with a more significant transfer of administrative, political and financial competencies. Stressing the critical function by the National Committee for the Decentralisation Reform as the centre of government (CoG) for driving the reform process, it discusses the need to further clarify mandates and procedures in order to define the future interaction across all levels in the day-to-day service delivery and the national planning and development process.

Following Parliament's approval of the new Municipality and Decentralisation Laws, and their subsequent ratification by Royal Decree in December 2015, Jordan is currently revamping the role of its subnational levels by re-allocating competencies to existing institutions, as well as creating new institutions in the municipalities and governorates to get policies closer to citizens.

This chapter assesses Jordan's decentralisation reform and the centre of government's (CoG) co-ordination capacity to successfully address the main challenges the country is facing, as identified in Chapter 1. It presents an overview of the decentralisation reform in Jordan and in particular, it analyses the Decentralisation and Municipalities Laws and the government's recent arrangements to lead and implement the reform under Jordan 2025.[1]

Since decentralisation is at the heart of this assessment, this chapter will first focus on defining the process and providing relevant international good practices. It will then determine the role of the centre of government in leading decentralisation reform and devising the mechanisms for an effective and efficient implementation that includes the active involvement and engagement of all key stakeholders.

Decentralisation and governance in Jordan

Jordan's country specific territorial reality is the result of its own political, social and economic history, described in Chapter 1. This section describes the territorial reality and constraints that have led to the current centralised state, and contrasts it with experiences of OECD countries.

A small country with great regional disparities

Jordan has 12 governorates, each headed by a governor appointed by the King through the Minister of the Interior. The governor and related bodies, who act as the executive organ for carrying out cabinet decisions at the subnational level, are essentially an extension of the central government, and are supervised by the Ministry of the Interior (MoI).[2] The municipal system is composed of 100 municipalities and breaks down into four sub-categories to reflect their different size: governorate centres (11 plus the Greater Amman Municipality, GAM), district centres (with a population of over 15 000), caza centres (with a population of between 5 000 and 15 000) and a fourth category for all other municipalities (Ababsa, 2013). Mayors and municipal councils were previously directly elected (but not the municipal council, under the new law) and supervised by the Ministry of Municipality Affairs, except for the mayor of GAM who is appointed by the King. GAM and the Aqaba Special Economic Zone are managed independently, under the Prime Minister.

The sizes and populations of governorates and municipalities have strong disparities. Among governorates, populations range from almost 2.5 million in Amman to fewer than 90 000 in Tafilah (Jordan Department of Statistics, 2017). Half of Jordan's population is concentrated within the Amman-Ruseifa-Zarqa conurbation (3 million out of 6.3 million inhabitants in 2011). Amman Jordan's major city, is four times bigger than the second, Zarqa, and seven times larger than Irbid, the third city of the country (313 800 inhabitants in 2013).[3] The country's population density is 86 inhabitants per square kilometre,[4] but 80% of the country has fewer than five inhabitants per km². The entire population lives in an area of less than 10 000 km², giving a true density ten times higher: over 650 inhabitants per km². The northern governorates, with less desert areas, have densities of over 300 inhabitants per square kilometre, this figure reaches 962 in Irbid. Kerak and Tafila are in the mountains and have suffered from population drift towards the capital; they have respective population densities of 68 and 39 inhabitants per km². In the cities, population density reaches world records, with over 30 000 inhabitants per km² in the poor areas of Amman and Zarqa (Figure 2.1) (Ababsa, 2013).

Figure 2.1. Jordan population density per governorate

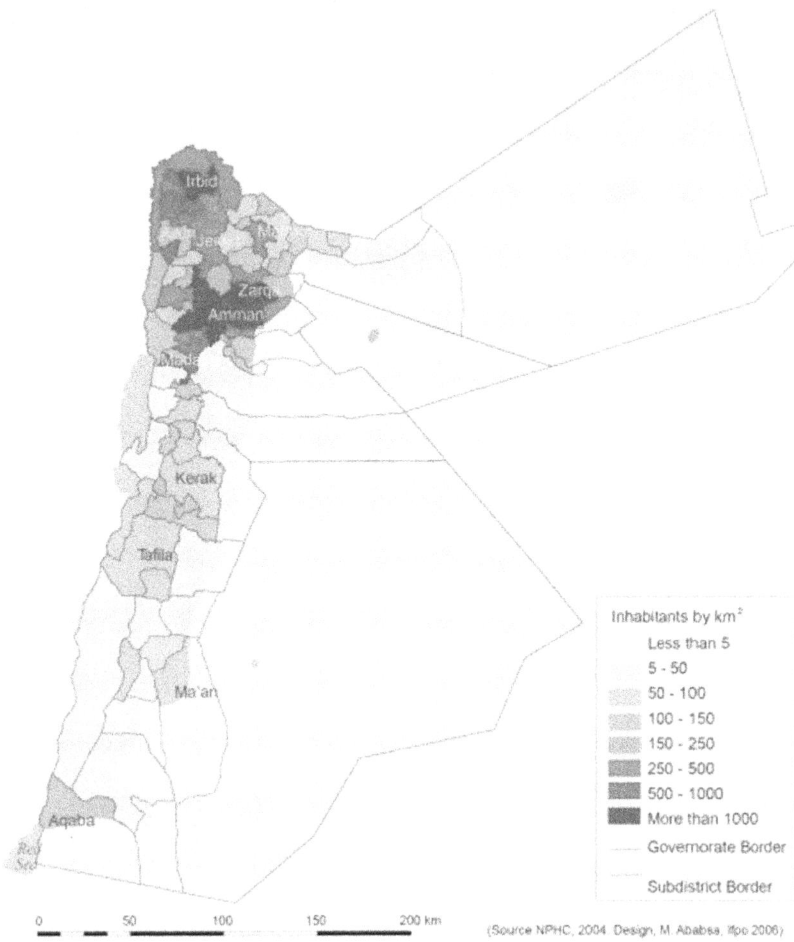

Source: Ababsa (2013), *Atlas on Jordan*, http://books.openedition.org/ifpo/5021?lang=en.

These significant differences of population density underline a territorial and country specific reality in Jordan. For instance, there is a big contrast between the north-west country, highly populated with the south-eastern desert area almost unpopulated. Jordan's Vision 2025 raises the need to promote decentralisation from a local development perspective to fight against unemployment and poverty to not only ensure public service delivery at the local level, but also to encourage local economic development (Figure 2.1).

Table 2.1. Challenges at the governorate level: GINI, unemployment and poverty in 2014

	GINI	Poverty rate in %	Unemployment in %
Ajloun	0.306	25.6	12
Amman	0.387	11.4	10.9
Aqaba	0.312	19.2	16.6
Balqa	0.333	20.9	15
Irbid	0.330	15	12.5
Jerash	0.254	20.3	11.8
Karak	0.317	13.4	18.6
Ma'an	0.28	26.6	20.1
Madaba	0.272	15.1	17.9
Mafraq	0.296	19.2	11.3
Tafilah	0.262	17.2	20.7
Zarqa	0.319	14.1	12.9

Source: Inform (2015), *Jordan 2025*, Ministry of Planning and International Cooperation, Amman, http://inform.gov.jo/en-us/By-Date/Report-Details/ArticleId/247/Jordan-2025.

There is a large disparity of territorial organisations in OECD countries, There are around 138 000 general purpose subnational governments in OECD countries, which are distributed in one, two or three government layers (Tables 2.2 and 2.3). Jordan is considered a highly centralised country, with a two-tier subnational government system that is made of 12 governorates and 100 municipalities.

Box 2.1. Subnational government structure in OECD countries

The multi-level governance structure of countries varies considerably in the OECD, with 9 federal states and 25 unitary states. Among OECD member countries, only eight have three subnational government tiers: the regional/federated level, the intermediary level and the municipal level. There are 18 countries, such as the Netherlands, with two subnational tiers (regions and municipalities), and 8 countries have only one subnational tier.

Table 2.2. Number of subnational governments* in the OECD in 2015, with figures on Jordan

2014-15	Municipal level	Intermediary level	Regional or state level	Total number of subnational governments
Federations and quasi-federations				
Australia	565		8	573
Austria	2 102		9	2 111
Belgium	589	10	6	605
Canada	4 014		13	4 027
Germany	11 116	402	16	11 534
Mexico	2 445		32	2 477
Spain	8 117	50	17	8 184
Switzerland	2 324		26	2 350
United States	35 879	3 031	50	38 960
Unitary countries				
Chile	345		15	360
Czech Republic	6 253		14	6 267
Denmark	98		5	103
Estonia	213			213
Finland	317		1	318
France	36 681	101	27	36 809
Greece	325		13	338
Hungary	3 177		19	3 196
Iceland	74			74
Ireland	31			31
Israel	252			252
Italy	8 047	110	20	8 177
Japan	1 718		47	1 765
Korea	227		17	244
Latvia	119			119
Luxembourg	105			105
Netherlands	393		12	405
New Zealand**	67		11	78
Norway	428		18	446
Poland	2 478	380	16	2 874
Portugal***	308		2	310
Slovak Republic	2 927		8	2 935
Slovenia	212			212
Sweden	290		21	311
Turkey	1 394		81	1 475
United Kingdom	389	27	3	419
OECD35	**130 005**	**4 111**	**514**	**134 630**
Jordan	**94**	**12**		**112**

Notes: The statistical data for Israel are supplied by and under the responsibility of the relevant Israeli authorities. The use of such data by the OECD is without prejudice to the status of the Golan Heights, East Jerusalem and Israeli settlements in the West Bank under the terms of international law. * Includes only subnational government with general competencies. **Netherlands: 403 municipalities as of 1 January 2014. *** The regional level in Portugal includes only two overseas regions: Madeira and Azores.

Source: OECD (2016a), *Subnational governments in OECD countries: Key data* (brochure), OECD, Paris, www.oecd.org/regional/regional-policy/.

Jordan's political, historical and geographic reality (described in Chapter 1) shows it to be a unitary state with a tradition of strong central power. Its administrative culture and background are very close to some OECD countries, such as France and Hungary, where the power is mainly concentrated at the central level, but a meaningful presence on the ground is ensured through prefects or governors and deconcentrated agencies from line ministries. The institutional organisation in OECD countries varies widely across member countries, with a vast majority being unitary states as shown in Table 2.3.

Table 2.3. Institutional organisation in the OECD, and number of subnational layers

	8 countries with only one level Municipalities		18 countries with two levels States/Regions Municipalities		8 countries with three levels States/Regions Intermediary governments Municipalities
9 federations and quasi-federations			Australia Austria Canada Mexico Switzerland		Germany Belgium Spain* United States
25 unitary countries	Estonia Finland* Ireland Island	Israel Luxemburg Portugal* Slovenia	Chile Korea Denmark Greece Hungary Japan Norway	New Zealand Netherlands Czech Republic Slovak Republic Sweden Turkey	France Italy Poland United Kingdom*

Note: * Spain is a quasi-federal country. Finland and Portugal have part of autonomous regions in part of the country. There is an intermediate level in United Kingdom.

Source: OECD (2016b), OECD Regional statistics, OECD, Paris, http://dx.doi.org/10.1787/region-data-en.

Middle East and North African (MENA) countries have a similar structure with regional and local level units. Although there are significant differences among big countries, such as Egypt and Algeria, and smaller countries, such as Jordan or Tunisia (Box 2.2).

Box 2.2. Territorial organisations in selected MENA Countries/Territories

Territories/ countries	Population, 2014, in millions	Regional level	Provincial Level	Local level
Algeria	39.9		48 provinces/wilayas, 160 districts/ constituencies (da'iras)	1,541 municipalities (communes)
Egypt	83.4		26 governorates, each divided into districts	217 towns + Luxor (with special status)
Jordan	7.5		12 governorates	100 municipalities
Lebanon	5		6 governorates (muhafazat), each (except Beirut) divided into districts (aqdaya)	930 municipalities and villages
Libya	6.3			
Morocco	33.5	12 regions	provinces and prefectures	municipalities
Palestinian Authority	4.4		14 governorates, 2 autonomous provinces	74 municipalities, 368 villages councils
Syria	22		14 departments	107 cities, 248 small cities, 207 villages
Tunisia	11.1		24 governorates (wilayat), each divided into districts	350 municipalities

Note: Western Sahara excluded.

Source: Author based on Bergh (2010) and GOLD REPORT 2010, UCLG country profiles, Population data from UNDP Human Development Report 2015; Journal Officiel de la République Tunisienne (2016) "Décret gouvernemental", www.legislation.tn/sites/default/files/news/tf20166003.pdf.

Although all MENA countries are unitary, territorial realities help to understand the different models and processes that each country is implementing to bring policies and public services closer to citizens. The next section of this chapter will provide a definition of decentralisation, stressing its differences with other models, such as deconcentration. This will be followed by an assessment of the evolution and current status of the decentralisation reform that Jordan under King Abdullah II, and his ambition to modernise Jordan while answering to citizens' needs for greater participation.

Decentralisation reform in Jordan

Defining decentralisation

Decentralisation is a complex and heterogeneous process. Decentralisation processes across the world have adopted a wide variety of forms, from the high level of decentralisation of certain federal states, such as Germany and some Spanish regions, to the more limited influence of regions in France or Hungary. Consequently, looking for a minimum common denominator is not a simple task.

The OECD broadly defines "decentralisation" (or devolution) as comprising a transfer of "public functions from higher tiers to lower tiers of governance. It can be administrative (transfer of civil servants and public functions to the local level), fiscal (devolution of fiscal resources and revenue generating powers), political (devolution of decision-making powers) or a mixture of these" (OECD, 2005). As such, the concept of decentralisation is often perceived in hierarchical terms, involving the top-down/vertical movement of administrative, fiscal and/or political/decision-making functions. Such functional movement can be intra-organisational (e.g. within government departments) or inter-organisational (e.g. from central to local administration).

For many years, international organisations like World Bank or UNDP have promoted decentralisation as a model to support policies closer to citizens. Decentralisation is directly linked to the principle of subsidiarity defined in article 5 of the Treaty on European Union[5] and the Council of Europe (with the European Chart of Local Self-Government)[6]. The rationale is based on the need to transfer competencies and responsibilities to authorities closer to citizens so as to be more adapted to the local reality and their specific needs. This implies a certain degree of autonomy to adapt to local realities but always complying with national laws and guidelines. Different degrees of autonomy at subnational level can bring to different models of decentralisation, as mentioned earlier, that can go from a complete devolution from the top to the bottom to transfer of some competences to a lower level.

Promoting decentralisation also brings the opportunity to enhance local governance, citizen participation and local democracy. Interaction between the State and civil society is essential and often easier to be created at local than at central level. Decentralised governments can become key actors to promote an active and vibrant civil society; in fact a greater degree of decentralisation can generate more opportunities for the emergence of new civil society organisations.

Box 2.3 details the different dimensions of decentralisation, and the differences between decentralisation, deconcentration and delegation of powers.

Box 2.3. Theoretic approach to decentralisation

Decentralisation: the transfer of responsibility to democratically independent lower levels of government, thereby giving them more managerial discretion, but not necessarily more financial independence. It usually includes:

- **Political decentralisation** refers to a situation in which political power is moved either to regional or local bodies that are elected, or to administrative actors who are appointed and supervised by elected bodies. Political decentralisation requires effective constitutional, legal, and regulatory frameworks to ensure accountability and transparency.
- **Fiscal decentralisation** is the most comprehensive form of decentralisation as it is directly linked to budgetary practices. It involves resource reallocation to subnational authorities. Fiscal decentralisation touches upon all forms of decentralisation; reallocating responsibilities without assigning sufficient levels of resources to the newly empowered units will not result in effective decentralisation.
- **Administrative decentralisation** aims to transfer the position of the decision-making authority and responsibility for the delivery of select public services from the central government to other levels of government or agencies.

Box 2.3. Theoretic approach to decentralisation *(cont.)*

Devolution is the moving of political power from the top to the bottom. It involves a permanent – legal or constitutional – transfer of responsibility, decision making, resources and revenues from a higher level of government to a lower, local level that enjoys substantial autonomy from the decentralising authority. In terms of education decentralisation, devolution transfers responsibility for education to lower levels of government, such as governorates, municipalities, or districts.

Deconcentration transfers decision-making authority – often by administrative decree – from a higher to a lower level of bureaucracy within the same level of government. The same hierarchical accountability is maintained between local units and the central government ministry or agency that has been decentralised. Deconcentration is often the first step undertaken by newly decentralised governments to improve service delivery, that is, the transfer of responsibility from central ministries to field offices or more autonomous agencies, thereby becoming closer to citizens while remaining part of central government.

Delegation assigns – usually by administrative decree – decision-making authority for specifically defined functions to local units of government or agencies that are not necessarily branches or local offices of the decentralising authority. In terms of education decentralisation, responsibility is transferred to elected or appointed education governance bodies, such as school councils or school management.

Sources: OECD (2005), "Decentralisation and Poverty Reduction: from Lessons Learned to Policy Action", Workshop OECD Development Centre and the OECD Development Assistance, Committee Network on Governance, OECD, Paris; OECD (2003), Managing Decentralisation: A New Role for Labour Market Policy, OECD Publishing, Paris, http://dx.doi.org/10.1787/9789264104716-en.

Under appropriate conditions, all of these forms of decentralisation and deconcentration can play important roles in broadening participation in political, economic and social activities in countries. Thus, decentralisation is not an end in itself, but is rather conceived to be "designed and evaluated for its ability to achieve broader objectives of […] equity, efficiency, quality and financial soundness" (Bossert, 1998). When the decentralisation process starts, the medium and long-term objectives to be achieved are at the heart of the reform.

The differences between federal and unitary systems might appear to be clear and well defined. However, a closer look at the practices reveals that even within each category there are numerous variations. In OECD countries, the unitary state model is the most common form of organisation, as previously shown in table 2.3.

Advantages and cost limitations of decentralisation

Decentralisation has advantages in two main areas: on the one hand, it is supposed to produce a reduction of administrative transaction costs and, on the other, to increase the proximity of decision-making, hence creating a more dynamic interaction with citizens. As for the former, a local administrations allows public and elected officials to be closer to the demands and needs of citizens and businesses, which gives them a greater capacity to react to them directly, without co-ordinating with intermediary and central institutions.

The second element is the greater interaction with citizens due to the proximity of decentralized institutions to their constituencies. Local government allows for a more direct and dynamic active interaction with citizens and can better take into account the political, cultural, ethnic and religious factors that are specific of their local communities. This interaction also implies more opportunities for consultation and participation of civil society in public affairs. This also improves public sector accountability as it enables citizens and CSOs to better supervise and monitor the use of public funds.

However, decentralisation is not a magic formula since it requires important efforts of co-ordination in the transfer of competences and also in assessing the performance and efficiency of management and delivery of public services by the lower levels. Giving more powers and resources to subnational governments will also be costly at least at the beginning when human and financial resources will be needed to ensure services are effectively and efficiently delivered by the new authorities. In fact, the lack of appropriate skills and capacities at the subnational level is known to be one of the main obstacles to successful decentralisation reforms.

Giving more competences at the subnational level can also entail risks on performance and accountability of the new authorities who will decide on how resources are to be used. This may also generate corruption from local elites if rigorous mechanisms of supervision are not put in place.

As stated before, there's not an optimal model of decentralisation. It's not an either-or choice[7]. For instance in different State models like Italy and Spain, subnational governments are kept under a tight financial discipline as enshrined in their Constitution. Governments must create or maintain the "enabling conditions" that allow local levels to take on more responsibilities when resources are available (see Chapter 3). (World Bank, n.d.).

Decentralisation is influenced by a country's size, population, political and institutional inheritance and diversity. These attributes have an important impact on the design and modalities of decentralisation, which are crucial for its success. The appropriateness of functions to be decentralised, adequacy of fiscal resources to be transferred to the subnational governments, effectiveness of administrative and legal set-ups, and sufficiency of technical/skilled personnel at all levels of government are important ingredients for a successful reform. The next section will provide a historic overview of Jordan's model and its evolution.

A historical overview of the decentralisation process in Jordan

Efforts to transfer competencies from the central level to lower tiers is a relatively recent process in Jordan, and has gone through several stop and go phases during the 2000s (see Chapter 1). Jordan has a long tradition of centralised power with limited scope of action to lower levels of governments.

The Constitution approved in 1952 only stipulates that municipal and local affairs are to be run by municipal or local councils. The details have been left to the Municipalities Law and other relevant laws. Governorates are part of the MoI, and their regulation is referred to in bylaws and the Administrative Divisions Law of 2000, where the 12 governorates are consolidated as administrative and deconcentrated administrations.

Municipalities were established by law three years after the Constitution was approved and were included in the 1955 Law on Municipalities. As outlined in Chapter 1, there were four categories of municipalities including the governorate centres, the district and caza centres and a fourth category for all other municipalities. The 1955 Municipal Law was inspired by the British system that gives wide responsibilities to mayors, but they have being declining in number progressively (Ababsa, 2016). In practice, the central government currently provides all basic services: water, electricity, gas, sewerage, primary education, healthcare, civil defence, public transport, housing and environment.

Municipalities are now only responsible for urban planning, waste collection, road maintenance and lighting, markets and building permits. They still have limited political power and few budgetary resources.

In the 1990s, the Ministry of Municipal and Rural Affairs created new administrative bodies in Jordanian municipalities aimed at promoting local development: the Local Development Units (further details in Chapter 3). They promoted forum and discussion with local communities on economic development and investment projects, however they had little impact due to the lack of competencies of municipal authorities (Government of Jordan, 2016b).

In parallel, during 1994-96, and under the auspices of international donors (mainly the United Nations Development Programme, UNDP, and the World Bank), 328 municipalities and 324 village councils were merged. In 2001, the number of municipalities was reduced to 99, and all village councils were dissolved and Amman, as the capital-city and surrounding communities were gathered in 1987 to form the Greater Amman Municipality (GAM). The considerable amalgamation of municipalities was intended to solve the problem of insolvency by cutting down on municipal staff while promoting greater citizen participation. It also forced minor tribes to create new alliances to keep some control over municipalities covering their traditional terrains (Ababsa, 2016).

The latest and most important drive towards strengthening local government emerged between 2004 and 2005 when King Abdullah II announced a plan to provide greater autonomy to local institutions, emphasising that "political development should start at the grassroots level, and then move up to decision making centres and not vice versa".[8] The initiative prioritised three regions (Northern, Middle and Southern), which were to create their own indirectly elected assemblies and regional capitals. The intention was that each region should manage its own services and decide on a policy to encourage local development. Local authorities were to be given greater leeway in guiding the implementation of development programmes at the local level.

To help draft a concrete proposal for decentralisation, King Abdullah II appointed a Royal Commission in January 2005 to examine the decentralisation scheme and make recommendations for its implementation. However, the creation of regions was not pursued, partly because of a lack of political preparedness, but also due to a lack of inter-ministerial co-ordination.[9] In a new speech in October 2008, King Abdullah II called for more public participation at the governorate level, and local development programmes were transferred from the Ministry of Planning to the MoI. In November 2010, King Abdullah II promised Parliament a draft law on decentralisation, including the creation of Governorate Councils. A ministerial Committee on Decentralisation was created and included four subcommittees (Legal, Institutional Framework, Finance, and Capacity Building); however, once again the government failed to reach consensus regarding concrete steps for implementation.

In parallel to these attempts, a new Municipal Law was approved in 2007 where an important democratic component was introduced by the direct election of municipal councillors, except for the GAM. This law enabled, for the first time, fully-elected municipal councils (half of which were previously appointed) and reached outstanding participation from citizens in the following municipal elections where voter turnout reached 50%[10]. The percentage of local elected women also increased dramatically due to the 20% quota included in the law. The last modification of the Municipality Law was in

2011, where the quota for women was increased to 25% and the "developmental role" of municipalities was introduced, this was further developed in the 2015 Law.

During the Arab Spring, the debate on strengthening the local level and improving citizen participation came back to the public sphere with democratic aspirations of the Jordanian population. Giving competencies to local authorities to engage the private sector in fighting unemployment was deemed an important part of the strategy. The creation of jobs across the country in both rural and urban areas was also part of a critical need to slow the exodus towards the capital (Inform, 2015). In some MENA countries, such as Tunisia and Morocco, this led to constitutional amendments to reinforce the role of subnational governments as drivers of socio-economic development and local democracy (Box 2.4).

Box 2.4. Decentralisation trends in MENA countries: Morocco and Tunisia

Morocco and Tunisia are at the forefront of decentralisation reforms in Arab countries. After the Arab Spring, both countries have amended their Constitution acknowledging local democracy and citizen participation as a key aspect for good governance. In both countries, administrative systems and even electoral codes have been modified to engage in local democracy.

The amendments introduced in the Constitution of Morocco in 2011 following the Arab Spring assign new responsibilities to Moroccan local and regional authorities and put citizens at the heart of public policies and service delivery at the local level (Articles. 135-144). This is aligned and in parallel with the "advanced regionalisation" (*Regionalisation avancée*) launched in 2007. Regional and local elections took place in 2015 with gender quota.

In Tunisia, the 2014 Constitution devotes a whole chapter to the local level where territorial decentralisation, local autonomy and administration are conferred. This is also linked to the creation of an intermediate level between regions and municipalities, the departments and the adoption of new electoral rules for local governments to promote local democracy. A Local Governments Superior Council is also to be created. Local elections have been postponed on several occasions and are expected to take place in 2017.

Sources: Based on OECD (2017a), *Guide des bonnes pratiques en matière de gouvernance locale au Maroc*, Paris, forthcoming ; Constitution de la république tunisienne (2014), www.legislation.tn/sites/default/files/news/constitution-b-a-t.pdf.

In 2013, the King asked again the government and parliament to start working towards the drafting of a new decentralisation law. Four draft laws were debated and revised and despite significant opposition to specific clauses in the law, the laws on municipalities and decentralisation were finally endorsed by Parliament on 23 August 2015.

The decentralisation and municipalities Laws: A centralised system also at the subnational level

Engaging in a decentralisation reform is a complex process that needs a strong political commitment as well as a sound administrative machinery ready to implement it. When a decentralisation reform is envisaged, not only its objectives need to be clearly spelled out but also the legal framework to achieve them. The creation of a strong legal framework is a priority to ensure the proper utilisation of public resources. This legal framework should clearly explain the rationale of the reform, the objectives to be achieved together with a clear description of the competences at different levels with the necessary resources. This should be accompanied with financial mechanisms to follow-up and evaluate the performance. This part is particularly relevant at the first stage of the process when the implementation of the new legal framework needs to be monitored and, if necessary, adjusted to the reality on the ground.

The Decentralisation Law (DL) and Municipality Law (ML) are the most significant step towards realising King Abdullah's vision of a political development process towards a better functioning democratic Jordan, which should starts at the grassroots level and moves up to higher decision-making centres (Inform, 2015). The reform takes places at a time when Jordan prepared its third National Action Plan for the Open Government Partnership, which highlights a new momentum for fostering the emergence of a culture of open, transparent, inclusive and accountable governance across the different layers of government.

The government of Jordan bases this reform on four pillars:

- Promoting citizen participation in decision making for democratic development.
- Promoting sustainable local development and equal distribution of benefits.
- Improving the efficiency and effectiveness of local administration and municipalities in providing services.
- Improving efficiency in planning and preparing local budgets.

While these pillars, for the first time, introduce important democratic components in the governorate and municipal levels, by creating elected local councils, they do not yet foresee the transfer of competencies and resources as core elements of the reform. Achieving these objectives would require a major and welcomed cultural change in the public administration in Jordan, however if the rationale of such reform remains clear, the means and tools to achieve it still need to be fully established. These ambitious goals need to fit into the core and yet scarce articles dedicated to governorates and municipal structural reform in both laws. The articles dedicated to administrations, structure, functions, funds and multilevel co-ordination barely represent 25% of the provisions of the DL (12 articles out of 47) and 41% of the ML (32 of 77 articles). The rest of the provisions of both laws are dedicated to electoral procedures. This implies that the laws are quite wide and just give the guiding principles, but that the concrete details for their implementation and their implications will have to be further developed by by-laws. At the time this report was written[11], only two by-laws from MoI on organisational structures had been approved. This could hamper and slow down implementation, as it will require more legislation to be approved by the national competent authorities.

According to interviews with government senior officials, the DL was originally conceived as a by-law of the Ministry of Interior (MoI) to rearrange the functioning and administrative competences of governorates. However, after intense internal debates, the Cabinet Office agreed to upgrade it to the rank of law.[12] Previous governorate regulations are MoI by-laws regulating the administrative functioning of governorates (number 46 and 47 from the year 2000). The rationale is to reinforce the relevance and importance of the reform and bring a more democratic dimension to the governorates, a deconcentrated administration strictly linked to MoI authority.

These two laws constitute the foundation for a legal framework aimed at promoting citizen participation and bringing policies closer to citizens. Other OECD countries have also engaged in recent reforms aimed at transferring more powers to the regional level to solve regional disparities and promote regional development by bringing public services and policies closer to citizens' needs (Table 2.4).

Table 2.4. Regionalisation trends in OECD countries

Types of regionalisation	Key characteristics	Country experiences
Creation of a new directly elected regional level. Czech Republic, Denmark, France, Italy, Spain, Poland, two Swedish regions since the late 1990s.	Clear competencies and accountability mechanisms regarding citizens	In **Italy**, regional reforms have taken place in several waves, from the early 1970s to the 2000s ("Bassanini" reforms). They are characterised by a broad allocation of competencies to regions, with the possibility to design differentiated autonomy for regions with an ordinary statute. In 2001, a constitutional reform markedly widened the competences of the regions, in particular concerning legislative powers, and abolished most state controls. In **Denmark**, a general reform of subnational authorities was carried out in 2007. The number of municipalities was reduced from 271 to 99. At the same time, five new regions replaced 14 former counties. The main objective of the reform was to produce efficiency gains based on economies of scale and to offer better and more specialised public services. Regions do not have many instruments to encourage municipalities to co-operate in implementing a vision for the region. It remains to be seen whether regions have enough sticks and carrots to encourage municipalities in their region to help implement the regional visions. In **France**, regions were created in 1982 with a specific focus on regional growth issues. The last reform was in 2014, which merged the regions from 22 to 13, and encouraged the creation of metropolitan areas (see Annex 1 of this report). The map of the new regions took effect on 1 January 2016. In **Poland**, regions were created in 1999 with the mandate to manage part of European Union funding and to elaborate regional development programmes.
Creation of a deconcentrated regional level, not elected. Greece, Ireland, Portugal, United Kingdom, Sweden to some extent since 1989.	Responsibilities to enhance co-ordination in specific areas across the national government and local authorities.	The **United Kingdom** has developed a hybrid structure that is based on a Regional Development Agency (RDA), set up and funded by the national government and overseen by a board of directors from the region and led by the private sector; and a regional Assembly, comprised of about 100 people from local government, academic institutions, business and voluntary organisations.
Creation of functional regions, with spatial planning functions. Korea.	Focuses mainly on spatial planning issues; has not led to the creation of a new layer of government.	In **Korea**, there is a strong regionalisation trend, but it focuses mainly on spatial planning issues and has not led to the creation of a new layer of government. In 2008, the Korean government announced the "five area-wide economic blocs" which divide the whole territory into five sub-economic blocs (except for two regions, the mountainous northeast area and Jeju Island). Each of these regions, with a population of more than five million, covers two or three provinces (or provincial cities) that share a similar historic, economic and social context. In order to guide co-operation among provinces in the same bloc, an autonomous regional headquarters, rather than a permanent supra-province body, will be installed in each region. This autonomous organisation will create a regional development plan for each bloc and promote horizontal co-operation among local governments in general.

Source: Author based on OECD (2010), *OECD Territorial Reviews: Sweden 2010*, OECD Publishing, Paris, http://dx.doi.org/10.1787/9789264081888-en.

One of the defining characteristics of this reform is the setting up of a legal framework into two laws: the Decentralisation Law, dedicated to the governorate level, and the Municipalities Law, dedicated to the municipal and district level. These will be assessed in the following sections.

The new role of the governorates

Governorates have long been the administrative and deconcentrated arm of the central government, headed by a governor and appointed by the Prime Minister. This is why some still consider Jordan as a one-tier of subnational government, as governorates are considered part of the central government and not another layer (UCLG, 2016). While the new decentralisation law introduces an elected council at the governorate level with increased competencies, in particular on strategic planning and promotion of socio-economic development, it still remains to be seen whether governorates are to get real autonomy from the central government.

The governorate is an administrative unit directly attached to the MoI,[13] which employs the personnel of the governorate and determines and allocates their budget. All ministries and agencies of public services (except the Ministries of Defence and Foreign Affairs) have departments or regional offices in the governorates.

Each governorate is managed by a Governor (*Mouhafiz*) who is designated by the Council of Ministers based on the recommendation of the Minister of the Interior, who may also have delegated duties directly from the Cabinet Office. Governors are responsible for maintaining public order and also have the roles of leading and supervising the work of government departments in the governorate and co-ordinate with the municipalities within its geographical boundaries (article 3 of DL). This figure is common in many OECD unitary countries such as the *Intendente* in Chile or the *Préfet* in France (Box 2.5).

Box 2.5. Role of the "Préfet" in France

Regional prefects (*préfets de région*) in France have become the linchpins for central government action in a region, and are responsible for co-ordinating the departments grouped around them and overseeing the coherence of the measures adopted in their territory. A prefect must also lead the dialogue and negotiations with elected bodies and their officers. They are appointed in the Council of Ministers by a Presidential Decree on the Prime Minister and Minister of Interior's recommendation.

French prefects are thus one response to a problem encountered in a large number of OECD countries – that of the inter-ministerial co-ordination of regional policies. They also exercise a vertical co-ordination function, not only between the various local players, but also between those players and the central government. However, while offering an undisputed advantage in terms of regional policy coherence, new reforms have increased the powers of the prefect in the regions.

Prefects in France and governors in Jordan have very similar roles in the implementation of the state's public policy, and the co-ordination between public institutions. However, this task appears more of a challenge in Jordan as deconcentrated units of line ministries depend on the governors, whereas some reforms in France – the "Charter of deconcentration" in 1992, renewed in 2015, and the "General Revue of Public Policies" (RGPP in French) – made it mandatory for local services of the sectorial ministries to obey the prefect's co-ordination. Although it is still difficult to break silos in France, and some ministries (such as Justice and Education) escape the authority of the prefect.

Box 2.5. Role of the "Préfet" in France *(cont.)*

The role of the regional Prefect has been reinforced with the latest deconcentration reform (Decree of 16 February 2010) and now plays a predominant role in reinforcing most national policies at regional level, except matters of safety and security, which are still managed at the department level. They also supervise and co-ordinate the department prefects.

Source: OECD (2012), OECD Public Governance Reviews: France: An international perspective on the General Review of Public Policies, OECD Public Governance Reviews, OECD Publishing, http://dx.doi.org/10.1787/9789264167612-en.

An innovation of the Decentralisation Law is the setting up of two councils in each governorate (Figure 2.2):

- The **governorate council**: a new elected body (with 85% elected and 15% appointed by the central government) approves the proposals of the Executive Council.
- The **executive council**: the existing board unit headed by the Governor (also appointed) and composed of representatives of the directorates (deconcentrated agencies from central government).

The governorate council introduces a democratic component at the highest level of the governorate administration in order to get closer to citizen's needs. However, the Law still limits the scope of its functions to approving draft key documents prepared by the executive Council, such as the strategic plans, governorate budget and governorates' need guide but with limited capacity to propose new initiatives except for investment projects and participating in joint projects with other governorates that will anyway require the validation from "the relevant bodies" (article 8 DL) of the central government. The DL also states that upon the recommendation of the MoI, the Cabinet will appoint a maximum of 15% of its members. For the time being, the criteria for choosing this 15% is yet to be clarified.

The governorate council enjoys a legal element with financial and administrative independence. In addition, while the governorate council is responsible for reviewing and approving proposals of the executive council, the final decision would not be placed in their hands in case of conflict, instead the final decision will be submitted to the Prime Minister. Along the same line, the law provides a system for conflict resolution where the elected body and the executive are at the same level of discussion in case of disagreement. The creation of the governorate councils will therefore introduce an unprecedented level of popular control and influence on which Jordan will have to build to make them more powerful and fully autonomous, in line with OECD good practices. The synergies and institutional arrangements to combine this elected body with the technical approach of the executive council will be a challenge especially as the funds remain at the central level and will need to be set in a very clear way to make them a fundamental piece of the decision-making process of the governorate.

Figure 2.2. New governorate structure

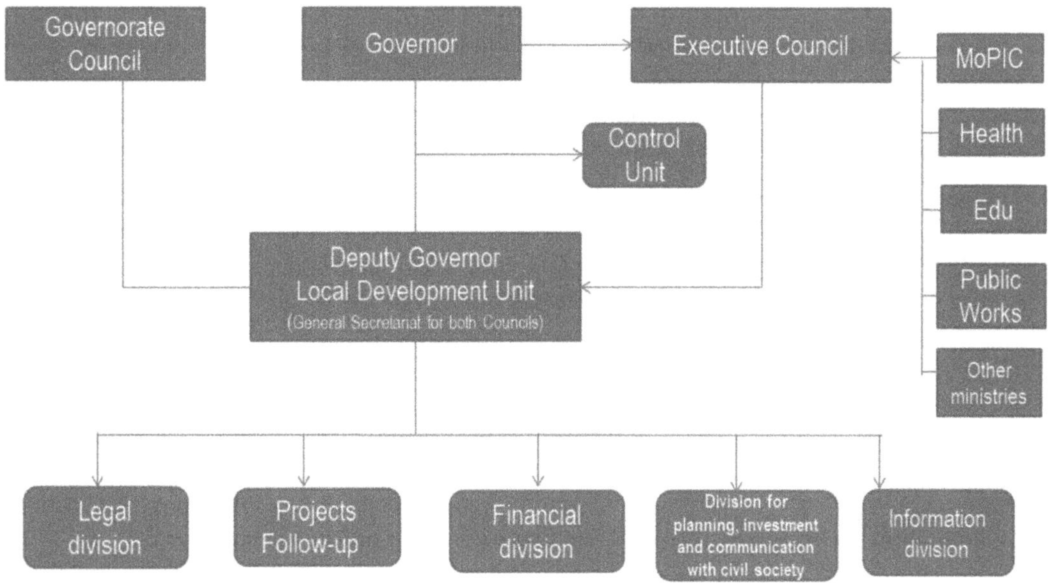

Source: Author based on Government of Jordan (2016a), Background report of the OECD Strategic Assessment of Jordan, unpublished working paper.

The executive council is in charge of the key programmes and initiatives of the governorate by preparing strategic and executive projects, the governorate budget (based on the sum allocated by the Ministry of Finance after proposal from the MoI), a yearly manual on the governorate and its municipalities' needs, as well as co-ordinating with municipalities and reviewing their strategies. It also takes decisions to address public issues in governorates, especially regarding public services (Article 5, DL). As shown in Figure 2.2, the duties of the executive council are fed from the line ministries present at the governorate level through to regional directors (mainly the Ministries of Planning and International Co-operation [MoPIC], Health, Education, Social affairs and Public Works), and with the Local Development Unit (LDU), which acts as the General Secretariat for both Councils.

The LDU occupies a key position at the heart of the administrative structure of the governorate. It holds the secretariat of both executive and governorate councils and reports directly to the Governor, head of the governorate (this figure will be further developed in Chapter 3).

The new regulation with the DL and ML is expected to contribute to enhancing co-ordination among the different bodies, however, the co-existence of different technical bodies with a hierarchical relation, from the LDU at the bottom, to the Manager, the technical official in charge of supervising the Development units and the Executive Council, and to the Governor and the Elected Council at the top is far from a simple organisational chart. Governorates will have to make a diagnosis and assessment to make the best of each part of the process and avoid overlapping and red tape.

This new administrative structure at the governorate level may generate some opacity in terms of responsibility and accountability. The coexisting mandate of the governor, who will be both a representative of the State and head of the Executive Council, may generate a problem of divided loyalty (to the central government and to the governorate) that could undermine the process of building place-based agendas. In fact, as the head of governorate, the governor will work on developing the territory from the local level perspective, while as the head of the Executive Council, he/she will be responsible for implementing national policies and guidelines. In most governorates, as a consequence of the centralised culture of the country and the predominant presence of line ministries, the deconcentrated hat that is under the authority of central government may prevail when implementing central mandates in the governorate against the new bottom-up approach.

One of the effects of the Decentralisation Law is to upgrade the level of legislation that rules governorates, whose functioning used to be under MoI decree (the latest was from 2000). However, the new framework does not foresee a transfer of competencies or functions from the central level, the executive council or the governor to the new elected body (i.e. the governorate council). Hence, governorate authorities will continue acting on the central government's behalf, with the governorate council performing limited democratic control and input provision functions. Although a democratic component has been introduced with the governorate council, this reform at the governorate level cannot be considered as decentralisation according to the OECD definition. The ambitious reform engaged by the Government of Jordan appears to set the goal of decentralisation as a medium-term objective, of which the first steps have just been established.

The municipalities in the reform

Municipalities are the lowest and one of the oldest administrative structures at the local level, together with the no longer existing villages.[14] As described earlier in this chapter, they were first regulated in 1955 and amended on several occasions (1988, 2001, 2007 and 2015).

Jordanian municipalities enjoy legal and financial autonomy since 1955 where key competencies are already described. They essentially include the traditional competences related to local governments[15] such as the provision of urban services (water, electricity, sewage) as well as town-planning and maintenance of road and public spaces, hygiene, public health (slaughter houses, prevent risks and epidemics) and public safety (prevention of fires, civil defence) and support on education, cultural and sports activities, assistance of fires.[16]

Municipalities are subject to supervision by the Ministry of Municipal Affairs (MoMA) on the legal and administrative side and on the financial oversight and guidance (further developed in chapter 3). However, many provisions of Municipalities Law (ML) limit the authority and autonomy of the municipalities and establish the basis for a relationship of dependence and subordination to the state. For instance, despite the theoretically large range of fields and competences previously mentioned, the functions and responsibilities attributed to the municipalities, except for urban planning (which is made in close co-operation with MoMA), are delegated or "deconcentrated" services from central government to deconcentrated agencies, or are responsibilities for the execution of work and services. An important part of the functions and services regulated by the law concern the responsibility of the various deconcentrated government departments or companies of public services represented in the municipal administration.[17]

The municipalities are neither involved nor consulted in the provision, and even less, in the design of the services related to these fields (Ababsa, 2016). In fact, municipalities currently don't have the power for policy making and decision making concerning the sphere of activities in which these services fit. They do not have the political autonomy to build local policy in response to specific local needs or a general local development strategy. The new bottom-up approach will bring the opportunity to change this dynamic. It is significant that social action, a traditional local competence that municipalities usually pay attention to (one of the closes policies to answer to basics citizens' needs) is only evoked by the law for assisting victims of fires and natural disasters.

While municipal competencies often seem to be under the supervision of MoMA, as well as other line ministries, the ML adds a new competency related to contributing to national development. This means that the local council will contribute to preparing the strategic and developmental plans and the "needs' guide" within its boundaries in co-operation with civil society organisations, and will submit them to the Municipal Council. The Municipal Council will prepare strategic and developmental plans for the whole municipality, as well as the municipal area needs' guide, and will submit them to the Executive Council at the governorate level. The co-ordination mechanisms to elaborate these plans remain unclear, as do the common criteria. However, the new bottom-up approach to the design of the national development plan, co-ordinated by MoPIC, can be the basis for more decentralised arrangements. In this context, citizen consultation mechanisms could be envisaged in a coherent manner to ensure a common approach (see Chapter 3).

Local administrations have the potential to develop other competences to provide concrete answers to local needs. In this sense, municipalities in OECD countries not only provide basic public services and strategic planning, but have also promoted innovation and local economic development to fight against unemployment. In some cases, such as Ireland, decentralisation reform has focused on clustering and promoting local economic development through a participatory approach (Box 2.6).

Box 2.6. "Putting people first - Action programme for effective and local government": Irish reform of local government

Putting people first - Action programme for effective local government set out reforms to improve:

- The delivery of services for the citizen.
- Deliver greater efficiency and effectiveness.
- Give local government a more central role in local development and community development.

It represents a significant change in government policy in relation to local government for the purposes of placing local government as the main vehicle of governance and public service at the local level; leading economic, social and community development, delivering efficient and good value services, and representing citizens and local communities effectively and accountably.

The Local Government Reform Act 2014, enacted on 27 January 2014, gives legislative effect to the commitments in "Putting People First" including the establishment of Local Community Development Committees (LCDCs) in each local authority administrative area.

LCDCs have now been established on a statutory basis in all 31 local authorities for the purpose of bringing a more co-ordinated and joined-up approach to local/community development at the local level. Membership includes local authority elected members and officials; State and non-State local development agencies; community and voluntary organisations; and other representatives of civil society, including business interests and farming interests.

Source: Government of Ireland (2012), *Putting people first: Action programme for effective local government*, www.housing.gov.ie/sites/default/files/publications/files/putting_people_first.pdf.

Municipalities will be managed by a municipal council, composed of a mayor, an undetermined number of members representing heads of local councils and an undetermined number of members of local councils who won the highest number of votes, except for Aqaba Special Economic Zone Authority (ASEZA) and Petra Tourism Developmental Authority (Article 3, ML). The creation of an elected body at the district level that is below municipalities called "local councils" within the boundaries of the municipality is one of the most relevant new aspects of the new law.

For the creation of local councils, a decree by the Minister of Municipality Affairs will determine the boundaries of the local council and the number of its elected members (at least five) that will be elected by popular vote.

Where local councils are created (everywhere except from GAM and Aqaba), the current directly elected municipal councils will be transformed into indirectly elected bodies. The Minister may, with the approval of the Cabinet, appoint two additional members in each Municipal Council who enjoy the same rights of elected members (Article 69, ML). The Greater Municipality of Amman presents an exception, as 25% of the council members and the Mayor are appointed.

The creation of local councils can contribute to come closer to people especially where the headquarters of the municipality are far away (like in the bigger cities or in remote areas). Yet, it can also contribute to a potential fragmentation of the political power by creating new structures at the sub-municipal level. In practice, this could also have a counter-productive effect after the major streamlining reform that Jordan undertook early 2000s by reducing the number of municipalities (from 328 municipalities and 324 village councils to 99 municipalities) and removing the villages. Jordan should pay attention on the effectiveness and real synergies between the municipal and local councils to make the most of both institutions.

In line with the King's vision of a grassroots approach to the national development process, elected local councils are tasked with proposing development projects and contributing to the preparation of strategic and development plans based on the identification of needs in co-operation with civil society organisations (Article 6, ML). Their work is then submitted to the municipal council. Figure 2.3 describes the organisational chart of Jordanian municipalities and local councils under the 2015 Municipalities Law.

Figure 2.3. Organisational chart of the municipality and local councils under the 2015 ML

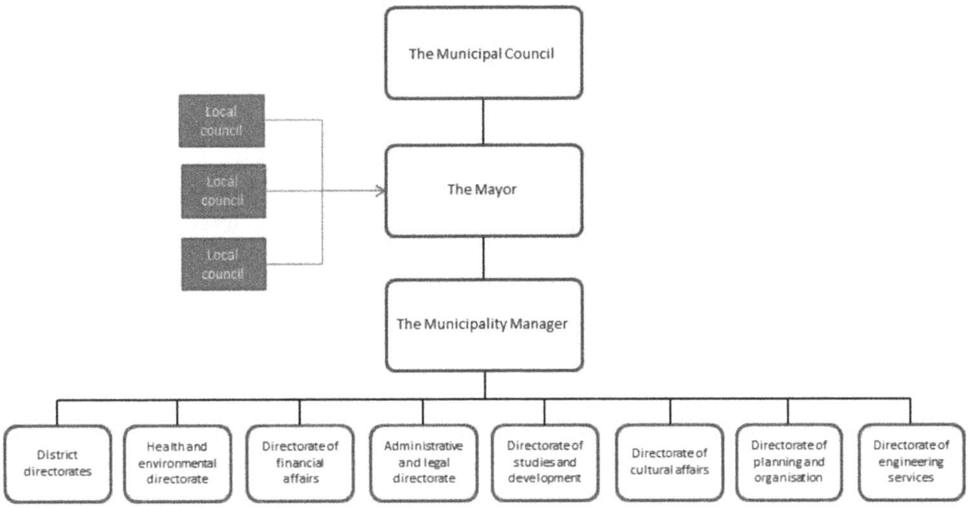

Source: Government of Jordan (2016a), Background report of the OECD Strategic Assessment of Jordan, unpublished working paper.

As mentioned earlier in this chapter, an important new aspect introduced by the law is a gender quota: 25% of municipal council seats are reserved for women (further explored in Chapter 4). This is an important step as the inclusion of women in representative bodies is still a challenge in the country (Box 2.7).

Box 2.7. Remaining barriers to women's participation in representative bodies in Jordan

Women's participation in representative bodies in Jordan has improved, yet it remains limited. Jordan introduced a quota system for the 2003 elections, which remains crucial to women's representation in the House of Representatives. In 2012, the number of seats reserved for women was raised from 6 to 15 seats out of 150. In the September 2016 elections, 5 additional women won in elections outside the quota, making women's representation in the Parliament 15%, compared to 12% in 2013.

On the municipal level, the quota grants women a share of 25% of seats in municipal councils, and the latest elections in 2013 witnessed a significant increase in female representation, from 28% to 36%.

Although there has been an overall improvement, a number of factors still seriously hinder Jordanian women's ability to fully participate in representative bodies on both national and local level. Based on the 2015 OECD Recommendation on Gender Equality in Public Life, the OECD supports Jordan in the framework of the MENA Transition Fund project "Towards inclusive and open governments: Promoting women's participation in parliaments and policy-making" and identified key obstacles for women's participation in national and local elections:

Box 2.7. Remaining barriers to women's participation in representative bodies in Jordan *(cont.)*

Enduring traditional power structures within political parties:

Despite the multiplicity of Jordanian parties and their various agendas, there is limited presence of women, in particular in leadership positions. Most parties do not include non-discriminatory articles or positive discrimination measures within their constitutions. While overall capacities to attract new members at the grassroots level are weak, a lack of gender sensitive outreach channels particularly hinder women's participation. Moreover, parties are still reluctant to support female candidates, fearing that voters from tribal or rural areas will refrain from supporting them.

Pre-eminent traditional gender roles supported by tribal structures:

Tribes continue to constitute major political actors in Jordan and remain crucial in mobilising support for candidates during elections. Prevalent traditional understandings of "the tribal representative as a male identity" prefer men as political candidates, while an emphasis remains on women's roles in the private sphere.

Barriers to achieving economic independence:

Economic independence is a prerequisite for political engagement. Women's economic participation in Jordan remains among the lowest in the Middle East region. Particularly in rural areas, women have limited access to sources of income, microfinance opportunities, loans and also limited access to even justice. In addition, traditional social constraints prevent women from enjoying their rights in ownership and inheritance. Mobility challenges, including both the absence of safe, inexpensive public transportation between Jordan's cities, further limit women's economic and political opportunities.

Lack of political experience in public life:

The historical weakness of female political and public participation naturally translates into a lack of political and electoral experience. With no female role models in positions of influence, the trust of Jordan's society in women's ability in political work is limited. Women's clubs and associations, as well as women's sections of professional unions, have proven successful in strengthening women's political participation through training and support networks for candidates. However, the majority are Amman-based and elite-led, and consequently disconnected from women at the grassroots level and from outside the capital.

Source: Based on OECD Project on Gender and OECD (2015), "OECD Recommendation on Gender Equality in Public Life", www.oecd.org/gov/2015-oecd-recommendation-of-the-council-on-gender-equality-in-public-life-9789264252820-en.htm.

In conclusion, similarly to what is happening at the governorate level, the ML has introduced a democratic component to the municipal management through Municipal and Local Councils, which is an important step toward a more participatory and place-based governance in Jordan that should not be underestimated. However, the lack of clarity in the distribution of powers between local councils and municipality councils and governorates' councils may create the risk of adding complexity to the current system and overlaps in the distribution of responsibilities and powers between municipal, local councils and institutions of the central government. In addition, the setting up of the local councils as foreseen by the ML is creating strong expectations among civil society and the private sector that popular participation will increase. However, in light of the lack of a major transfer of actual competencies and powers to the local level, the label of "decentralisation reform" may be misleading. The engagement narrative provided by the Royal Court and the government may more adequately reflect the main intention of the reform, that is, to strengthen popular participation in the national planning and development process.

The current institutional arrangements established in both laws create a complex system that will require strong co-ordination mechanisms and clear definition of roles, mandates and deadlines for every step. Figure 2.4 shows a tentative outline of these arrangements according to the laws. The co-ordination mechanisms between the MoI and MoMA, either at the central or subnational level, remain unclear. There are many points of connection across the governorate and municipal level, especially on budget, strategic planning and governorate and local development units that would need common procedures and alignments that need to be settled from the beginning by both ministries.

Figure 2.4. Institutional arrangements at the governorate and municipal level

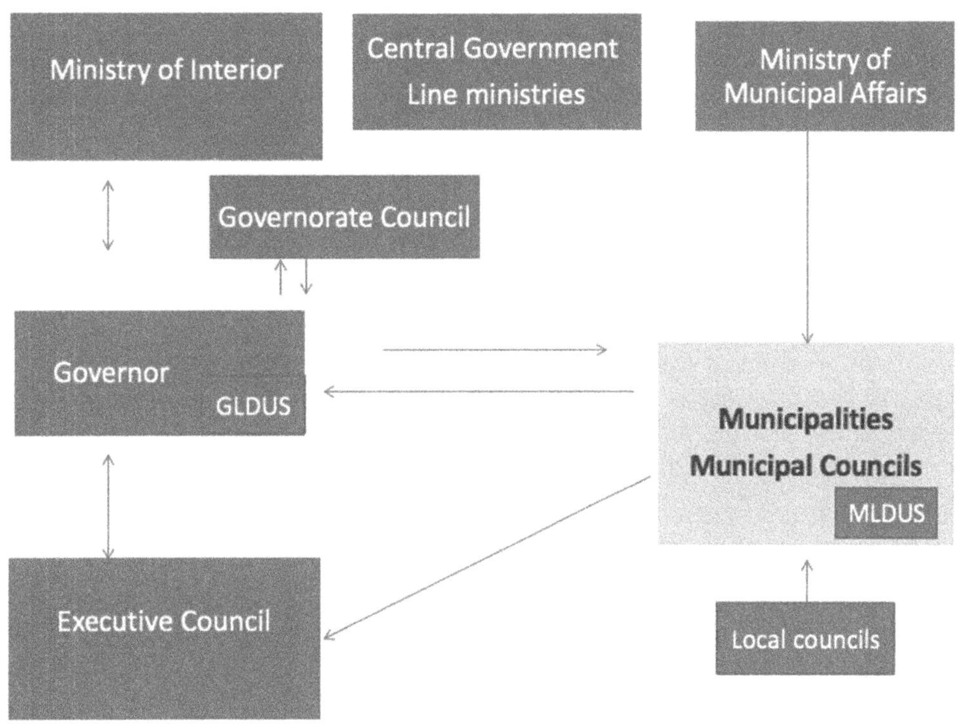

Source: Author's own work.

The role of the central government will be determinant in translating and putting into practice the Laws. A well-articulated implementation strategy requires a strong and well-defined Centre of Government leading the reform and marking the path towards the objectives set in consultation with key stakeholders.

Centre of government in Jordan

According to the traditional OECD definition, the Centre of government (CoG) is the body or group of bodies that provides direct support and advice to the head of government and the Council of Ministers. The CoG is known under different labels in different countries, such as the Chancellery, Cabinet Office, Office of the President, and Presidency of the Council of Ministers. From its traditional role of serving the executive from an administrative perspective, the CoG is now playing a more active role in policy development and co-ordination across OECD members. The centre in many countries now provides services that range from strategic planning to real-time policy advice and intelligence, and from leading major cross-departmental policy initiatives to monitoring progress and outcomes (OECD, 2014a).

More recently, OECD countries have widened the scope of the CoG that not only refers to the presidency or its equivalent but also includes ministries with a key and leading role in defining, implementing and follow-up strategic policies. This new definition integrates the Ministry of Finance (where policy priorities are matched with resources) and the Ministry of Planning, when it exists (with an important role in designing policy priorities across the administration and how these contribute to an overall strategic plan). In other cases, and depending on the institutional situation of a country, other ministries or key strategic organisations can also be considered as part of the CoG for their whole-of-government and cross-governmental co-ordination role. It can be the case of Ministries of Public Administration or governmental bodies in charge of Human resources Management, digital government or regulatory policy (OECD, 2015a).

After the analysis of the decentralisation reform and its challenges, this section examines the strength and agility of Jordan's centre of government institutions to lead the implementation of the government's national vision and plan for decentralisation across central government and with its subnational partners.

Centre of government in Jordan: The institutional set-up

According to the experience of OECD member countries, in the past, the functions of the centre of government were often limited to serving the executive on administrative matters. Today, the CoG is playing a much more active role in policy development involving other strategic stakeholders to ensure cross-government co-ordination and strategic foresight (OECD, 2015d).

The top four priority tasks of the CoG, as identified by the OECD Questionnaire on the Organisation and Functions of the Centre of Government (OECD, 2013), are:

- Supporting decision making by the head of government/cabinet, which in almost all countries involves blending dual streams of political and non-partisan advice.
- Policy co-ordination across government, which increasingly includes leading cross-departmental priority strategies.
- Monitoring progress with policy reform, which means developing new mechanisms that emphasise outcomes rather than just tracking expenditures.
- Strategic planning, which is being redefined post-crisis to be more closely aligned with policy development and resource allocation.

Other highly valued functions include handling government communications and its media strategy, managing relations with the legislative branch, and preparing and operationalising the government programme. The 2013 OECD questionnaire gives an overview of the centre's main responsibilities in OECD countries (see Figure 2.5).

Figure 2.5. Centre of government's main responsibilities

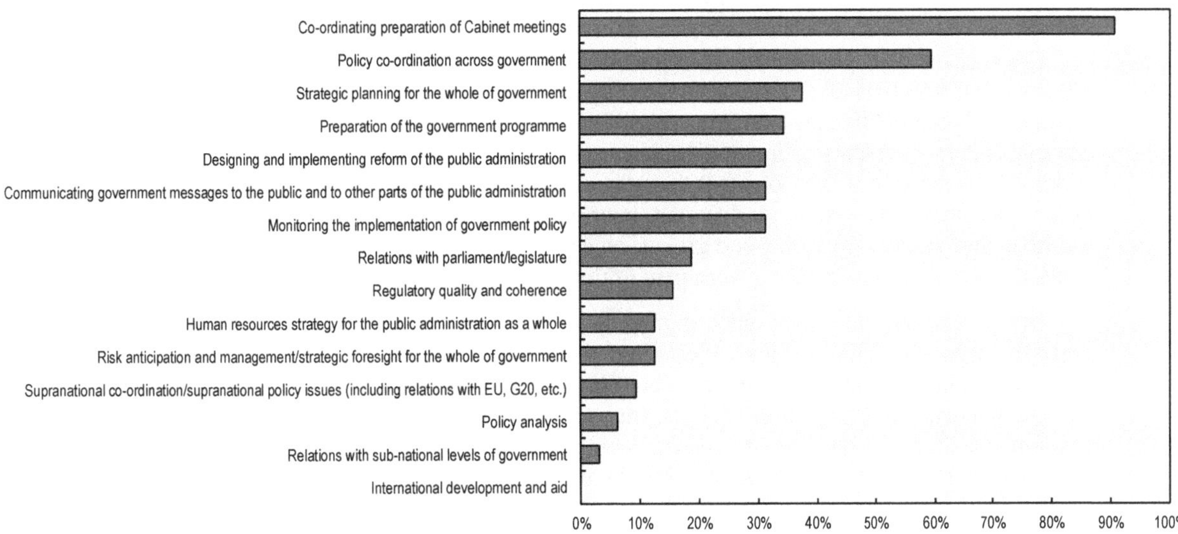

Source: OECD (2013), "Questionnaire on the Organisation and Functions of the Centre of Government", www.oecd.org/officialdocuments/publicdisplaydocumentpdf/?cote=GOV/PGC/MPM(2013)3&docLanguage=En.

Strengthening the centre of government may seem to monopolise government's power. On the contrary, it is aimed at giving support to ministries and agencies and prevent them from working in silos. The centre of government offers a common strategic framework with agreed outcomes and guidelines on how to achieve them that can actually help them. In this sense, "the centre's role should be a supportive and enabling one, encouraging line ministries to plan and implement their initiatives in line with whole-of-government policy, and contributing to setting and steering government-wide strategies" (OECD, 2015b).

Generally speaking most OECD countries either in presidential, parliamentary and other systems, the three key roles of the centre are:

1) Supporting quality decision making by the head of government.

2) Policy co-ordination across government.

3) Monitoring the implementation of government policy (OECD, 2015b).

With declining trust figures across countries in the aftermath of the 2008 crisis, the CoG's leadership and innovative decision-making capacity is more decisive than ever before to ensure that government has a clear vision for a country's future, is capable of engaging in a dialogue with the administration and citizens on this vision, and manages to deliver so as to foster sustainable long-term growth and well-being (OECD, 2013).

Box 2.8 provides a more detailed overview of CoG's trends and how vision, leadership and innovation are central to its daily business. Across these three areas, the capacity of bridging the (potential) gap between political staff (ministries, state secretaries, political advisors and senior civil servants in certain cases) and the civil service is one of the challenges of incoming governments (OECD, 2015b).

Box 2.8. CoG: Observations and trends in 2014, vision, leadership and innovation

The success of a government rests on its ability to define a vision for the country that reflects an electoral mandate and that is typically designed to increase well-being, prosperity and international competitiveness. In the years following the economic crisis, budget concerns dominated in most countries, crowding out any other vision. However, and governments are now seeking to be more forward-looking and strategic, and most OECD Members have some form of vision document. This vision has different, interlinked dimensions, including a long-term vision for the nation, usually going beyond growth objectives to embrace well-being and sustainability goals, and a vision for what the government of the day wants to achieve.

The government no longer has a monopoly on defining the **vision**. While efforts to gather citizens' views could risk raising expectations that cannot be fulfilled, such bottom-up visions can help validate and legitimise government policy. Vision depends on two crucial factors that were mentioned repeatedly in the debate: trust and communication. If citizens do not trust the government, they will not trust its vision. Taking steps to strengthen trust in government more generally will help to ensure greater buy-in on more strategic goals. Communication and ownership are also important. If the vision has a strong narrative, connects to citizens' lives and is well communicated, then it can help generate support for difficult reforms. A particular problem faced by policy makers is that the reform process and its translation into real benefits for citizens are often too slow, undermining confidence and enthusiasm for longer-term visions.

Leadership is crucial to drive policies that contribute to a strategic vision. In a complex and challenging policy environment, characterised by low levels of trust in government, leadership is an essential attribute of effective government. Room for manoeuvre of governments has probably diminished at both the national level, because of budgetary pressures, and at the international level, because of globalisation. Nevertheless, the centre guides in terms of substance and helps departments understand how to align policies with broader objectives. The centre also has a role to play in leading by example, promoting efficiency and good policy management by departments. A key issue is to ensure that the civil service and political staff do not become disconnected, working as separate entities at the centre.

Many centres of government actively promote **innovation** in their public services, with an emphasis on encouraging a culture of innovation in public services and providing a stable frame for policy innovation and creativity. The centre can provide an impetus – particularly when it partners with specialist agencies that can identify talented people, good ideas and roll-out techniques. Some countries have successfully used innovation focal points or dedicated units to drive public sector innovation; at the same time, being the innovation leader requires appropriate financial and human resources.

Sources: OECD (2014b), "Vision, leadership, innovation: Driving public policy performance", 33rd Meeting of Senior Officials from Centres of Government, OECD, Paris, www.oecd.org/gov/summary.pdf; OECD (2015c), *Costa Rica: Good Governance, from Process to Results*, OECD Publishing, Paris, http://dx.doi.org/10.1787/9789264246997-en.

Another important element and distinctive feature of the CoG is its capacity to give the country's strategic vision its specific shape, to secure its coherence, and to make it operational. A starting point is likely to be the government's programme or its equivalent. It can also be a broader document providing strategic foresight of what are the key objectives to be achieved on a medium term, the obstacles or challenges to overcome and an action plan to implement those objectives (i.e. a national development plan). For instance Sweden created "the Commission on the Future" where country key challenges in the long term (2020 and 2050) were identified.

Jordan 2025 is the starting point with its ten-year strategy which calls for a transformation of the country's socioeconomic model of development to achieve growth and prosperity based on competitiveness and providing more employment opportunities. The vision's framework addresses five main pillars: human resource development, social development, economic development, decentralisation and governorate development, and infrastructure. It also includes a road map with short and medium-term objectives that the country aims to achieve in the following years. Decentralisation appears to be one of the six core priorities of the axes on Government Priority Initiatives (Figure 2.6).

Figure 2.6. Core priorities for Government in Vision 2025

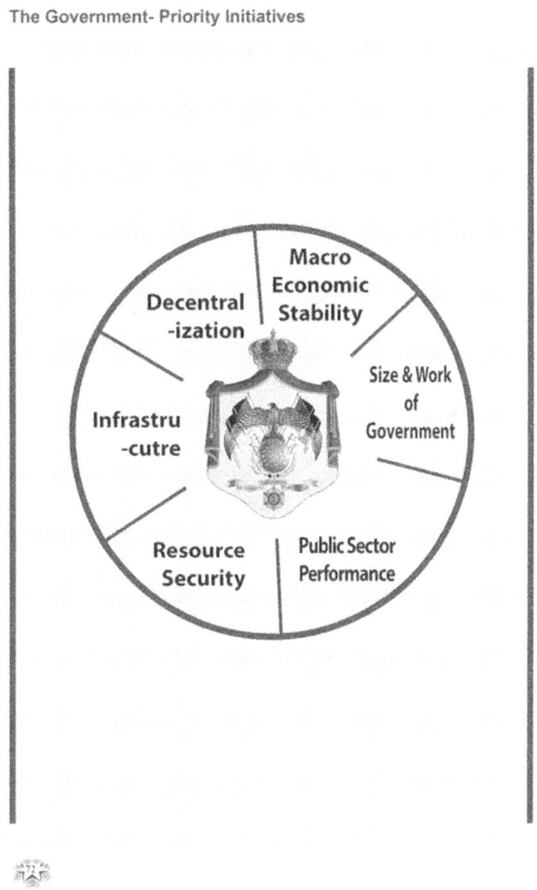

Source: Inform (2015), *Jordan 2025*, Ministry of Planning and International Cooperation, Amman, http://inform.gov.jo/en-us/By-Date/Report-Details/ArticleId/247/Jordan-2025.

Decentralisation reform is included in the Government Priority Axe but conceived as a separate objective and not directly linked to the "Public Sector Performance" neither to the "Size and Work of Government". In fact, the decentralisation reform is described in general terms as the Laws were still to be drafted when the Jordan 2025 was published. As described in Table 2.5 the targeted scenario does not specify the strategic objectives of the decentralisation reform and just mention in broad terms, the need of a first diagnosis of the current situation and to strengthen the financial and human capacities and transparency and accountability of local governments. Those priorities are directly linked to those on local development included in the Society Priority Axe where governorates and municipalities are mentioned as key actors to support investment and development projects.

Table 2.5. Decentralisation priorities in Jordan 2025

Targeted scenario	Priority Initiatives
Issuing the decentralisation law for 2014 and formulating a national strategy and plan to implement the decentralisation law and the reforms necessary	• Conduct surveys for the National legislative system that may conflict with the decentralisation law, if passed • Conduct survey studies to analyse all local services provided by the central government to find a mechanism to delegate service delivery to local administrations in the governorates to be in line with the powers that will be granted to these administrations under the Law • Implement programs to strengthen the financial decentralisation and public expenditure management and find the necessary funding for the financial cost of the application of the law. • Prepare and implement programs to build the capacity of workers in the local administration, the executive departments and the elected structures in line with the reform of the decentralisation system. • Implement programs and workshop to raise awareness about decentralisation and local administration and programs to enhance local control and promote transparency and accountability • Analyse the current reality of local administration system and local development • A national dialogue at all levels that include all categories • A policy paper for the reforms of the decentralisation system • Develop a set of sub-executive programs for all sectors targeted for reform of decentralisation system
Promoting local development	• Enhance the governorate's production capacity and reduce development disparities between them and focus on local economic development • Strengthen local partnerships between government, agencies, municipalities, civil society institutions and the private sector • Build the institutional capacity of active partners in local development sector • Enable municipalities in the area of planning and development and improve the quality of their services to perform their role in development. • Increase funding for job-generating institutions in the local development sector • Set up a fund in municipalities to support municipalities that are implementing projects in partnership with private sector • Direct technical support programs towards projects implemented by institutions in the local development sector during the setting-up phase to ensure the sustainability of these projects and that they will create job opportunities. • Improve the mechanisms of collection of receivables and financial rights of municipalities • Conduct economic feasibility studies of the outputs of the investment map of governorates.

Source: Inform (2015), *Jordan 2025*, Ministry of Planning and International Cooperation, Amman, http://inform.gov.jo/en-us/By-Date/Report-Details/ArticleId/247/Jordan-2025.

Following this logic, the key performance indicators for decentralisation are directed liked to the ones related to Communities and local development and do not set concrete data on the effectiveness or impact of the decentralisation reform on the administrative structure. Table 2.6 shows that indicators only refer to the provision of ICTs in local governments, an objective that is supposed to be achieved in the first year of evaluation, 2017.

Table 2.6. Key performance indicators on Decentralisation reform in Jordan 2025

Indicator	2017	2021	2025
Number of governorates where poverty exceeds the national average	7	5	3
Number of investment projects through the partnership between the municipalities and the private sector	60	150	275
Number of municipalities benefiting from integrated computerised financial system project	100	100	100
Economic feasibility studies of the outputs of the investment map of governorates	70%	85%	100%
The contribution of the organised private sector in meeting housing needs	50%	55%	60%

Source: Inform (2015), *Jordan 2025*, Ministry of Planning and International Cooperation, Amman, http://inform.gov.jo/en-us/By-Date/Report-Details/ArticleId/247/Jordan-2025.

The fact that Decentralisation and Municipalities Laws were only approved two years later also explains that the new elected councils at governorate and local level are not mentioned in Jordan 2025 and therefore the link to citizen participation can be found only in the Executive Programme 2016-2018. This operational and strategic document develops Vision 2025 and describes its core priorities, expected outcomes and activities during 2016-2018. It includes the missing information on the decentralisation reform by highlighting the key challenges and some of the expected outcomes on the institutional arrangements and citizens' participation issued from the decentralisation reform passed in December 2015.

Jordan's national reform on decentralisation requires a strong and well-defined centre of government able to identify the key steps, as well as follow-up and implementation mechanisms to ensure it is successfully carried out. In addition to help defining and implementing the national strategic vision, the CoG needs the capacity to communicate its objectives and achievements in a way that citizens can understand and appreciate. Transparency and openness help to promote a shared sense of purpose for stakeholders outside and inside the government. Good communication flows within the administration is also important so that, for example, all concerned institutions can understand the vision, share in its construction, and understand their role, responsibility and accountability for results. In Jordan, this appears to be one of the main challenges that the central government will have to face as it implements the decentralisation reform. The Jordanian CoG provides support to the Prime Minister and the Cabinet Office and is distributed across the following institutions:

- **Prime Minister (and Cabinet)**: The Prime Minister acts as head of government and, together with the Cabinet minister, has the following functions: to appoint and remove employees who hold "positions of trust"; the initiative to enact laws and the right of veto; the collection and expenditure of the national revenues; and oversight of the proper operation of administrative services and agencies, among others. In practice, the Cabinet Office serves the purpose of a co-ordination body, where the Prime Minister can monitor progress on strategic issues. Among the objectives set in Jordan 2025, the strengthening of the Delivery Unit to support ministries in achieving the Prime Minister's priorities initiatives and the creation of a Department of Strategic Policies are also aligned with the CoG and a whole-of-government approach.

- **Ministry of Planning and International Co-operation (MoPIC)**: its primary duties include the preparation and follow-up of the national development plan (Jordan 2025); and verification that public investment projects across government entities are aligned with priorities set forth in the plan. Through these functions, the ministry gives technical and political advice to the Cabinet and other public institutions, while it formulates, co-ordinates, monitors and evaluates the strategies and priorities of the government. This ministry is also in charge of co-ordinating international donor community and civil society organisations, in particular through the Open Government Partnership. MoPIC is the national focal point for the Open Government Partnership,[18] and the Minister heads the ad hoc committee composed of representatives from the public and sector and CSOs.
- **Ministry of Political Development and Parliamentary Affairs (MoPDPA)**: this is the interface between the executive and the legislative branch, and is also in charge of relations with citizens, media and CSOs. It has a crucial role in the drafting of laws (as interface with Parliament), and has been assigned the specific task of raising awareness and campaigns on the Decentralisation and Municipalities Laws.
- **Ministry of Finance** (MoF): co-ordinates the budgetary cycle for the central government budget (i.e. ministries and their subsidiary bodies). The Ministry of Finance has competences regarding central government budget, public accounting, management of state property and management of the internal and external debt, public procurement, among others. Responsibilities also include its contribution to the stability and economic growth for social development through the collection, management, allocation, accountability and proper use of financial resources.

National Decentralisation Committee

A National Committee was created to co-ordinate, implement and follow-up the decentralisation reform in the DL and ML. Consequently, both the MoI and MoMA have a leading role in their respective competencies: MoI is in charge of the implementation of the DL, whereas MoMA has competencies for the ML.

The committee is composed of:

- **The Ministry of the Interior (MoI)** was established since the formation of the first central government in Transjordan in 1921, and is traditionally associated with the tasks of maintaining security and public order, as well as representing central government in the governorates. The MoI designate governors and co-ordinate the Decentralisation Law and the tasks developed by governorates. MoI is also in charge of the implementation strategy of DL and the by-laws regulations.
- **The Ministry of Municipal Affairs (MoMA)** is responsible for overseeing and giving support to municipalities and joint service councils, the Higher Planning

Council and the Cities and Villages Development Bank. It is responsible for drafting all legislation related to municipalities and the subsequent by-laws.

In addition to being "heads of the reform", MoPIC and MoPA also play a key role due to their position at the CoG. The Ministry of the Public Sector and Ministry of ICT are also members of the Decentralisation Commission.

- **The Ministry of Public Sector Development** (MoPSD) co-ordinates the government's strategy and management of its public sector, particularly regarding service delivery improvement, institutional streamlining, human resource management and programme management.

Figure 2.7. Centre of government for decentralisation reform in Jordan

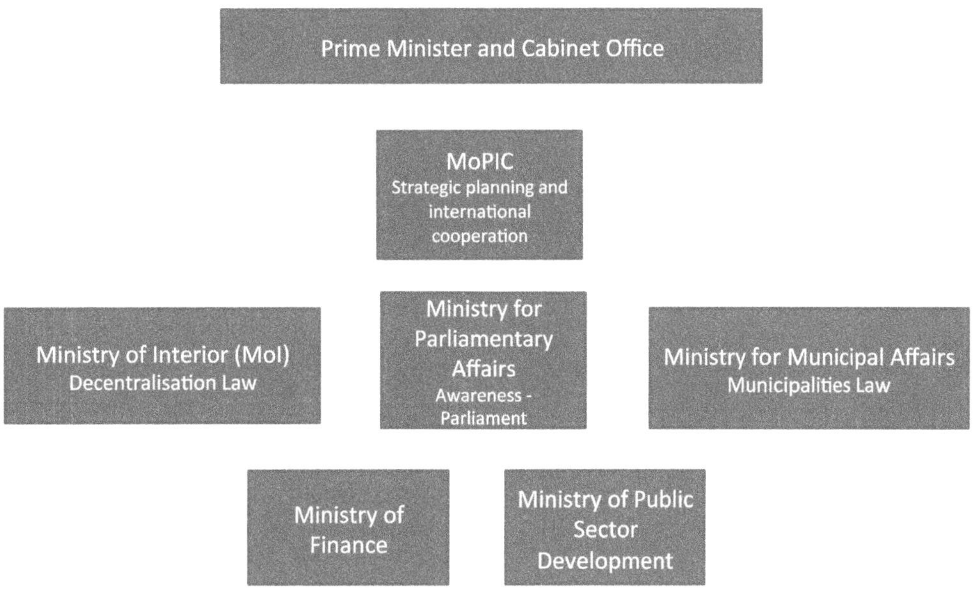

Its executive arm, the Executive Committee, is chaired by the Secretary General of the Ministry of the Interior and Ministry for Municipal Affairs. It includes among its members, the secretary generals of the ministries of: Planning and International Co-operation, Public Sector Development, Finance, Communications and Information Technology, Political and Parliamentary Affairs and the Director General of the budget department, in addition to a number of directors of departments at the MoI and MoMA. The executive committee is also in charge of starting the preparatory procedures for the governorate and municipal elections in 2017 and for the implementation of both laws.

While good working relations between these institutions appear to be the norm, their interaction seems to lack institutionalisation and a strategic dimension. There appears to be a theoretical common understanding or willingness to engage collectively in steering the design and implementation of the government's decentralisation that it is not put into practice. The MoI and MoMA, together with MoPIC and MoPol Affairs and overall government co-ordination, could benefit from involving the other institutions more closely. It would be particularly relevant to have the Ministry of Finance actively contribute to whole-of-government steering, as it controls the fiscal framework and appears to be leading improvements in the government's analytical capacity.

The new competences on strategic development could also create some misunderstandings and overlapping at the subnational level. At the central level, MoPIC has been in charge of elaborating the governorate developments plans. With the new regulations, the governorate and municipalities have competencies and will have to co-ordinate with MoPIC, although they first rely on the MoI and MoMA. Ministries in central government will have to make efforts to ensure aligned policies and coherence, particularly regarding in such an important topic as strategic planning.

Significant silos remain regarding the effective follow-up, monitoring and evaluation of the decentralisation policy performance, which are undertaken to assess performance against the achievement of results and the improvement of outcomes. Reporting to the public regularly on performance can help enhance government transparency and accountability, while reducing overlap and duplication in roles and responsibilities among CoG institutions and between the CoG and line ministries. This will ultimately improve public trust in the government and its institutions. The example of Spain's Commission for the Administrative Reform (CORA) and OPERA could serve as inspiration (Box 2.9).

Box 2.9. The strategic role of the CoG in the implementation process: The case of Spain

In the course of discussions that the review team had with various stakeholders, it has been noted that many of the interlocutors – notably those charged with implementing the reform – were aware of the challenges and difficulties between some of the targets and the pace established for DL and ML on the one hand, and the financial allocation necessary to achieve them on the other. For instance, many actions included in the implementation draft strategy (facilitated by the MoI) relied on expected grants from international donors in the near future, whereas the foreseen time horizon set longer implementation targets. In these cases, the government is thus supposed to step in with its own resources. However, these do not always seem to be readily available.

The suboptimal monitoring and reporting mechanism has not allowed for these identified discrepancies to be reported in a timely manner to the steering and co-ordination function of the reform, or to efficiently act upon them if appropriately communicated.

In general terms, a weak monitoring and reporting system puts the accountability of the whole reform at risk, as well as the pace and quality of its implementation, as it makes it difficult to intervene with incremental corrections on the direction and pace of the reform.

An example of administrative reform and reporting on the implementation process is provided by Spain, where a Commission for the Reform of the Public Administration (CORA) embodied a process of data collection, dialogue among practitioners and diagnosis about the weaknesses of Spain's public administrations. This was part of a broad public administration reform plan aimed at improving the efficiency of the public administrations, enhancing the quality of services provided to citizens and business, and making the public administrations more accountable and transparent.

The CORA report was presented in June 2013 and included 217 proposals, 139 of which addressed both the central administration and regions (autonomous communities), while 78 concerned only the central administration.

Box 2.9. The strategic role of the CoG in the implementation process: The case of Spain *(cont.)*

The Office for Execution of the Administrative Reform (OPERA) was created, which is a dedicated structure that monitors the implementation of CORA's recommendations. OPERA also engages with the regional level (autonomous communities) in the follow-up process. An ad hoc group was also established within the Council on Fiscal and Financial Policy, which is the main sectoral conference where central government and the autonomous communities co-ordinate their fiscal and financial policies. OPERA publishes quarterly and annual monitoring reports on updated implementation progress and the co-ordination mechanisms that have been newly initiated.

Note: Quarterly and annual reports are available on the website of the Spanish Ministry of Finance and Public Administration, see: www.seap.minhap.gob.es/web/areas/reforma_aapp.html.

Sources: OECD (2016c), *OECD Public Governance Reviews: Spain 2016: Linking Reform to Results for the Country and its Regions*, OECD Publishing, Paris, http://dx.doi.org/10.1787/9789264263024-en;
OECD (2014c), *Spain: From Administrative Reform to Continuous Improvement*, OECD Publishing, Paris, http://dx.doi.org/10.1787/9789264210592-en.

The role of Parliament

The role of Parliament has been crucial in decentralisation reform in Jordan. Once the Law of Municipalities was submitted, many amendments were introduced by members of Parliament. In particular, the King solved the controversial issue of keeping the legal and financial autonomy of the Governorate Councils, like municipal and local councils against the Parliament's approach of limiting the scope of this elected council.[19] In OECD countries, decentralisation reform have been opportunities for intense interaction between citizens and the government on the most appropriate institutional set up of the state, often involving debates on the historical and cultural territorial identifies of the various communities at subnational level, as well as fundamental national policy concerns such as fight against corruption or what an equitable redistribution of financial resources to under-privileged areas.

Debates over the draft law in Parliament lasted for almost a year. Supporters of the law argued that the bill would speed up reforms and trim bureaucracy, as well as improve the democratisation efforts. They emphasised the wider possibility for citizens at the local level to participate in decision making as the country is fragmented and many groups remain under-represented. Opponents pointed out that the implementation of the law will be costly while the economic situation is poor, and may cause problems regarding transparency and corruption, as well as the risk of power capture by local elites.

As anticipated, the Decentralisation Law was originally conceived as a MoI's by-law and was only subsequently upgraded to a law following controversy between central government and the Parliament (conflict on approving the law under the basis of Articles 120 or 121 of the Constitution).[20]

The interest and reactions showed by the Jordanian Parliament towards the decentralisation reform is an opportunity to improve relations between the executive and the legislative branch. Jordan 2025 also highlights Transparency and accountability towards Parliament and citizens as one of the key priorities for an "effective and efficient Government" (Inform, 2015). The follow-up and implementation phase can be also an opportunity to improve Parliament's role, as well as the government's accountability towards citizens through the legislative.

Jordan's approach to the decentralisation reform will bring elections to the lower levels, from governorates to municipal and local level. This new phase will be the opportunity to create more synergies between citizens and politicians, as they will run for elections at subnational level. It can have an indirect impact on Members of Parliament's activities and interests, as they usually come from different territories, villages and cities from all over the country, which they usually and informally represent. King Abdullah already raised this issue in one of his discussion papers stressing the need for Members of Parliament to balance their role of presenting the "needs of local constituencies" as well as "the interests of the Kingdom as a whole"[21]. New local elected may also create their own "networks' and connect the citizens 'needs through lobbying with Members of Parliament.

In fact, the narrative of the reform is sustained on citizen participation and bringing policies closer to citizens, however, both laws have been drafted and approved without formal and prior consultation with citizens. CSOs voiced their concern about the lack of consultation before the laws were sent to Parliament[22]. The arrival of new elected representatives at subnational level may contribute to make citizens 'voice better heard.

Assessment and recommendations

This chapter has described decentralisation trends and the place of Jordan's reform. Decentralisation needs to be a flexible process adapted to the country's reality and conditions. The 2015 Decentralisation Law and Municipality Law reflect the commitment of the Government of Jordan to move forward towards a new culture popular participation at the subnational layers of government and local democracy. However, for King Abdullah II's vision of a political development process that starts at the grassroots level, and then moves up to higher decision-making centres to fully materialise, a number of key challenges needs to be addressed.

Government has a strong political commitment towards decentralisation reform that allows central/local dynamics to evolve, and that takes into consideration the potential instability of the political framework. Decentralisation requires not only a strong political commitment from the central government but also a social consensus based on the populations' demands and needs. In that sense, constant changes in the political framework can hinder the building of support for decentralisation (Work, 2012). Although Government of Jordan has a high rotation of high officials because of frequent cabinet reshuffling, Ministers of Interior and Municipal Affairs keep certain stability been among the most stable Ministries which impact in long term reform like the decentralisation one[23].

Jordan is at the first stage of a long path towards decentralisation. The official discourse on decentralisation needs to take into consideration all the political, financial and administrative components that such a reform requires. The introduction of the democratic component by including elections at governorate and local level is an important step that will also bring responsibilities and duties to the Jordan Administration. The establishment and consolidation of local democratic administrations will require a profound change in administrative, working and regulating culture between government and constituencies.

One of the major challenges can be to find the right balance between the institutional and traditional role of the Governor and indirectly of the Executive council together with the new political powers conferred to the Governorate elected council that will need support at a first stage to develop all its potential. Promoting a culture of institutional co-operation among the key bodies, Governor, governorate council and executive council will be essential to ensure a fluent dialogue and partnership for better service delivery to citizens.

The current centralised system is characterised by providing basic services to the citizens and by carrying out extensive social investment. These characteristics explain the resistance of national government institutions to transferring functions to other levels. The culture that has developed around the centralised system in Jordan for more than 50 years has sometimes rendered Jordanian municipalities not visible enough to develop their role and potential and has prevented citizens from perceiving local governments as the provider of services or the promoter of local development.

At the same time, the current reform in Jordan provides a major opportunity for redefining roles and responsibilities in line with the principle of bringing services closer to the citizen, which makes political, economic and administrative sense. Several OECD countries can serve to inspire this process. For example, France, Germany and Poland provide models of functional assignment that reflect this principle (Box 2.10).

Box 2.10. Allocation of responsibilities to the lower tiers of government: France, Germany and Poland

France

In France's administrative system, each tier of government below the national government is granted specific responsibilities, which are defined in legislation.

The responsibilities of regions include:

- Regional economic planning and policy, industrial development.
- Professional education and high schools (but not the management of the teachers and the school programmes), professional education for the unemployed.
- Transportation outside of cities (interurban buses, regional trains, school buses for high schools). Some regions have also been assigned responsibility for local ports and airports.
- Environmental protection with some special plans organisation.

The responsibilities of departments include:

- Intercity roads (routes départementales).
- Some social policies and welfare allowances.
- Secondary (or middle/junior high) school (except teaching and school programmes/curriculums).

In addition, regions and departments share responsibilities over:

- culture
- sport
- tourism

Box 2.10. Allocation of responsibilities to the lower tiers of government: France, Germany and Poland *(cont.)*

- regional languages.

Communes (municipal governments)[1] are responsible for almost all matters regarding municipal affairs, including:

- primary schools and pre-school
- local roads
- local police and public order
- urbanism
- local ports and canals
- housing
- cemeteries
- culture and sport facilities and incentives policies
- local social services
- local transportation
- gas and electricity networks.

Poland

In Poland's administrative system, each tier of government below the national government is granted specific responsibilities, which are defined in legislation.

The responsibilities of districts include:

- secondary education
- healthcare (districts manage only hospital and polyclinic buildings, while current expenditures are covered by separate health authorities)
- roads of district importance
- several social services
- labour offices (coping with unemployment)
- protection against natural disasters
- consumer protection
- land surveying
- various inspections, such as sanitary and building.

The responsibilities of municipalities include:

- pre-school and primary education (for children up to 15-years-old)
- "communal services" including: water and sewage, solid waste collection and disposal, street lighting, local parks and green areas, central heating
- local roads and streets maintenance
- local public transport in cities
- communal housing

Box 2.10. Allocation of responsibilities to the lower tiers of government: France, Germany and Poland *(cont.)*

- voluntary fire brigades
- various social services, including social benefits for the poor
- local culture (including local libraries and leisure centres)
- local physical (spatial) planning.

Germany

In Germany's administrative system, local authority administrations make up the third pillar of the administration. Their tasks include the administration of town planning, road building and housing, social and health services, and public facilities (swimming pools, libraries, day-care centres and sports facilities). Local authorities are also responsible for providing local public transport and refuse disposal and for ensuring the supply of water, gas, electricity and community heating. These utilities are largely operated as enterprises organised under private law.

Sources: Association des administrateurs territoriaux de France (2016), "The French experience of decentralization"; Swianiewicz , P. (2015), "Territorial consolidation reforms: European experiences of the 21st century", Geobalcanica, pp. 379-388, http://geobalcanica.org/wp-content/uploads/2016/04/GBP.2015.48.pdf; Federal Ministry of the Interior (2014), "The federal public service: An attractive and modern employer", www.bmi.bund.de/SharedDocs/Downloads/EN/Broschueren/2014/federal-public-service.pdf?__blob=publicationFile; OECD (2017b), Decentralisation and Multi-level Governance in Kazakhstan, OECD Publishing, Paris, forthcoming.

Sustaining high-level political support is key to ensuring the success of the reform; the reform and donor attention to decentralisation reform speaks of the political commitment to carry it out. The fact that the leading body is in the Centre of Government also illustrates political support from the top level, and grants authority to request the participation of line ministries and agencies.

Given the importance of making the decentralisation reform happen, and to ensure a long-lasting reform, the government could consider the following recommendations:

The need of clarifying roles, competences and the relevance of the implementation process of the decentralisation reform:

- **Clarify roles and responsibilities at the national, governorate and local level.** This could include a clearer identification of services to be provided by each level of government, the line ministries' role, and the opinion of governorates and local governments that share competencies. This would be complemented by a comprehensive list of competency distributions across the different levels. Organisational charts would be published on line in the websites of each administration.
- **Publish guides and materials on the Decentralisation and Municipalities Laws,** their implications and effects at the national, governorate and local level, with a focus on the forthcoming elections at the governorate and local level. These guides will be an important working tool for public servants and employees

at the national, governorate and local level, and will ensure a common understanding of the implications and expected outcomes of the reform.

- **Promote a general and comprehensive debate on the new role of governorates, and in particular of the governor, Governorate Council and the Executive Council, especially before the 2017 elections**. Clarify the relationship between governors and the Executive Council (and line ministries in Amman), as well their co-ordination role with municipalities.
- Once the elected bodies take up their duties, **council member will need support to understand the dynamics of each administration.and how to contribute to them.** Government of Jordan will need to concentrate on reinforcing the capacities of the members of the newly elected bodies to ensure that the citizens' expectations on their role and functions will be appropriately met.
- **A follow-up committee should be created to bring updated and evidence-based information to the Cabinet on a regular basis**. Such a committee will also help promote a more integrated approach between the MoI and MoMA to ensure that a "subnational dimension" is fully integrated on the implementation strategy and the road map.

A stronger and more co-ordinated centre of government (CoG)

- **Consolidate and reinforce the role of Jordan's centre of government on implementing the decentralisation reform**, recognizing that the Cabinet Office, MoI, MoMA, MoPIC and MoPPA will all play key roles.
- **Strengthen and reinforce co-operation and co-ordination among the CoG institutions implicated in the decentralisation reform** as well as with the rest of the public administration. Crucially, this could contribute to overcoming the existing silo-based approach to service delivery at the local level (as outlined in Chapter 3), while ensuring that policy and spending are better linked and potential overlap and duplication reduced. The GoJ must also ensure effective communication and co-ordination between CoG institutions and collectively with line ministries and citizens by developing a clear communication strategy towards citizens to explain the decentralisation reform through seminars and a dissemination campaign across the country. Some initiatives such as the national dialogue launched by the Ministry of Political and Parliamentary Affairs together with the Jordan NGOs coalition is an initiative that could be replicated even prior to the elections.
- In so doing, **the Decentralisation Committee needs to follow an implementation road map agreed and approved by the Council of Ministers that includes a set of short, medium and long-term objectives**, as well as expected outputs and outcomes. These outputs and outcomes should include performance indicators and should be published and disseminated regularly.
- **Develop a centralised monitoring mechanism** to evaluate and make adjustments during and after the implementation of the decentralisation programme.
- **Strengthen capacity to implement decentralisation reform in the structures within the CoG by reinforcing the human and financial resources of the MoI, MoMA and MoSPD** so that they can work closely with governorates and municipalities on designing and implementing decentralisation strategic policy

and assessing and monitoring progress, and feed this information into governorate programmes.

- **Reinforce the working relationships between the MoI and MoMA** so that all are working to achieve the same strategic decentralisation objectives and to mainstream decentralisation within the Jordan 2025. These ministries could work with MoPIC, which is responsible for integrating all strands of national development strategy, including decentralisation and regional development, inclusive growth, and public administration reform at the subnational levels into the Biannual Development Programme (currently 2016-2018).
- **Parliament should play a greater role in the follow-up of the implementation of the reform.** The Government of Jordan (through the Ministry of Political and Parliamentary Affairs) could consider submitting annual decentralisation reports to the Parliament by developing performance indicators on decentralisation and their impact against the objectives of the reform.

Notes

1. www.jordantimes.com/news/local/decentralisation-meant-give-citizens-stronger-voice%E2%80%99.
2. www.kinghussein.gov.jo/government2.html.
3. www.citypopulation.de/Jordan.html.
4. http://data.worldbank.org/indicator/en.pop.dnst.
5. http://eur-lex.europa.eu/legal-content/en/txt/?uri=celex:12012m/txt.
6. www.coe.int/en/web/conventions/full-list/-/conventions/treaty/122.
7. www.ciesin.org/decentralization/english/general/different_forms.html.
8. King Abdullah's Speech on decentralisation plan in 2005, http://kingabdullah.jo/index.php/en_US/speeches/view/id/76/videoDisplay/0.html.
9. Internal report.
10. www.al-monitor.com/pulse/politics/2013/08/jordan-elections-low-turnout.html.
11. February 2017.
12. According to Hamdi and information from the Ministry of the Interior.
13. Administrative Divisions Bylaw No. 46 of 2000.
14. Villages were extinct and merged in the amalgation reform approved in 2001.
15. www.mota.gov.jo/Documents/Municipal_sector.pdf.
16. Ibid.
17. Ibid.

18. http://inform.gov.jo/en-us/By-Date/Report-Details/ArticleId/78/The-Open-Government-Partnership-Jordan-National-Action-Plan and www.mop.gov.jo/Default.aspx.

19. www.jordantimes.com/news/local/king-rejects-decentralization-bill-unconstitutionality.

20. www.jordantimes.com/news/local/lower-house-removes-constitutional-flaw-decentralisation-bill; www.jordantimes.com/news/local/king-rejects-decentralization-bill-unconstitutionality.

21. https://kingabdullah.jo/en/discussion-papers/each-playing-our-part-new-democracy.

22. www.hayatcenter.org/uploads/2015/02/20150218140127en.pdf.

23. For the Ministry of the Interior: Awad Mohammad Khleifat (11/10/2012 - 30/3/2013), Hussein Hazza Al Majali 30/3/2013 – 29/5/2016, Salameh Hammad (1/6/2016-15/1/2017) and Ghaleb Al Zu'bi (15/1/2017- Present). For Ministry of Municipal Affairs: Ahmad-Maher Abu Al Saman, (11/10/2012 - 30/3/2013), Hussein Hazza Al Majali 30/3/2013 – 29/5/2016 and Waleed Al Masri (1/6/2016- present).

References

Ababsa, M. (2016), *Decentralisation in the Mashrek region: challenges and opportunities. (The cases of Jordan, Lebanon and Yemen)*, Platforma, Bruxelles, www.academia.edu/24731610/Decentralization_in_the_Mashrek_region_challenges_and_opportunities._The_cases_of_Jordan_Lebanon_and_Yemen_.

Ababsa, M. (2013), *Atlas on Jordan*, http://books.openedition.org/ifpo/5021?lang=en.

Ahmaro I.H. (2014), "Controlling the Financial Performance of Jordanian Municipalities by Improving Financial Regulations An Analytical Study", Journal *of Business Studies Quarterly 2014,* Vol. 6, No. 2.

Bergh, S. (2011), "Decentralisation and Local Governance in the MENA Region", *Med2010*, IeMed, Barcelona.

Bossert, M. (1998), "Analyzing the decentralization of health systems in developing countries: decision space, innovation and performance", *Social Science and Medicine*, Vol. 47, No. 10, www.hsph.harvard.edu/ihsg/pdf/science.pdf.

Constitution de la république tunisienne (2014), www.legislation.tn/sites/default/files/news/constitution-b-a-t.pdf.

Government of Jordan (2016a), Background report of the OECD Strategic Assessment of Jordan, unpublished working paper.

Government of Jordan (2016b), Executive Development Programme 2016-2018, www.mop.gov.jo/pages/viewpage.aspx?pageid=103.

Government of Ireland (2012), *Putting people first: Action programme for effective local government*, www.housing.gov.ie/sites/default/files/publications/files/putting_people_first.pdf.

Harb, M. and Atallah, S. (2015), *Local Governments and Public Goods: Assessing Decentralisation in the Arab World*, The Lebanese Center for Policy Studies, Beirut.

Hossain, A. (n.d.), Administrative Decentralization: A Framework for Discussion and Its Practices in Bangladesh, http://unpan1.un.org/intradoc/groups/public/documents/unpan/unpan019445.pdf.

Inform (2015), *Jordan 2025*, Ministry of Planning and International Cooperation, Amman, http://inform.gov.jo/en-us/By-Date/Report-Details/ArticleId/247/Jordan-2025.

Jordan Department of Statistics (2017), Statistics homepage, http://web.dos.gov.jo/?lang=en (accessed 12 February 2017).

Law on Municipalities (2015), Law No 41 of 2015, www.iec.jo/sites/default/files/2015%20Municipalities%20Law%20EN.pdf.

Law on Decentralisation (2015), Law No 49 of 2015, www.iec.jo/sites/default/files/2015%20Decentralisation%20Law%20EN.pdf.

OECD (2017a), *Guide des bonnes pratiques en matière de gouvernance locale au Maroc*, Paris, forthcoming.

OECD (2017b), *Decentralisation and Multi-level Governance in Kazakhstan*, OECD Publishing, Paris, forthcoming.

OECD (2016a), *Subnational governments in OECD countries: Key data* (brochure), OECD, Paris, www.oecd.org/regional/regional-policy.

OECD (2016b), OECD Regional statistics, OECD, Paris, http://dx.doi.org/10.1787/region-data-en.

OECD (2016c), *OECD Public Governance Reviews: Spain 2016: Linking Reform to Results for the Country and its Regions*, OECD Publishing, Paris, http://dx.doi.org/10.1787/9789264263024-en.

OECD (2015a), "Centre Stage: Driving Better Policies from the Centre of Government", *GOV/PGC/MPM(2014)3*, OECD, Paris, http://olisweb.oecd.org/vgn-ext-templating/gov-pgc-mpm(2014)3-eng.pdf?docid=jt03363892&date=1413295920073&documentid=621867&organisationid=1&filename=jt03363892.pdf.

OECD (2015b), *Slovak Republic: Better Co-ordination for Better Policies, Services and Results,* OECD Publishing, Paris, http://dx.doi.org/10.1787/9789264247635-en.

OECD (2015c), *Costa Rica: Good Governance, from Process to Results*, OECD Publishing, Paris, http://dx.doi.org/10.1787/9789264246997-en.

OECD (2014a), "Centre stage: Driving better policies from the centre of government", GOV/PGC/MPM(2014)3/FINAL, OECD, Paris, www.oecd.org/gov/Centre-Stage-Report.pdf.

OECD (2014b), "Vision, leadership, innovation: Driving public policy performance", 33rd Meeting of Senior Officials from Centres of Government, OECD, Paris, www.oecd.org/gov/summary.pdf.

OECD (2014c), *Spain: From Administrative Reform to Continuous Improvement*, OECD Publishing, Paris, http://dx.doi.org/10.1787/9789264210592-en.

OECD (2013), "Questionnaire on the Organisation and Functions of the Centre of Government", OECD, Paris, www.oecd.org/officialdocuments/publicdisplaydocumentpdf/?cote=gov/pgc/mpm(2013)3&doclanguage=en.

OECD (2010), *OECD Territorial Reviews: Sweden 2010*, OECD Publishing, Paris, http://dx.doi.org/10.1787/9789264081888-en.

OECD (2005), "Decentralisation and Poverty Reduction: from Lessons Learned to Policy Action". Workshop OECD Development Centre and the OECD Development Assistance, Committee Network on Governance, OECD, Paris.

OECD (2003), *Managing Decentralisation: A New Role for Labour Market Policy*, OECD Publishing, Paris, http://dx.doi.org/10.1787/9789264104716-en.

Swianiewicz, P. (2015), "Territorial consolidation reforms: European experiences of the 21st century", Geobalcanica, pp. 379-388, http://geobalcanica.org/wp-content/uploads/2016/04/gbp.2015.48.pdf.

UCLG (2016), *Jordan Country Profile. Global Observatory on Local Finance*, United Cities and Local Government, www.uclg-localfinance.org/sites/default/files/jordan-mewa-v3.pdf.

Work, R. (2012), Overview of Decentralisation Worldwide: A Stepping Stone to Improved Governance and Human Development. UNDP, New York http://biblioteca.unmsm.edu.pe/redlieds/Recursos/archivos/gestionestado/overview-decentralisation-worldwide-paper.pdf.

World Bank (n.d.), *Decentralization Thematic Team, Defining Decentralization* www.ciesin.org/decentralization/English/General/Different_forms.html.

Chapter 3.

Enablers for an effective and efficient public service delivery at the local level in Jordan: Overview of good practice

The decentralisation reform has raised high expectations that public policies will be brought closer to citizens and that public service delivery will become better tailored based on a bottom-up approach. For this promise to materialise, and indeed have a positive impact on local communities and economic activity, this chapter identifies four conditions that should be fulfilled: 1) a transformation of Local Development Units (LDUs) to act as cornerstones of the public administration at subnational level and for local development; 2) a clarification of the administrative and financial autonomy of subnational government institutions in addressing day-to-day service demands; 3) a co-ordinated dialogue between the central, governorate and the municipal levels in the identification of citizens' needs and in rolling out Governorate Development Plans; and 4) a strategic approach to reinforcing capacities and training among local civil servants and elected officials.

The previous chapter focused on the different models of decentralisation and on describing how decentralisation reform is not an end in itself, but is conceived as a way to bring policies and services closer to the people. Some decentralisation reforms include approaches that increase the supply and quality of local government services, while others stimulate their demand and the community oversight of them.

Public services at local level can either be delivered directly by local governments from their own competences or delegated from other administrations or by deconcentrated bodies from the central government. In many countries, such as Jordan, central government ministries responsible for service delivery have created field offices and delegated more decisions and resources to their local staff. In principle, a well-deconcentrated government system is able to increase and better allocate the total amount of resources available for universal access to basic public services (Work, n.d.).

Yet, it is important that the government considers the key role of local authorities, not only as the channel for citizen participation in strategic planning, but also as a service provider on the ground. In the Netherlands, for example, there is an ongoing debate on the positioning of local government as a decentralised government or as a service desk for all central government bodies[1] at the local level. Both approaches, the deconcentrated or the decentralised, have their merits; however the role of the local government in providing public services at the local level needs to be clarified if Jordan is to identify its specific way towards decentralisation.

For Jordan, four key issues should be taken into consideration as enablers for effective public service delivery at the subnational level:

- the legal and policy framework for service delivery
- strategic planning
- inter-institutional dialogue
- building local capacities.

The framework for service delivery at the subnational level: The key role of Local Development Units

The role of the public administrations in providing good services to citizens and businesses that meet and give an answer to their essential needs and demands is one of the key functions of the central and subnational governments. In so doing, public administrations need to provide themselves with a sound and performing institutional, administration and financial structure to ensure the conditions necessary to enable good public service delivery.

Promoting service delivery at the local level requires a bottom-up approach to identify and answer the needs of citizens, as well as a clear vision from the highest levels to ensure that services are delivered in an efficient manner and at the most appropriate level. In this sense, strategies for service delivery can vary across different regions or territories in the country. This is the case in the United Kingdom (Box 3.1), where through a single government approach the strategies to better provide services at the local level are adapted to each reality.

Box 3.1. Strategies for local service delivery in the United Kingdom

The United Kingdom has longstanding experience in promoting service delivery that is adapted to each territory at the local level. In England, the government is committed to working with local areas to redesign public services to deliver better outcomes and value for money for the public. In October 2011, the Department for Communities and Local Government (DCLG) set out a new programme where the key focus is on outcomes and how best to deliver them, rather than being limited by existing organisational responsibilities.

This initiative has recently received a number of significant boosts. First in November 2014 with the devolution of significant powers to the Greater Manchester Combined Authority, and second in February 2015 with the announcement of a devolution of control over National Health Service spending in the area. The 2015 Queen's speech also included the Cities and Local Government Devolution Bill to enact these changes and enable similar changes in other areas.

Sources: OECD from CIPFA (2017), Aligning local public services website, www.cipfa.org/cipfa-thinks/aligning-local-public-services (accessed 14 February 2017); DCLG (2017), Department for Communities and Local Government Website, www.gov.uk/government/organisations/department-for-communities-and-local-government (accessed 14 February 2017).

Local governments in OECD member countries are usually responsible for managing and delivering numerous services to their communities, ranging from public health to recreation facilities, local road maintenance and public libraries. In the case of Jordan, Local Development Units (LDUs) and the fiscal environment are two key features that lay the foundations of a sound and effective decentralisation reform.

Reinforcing a subnational administrative and financing structure to ensure sustainable public services in Jordan

Service delivery in Jordan is highly centralised, "with only limited delegation of authority in decision making on financial matters and service design and delivery delivery"(Work, 2012). The role of deconcentrated units is usually focused on the implementation of decisions made by central ministries. Even following the recent reform, governorates and municipalities still have relatively few new competencies, if compared to OECD countries, and in practice play a support role in public service provision. The law entrusts municipalities with some competencies and functions, such as street and road construction, public lighting, sewage systems, market infrastructure and organisation, refuse collection, issue of licenses, management of handcraft, public parking places, and control of local economic activities (as shown in chapter 2). Major public services that still belong to the central level include: defence, public order and safety, economic affairs, protection of the environment, housing and community amenities, health, education, social protection, and recreation, culture and religion.

The potential of Local Development Units as a cornerstone for local development in Jordan

Local Development Units were created at governorate level in 2003 "with the aim of developing participatory mechanisms to engage local stakeholders in local development processes" (Ababsa, 2015). In February 2008, 92 functions were transferred from the level of line ministries, to governorates to "make public services more accessible to the population, however, these services were limited in scope and neither the governorates,

LDUs nor the local authorities were sufficiently empowered to adopt more proactive roles" (Ababsa, 2015).

In this context, the new institutional set up due to the DL and Municipal Law (ML) gives an important role to Local Development Units as they are located at the heart of the governorate and municipal level, and called to be a cornerstone of governorate and municipal public administration. The main role of LDUs is to act as general secretariat at the governorate and municipal level and as an interface with local community stakeholders, civil society and private sector.

Governorate Local Development Unit (GLDUs)

Governorate Local Development Unit (GLDUs) act as a secretariat of the governor to study, examine, and evaluate central socio-economic policies that are relevant for the region, as well as to develop proposals for co-ordinated policies (Article 10, DL). They have functions in programming and project follow-up, as well as on data collection and research.

However, GLDUs seem to continue to operate within a deconcentrated system. While they have, in theory, assumed a position where they can play a major role in the preparation of local development strategies and local development action plans for their respective governorates, in practice their primary focus is on reporting to the centre on the implementation of projects by other government authorities at the governorate level. The legal and institutional framework presents a complex picture within which the roles of LDUs are not clearly defined in relation to the governorates, governors, executive and the new Governorate Council, as well as line ministries. The problem is the same at the municipal level.

According to the interviews and information gathered during the OECD peer review mission, as well as through the OECD Review's questionnaire, GLDUs seem to be heavily influenced by the institutional framework in which they operate. As shown in Figures 3.1 and 3.2, GLDUs' position in relation to the governor, as well as the executive (i.e. line ministries) and the Elected Council, is of particular importance. Discussions with local public officials suggested limited interactions between GLDUs and other divisions within the governorate. Deeper co-operation with other divisions with an external (e.g. general safety and environment, political affairs, social affairs) and internal (IT, human resources and finance) focus would ensure a more effective integration between the new horizontal competences of GLDUs and the existing divisions with vertical responsibilities within the governorates. Furthermore, since line ministry departments at the level of the governorate are not strictly situated under the governor's supervision, GLDUs have very few opportunities to influence them, beyond data collection roles.

Figure 3.1. Local Development Units at the governorate level

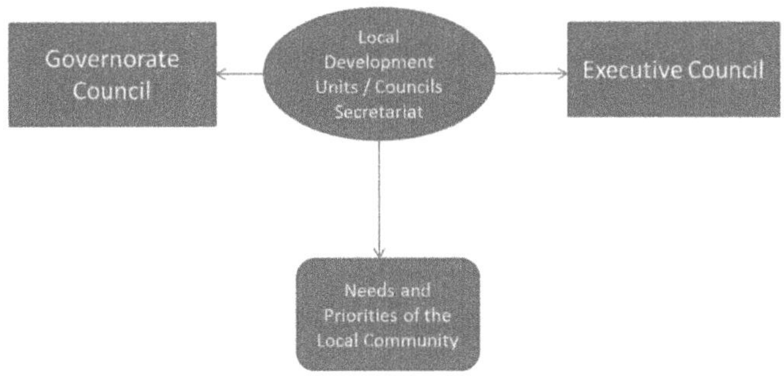

Source: Information provided by the Ministry of the Interior through the OECD questionnaire.

Figure 3.2. Proposed structure of the local development unit in the governorates

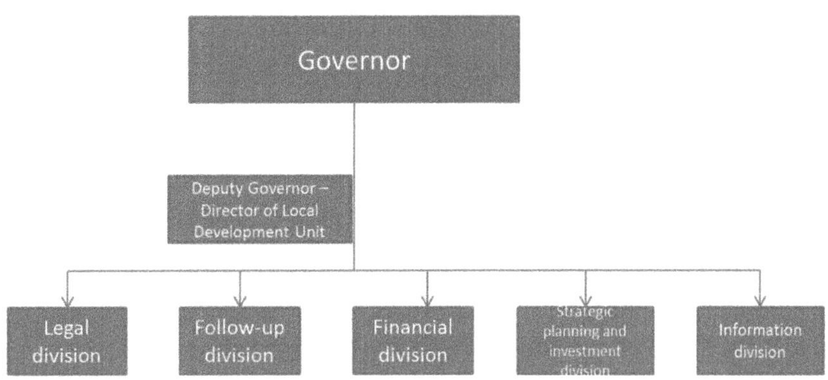

Source: Information provided by the Ministry of the Interior through the OECD questionnaire.

In fact, the legal framework for GLDUs appears confusing as it is composed of an amalgamation of different bylaws and circulars.[2] The DL would have been a good opportunity to recast all existing legislation on LDUs in a single text. In addition, some GLDU roles have been performed on a case-by-case basis in response to specific instructions from the Ministry of Interior's Local Development Directorate, but also to a limited extent, the governor. Some GLDU staff interviewed during the country visits expressed concern that they currently work in a reactive rather than proactive mode, with limited vision on the needs of the governorate as a territory and on how to identify and address its strategic priorities.

Despite the difficulties, thanks to the new law, GLDUs have expanded their role as to add additional functions, such as actively participating in the strategic planning processes as well as the preparation and follow-up of Governorates Development Programmes. This also includes co-ordination with CSOs and municipalities, and in-depth analysis of socio-economic data (as opposed to daily requested data collection). Several GLDUs have been active in carrying out field visits to assess local demands and needs. Some have even been involved in reviewing citizen complaints as part of this assessment. In some cases (e.g. Ajloun, Tafilah), GLDUs have been involved in local development planning that goes beyond capital infrastructure projects, for example in examining the local economic development potential of the governorate, in co-ordination with private sector interest groups and environmental impact analysis.[3]

The presence of external donor financing has often had a positive impact on the role of GLDU staff, particularly when they focus on facilitating the implementation of development projects involving local communities. In some cases (Irbid, Mafraq, Zarqa), GLDUs have also been engaged in projects concerning Syrian refugees and their impact on host communities.[4]

While it is too early to assess the role that GLDUs will perform under the new arrangements foreseen in the DL, interviews and data collected show that they are currently performing mostly basic functions in line with the regulations of the Ministry of the Interior (MoI). However, some of them are expanding their role and are starting to perform more advanced support functions to the office of the Governor, horizontal co-ordination, data driven monitoring and evaluation activities, project co-ordination and citizens' outreach and consultation. While these tasks are being performed to varying degrees of intensity and quality, they clearly suggest a set of potential roles and functions GLDUs could play in the near future and how strategic they would be in supporting the decentralisation aspirations of the Jordanian Government.

Municipal Local Development Units (MLDUs)

Mutatis mutandis, the situation at the municipal level appears similar. Since 2008, every municipality has been expected to create a local development unit (MLDU), however many do not seem to be yet operational and most municipalities complained about the lack of sufficient resources to dedicate staff to them.[5] As for the GLDUs, the most active MLDUs are those that participated in international donor projects[6], which resulted in municipalities with a good experience of producing municipal development plans, under the Ministry of Municipal Affairs (MoMA) supervision.

MLDUs have started to establish more viable institutional relationships with other ministries and national authorities, as both represented in deconcentrated offices at local level as well as in the capital, although they remain somewhat isolated due to the lack of a formal mandate to co-ordinate with them. In this context, MoMA still plays a crucial role as an intermediary between municipalities and line ministries. The new legal framework and institutional set-up should encourage further autonomy and room for manoeuvre adapted to local needs.

MLDUs are accountable to the municipality manager and have the following tasks: (Figure 3.3):

- Draft and prepare a database for the municipality, official institutions and civil society organisations.
- Co-ordinate between the municipality and civil society organisations on issues regarding sustainable development.

- Propose projects and prepare initial studies for the economic development of the community and municipality to present to the donors.
- Strengthen the role of the municipality in the cultural sector.
- Prepare studies on the social and economic realities of the local community, conduct surveys and prepare relative questionnaires.
- Hold training courses for employees and human resources in the municipality.

Figure 3.3. Institutional set-up of MLDUs - The example of Ajloun

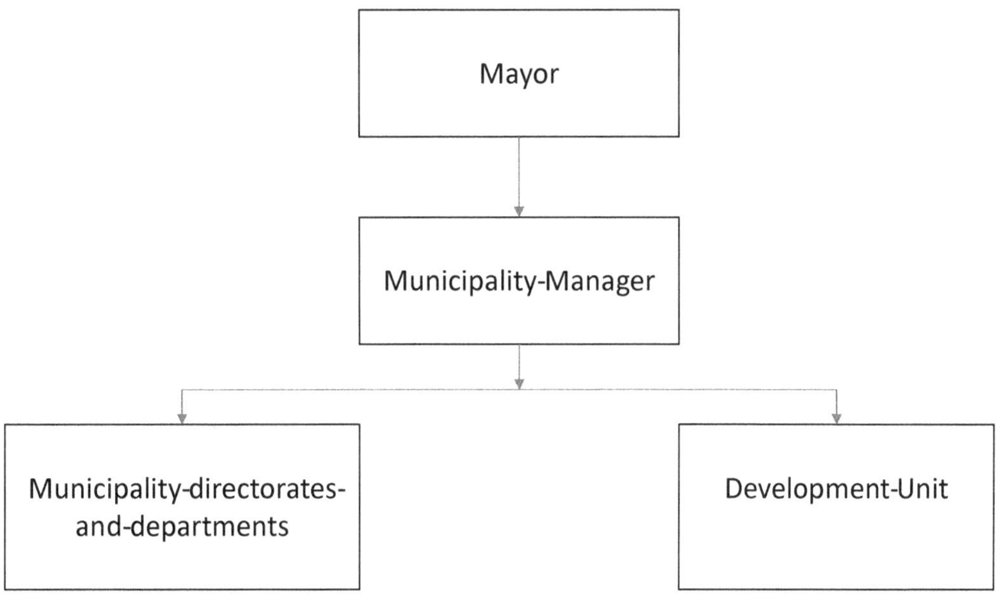

Source: Government of Jordan (2016), Background report of the OECD Strategic Assessment of Jordan, unpublished working paper.

Similarly to GLDUs, OECD assessment based on interviews and answers to the Review's Questionnaire and an analysis of relevant reports prepared by the international donor community7 reveals that currently MLDUs still play a relatively marginal role in the development aspects of local communities. The lack of proper communication channels amongst LDUs in each municipality and the council limits their capacity to provide inputs to and influence policymaking and service delivery mechanisms of the municipalities. Moreover, MLDUs often lack the skills and capacities to develop their roles and responsibilities`, as well as the necessary financial resources to develop the assigned functions. However, despite the denounced lack of resources and capacities, LDUs often end up developing functions beyond their assigned tasks and are successful in performing them. This is particularly the case in areas with a high number of refugees, where the demand and supply of public services is higher than in other regions of the country (Mafraq).

From a vertical perspective, co-ordination between GLDUs and MLDUs in the same governorate seems to be only informal and on an irregular basis. MLDUs provide GLDUs with data, but no specific mechanism or common procedures have been approved to ensure good data collection that gives support to territorial development. There's even no evidence if the methodology used to collect data at municipal and at governorate level is the same and if the same administrative procedures are followed to collect and use those data. While some GLDUs may be involved in the follow-up development issues of the municipal councils through their work in relation to the Executive and Advisory Councils, there are very few occasions where GLDUs have played a proactive and consultative role towards MLDUs.

Box 3.2 shows that in the case of Spain, the Technical Assistance Service for Municipalities provided by Provinces (that can be compared to Jordan's Governorates) to municipalities is an interesting tool to establish common procedures and collect data in an effective manner.

Box 3.2. The Spanish Technical Assistance Service for municipalities

The main feature of the Spanish local government system is its fragmentation: there are around 5 700 municipalities and over 75% have below 1 000 inhabitants. Because of this, Provincial Councils (*Diputaciones Provinciales*) play a major role as an intermediate local government. In the organisational structure of the Provincial Councils, the "Technical Assistance Service" develops technical and bureaucratic functions to support small municipalities in each province, particularly those with more limited economic and managerial resources.

Support for establishing common administrative procedures (back office and front desk) and digital administration (software tools) are among the most requested services from small municipalities to Provincial Councils. Other widely used technical assistance services are support and advice to accounting and optional technical assistance, both for public works and urban planning.

Source: Orduña, E. (n.d.), Annex 2, www.famp.es/famp/programas/seminarios_cursos_jornadas/14_AdmonLoc/informe.pdf.

Figure 3.4. Institutional arrangements in the new decentralisation framework

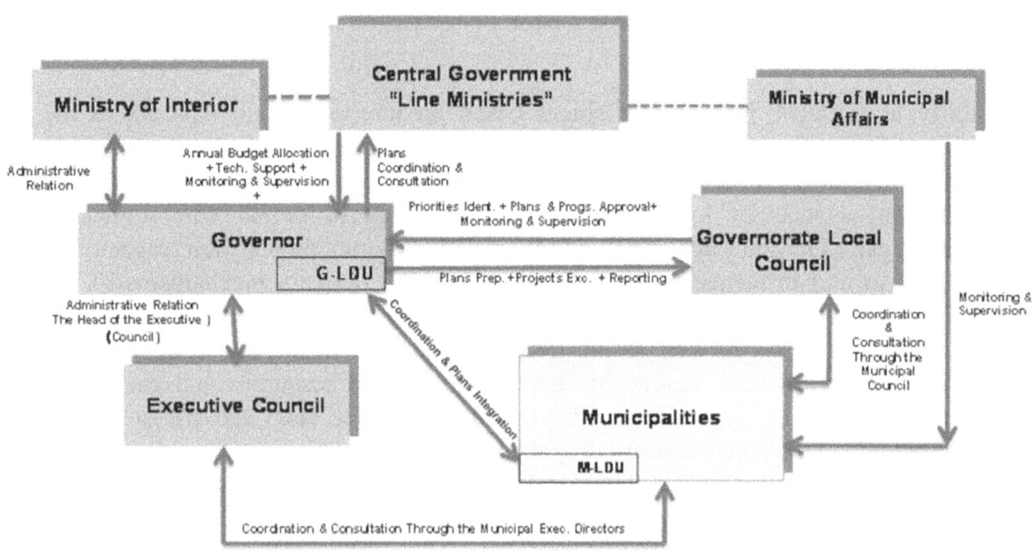

Source: UNDP (2010), *Capacity Building for Decentralization, Jordan: Focus on Governorate LDU*, Draft Final Report prepared for UNDP and MoPIC, internal document.

Although GLDUs and MLDUs do not yet play a key role as facilitators of local development, it is clear that they have the potential to do it, provided that there are given the necessary human and financial resources.

The Fiscal Dimension

Fiscal systems are essential for making decentralisation work (OECD, 2013). Any substantial reform requires the necessary resources to be carried out. If decentralisation is the aim of the reform, that is giving more competencies and autonomy to the lower levels, subnational governments would also require the financial resources to develop the new functions allocated in the Law. This section will describe and assess Jordan's fiscal arrangements at the subnational level in the context of the decentralisation reform. As mentioned in Chapter 2, the Mashreq region inherited a tradition of centralised taxation from both the Ottoman Empire and the colonial states. In most countries, the transfer of some responsibilities to lowest subnational levels has not been accompanied by fiscal reforms that either ensure adequate central transfers or grant local administrations the ability to collect their own revenues (Bergh, 2010).

Jordan is also a centralised country at fiscal level. Compared to the OECD, subnational governments have limited income, a high level of spending, and the degree of investment is below OECD levels (Figure 3.5). The limited autonomy of subnational governments in fiscal terms contrasts sharply with the country's regional disparities. The fiscal and investment needs are in fact very different for a.2.5M inhabitants like Greater Amman Municipality (GAM) and a smaller but very remote territory like Ma'an (121 000 inhabitants) but also with important transport and infrastructure deficits.

Figure 3.5. Subnational government expenditure as a percentage of GDP and total public expenditure in OECD countries, 2014

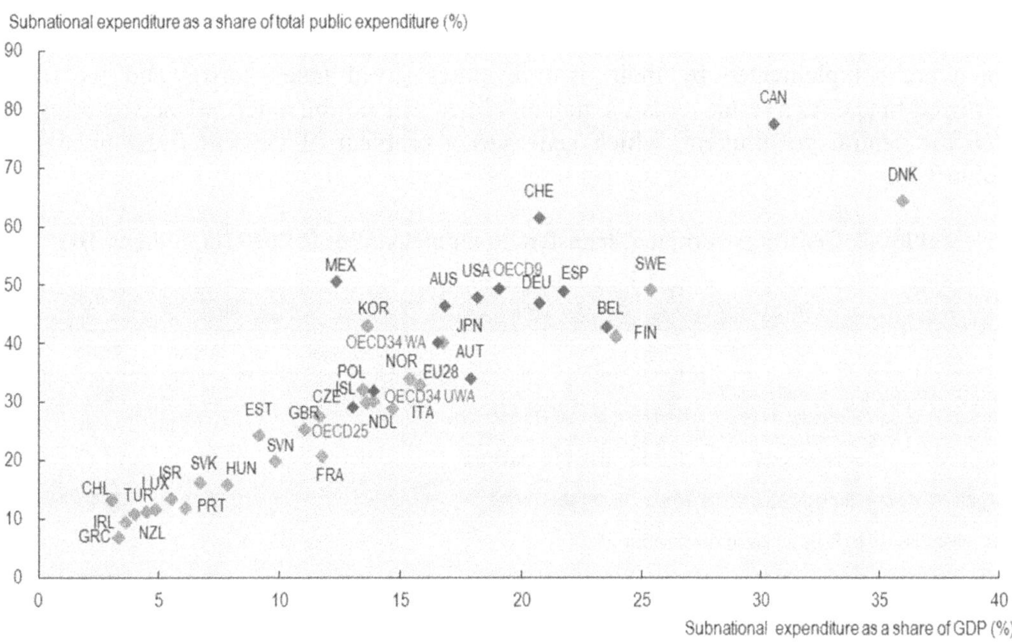

Note: 2013 Mexico, Chile and New Zealand; 2012 Australia; 2011 Turkey. Federal countries: dark markers. Latvia is now also member of the OECD.

Source: OECD (2016d), OECD Subnational government Structure and Finance (database) http://dx.doi.org/10.1787/888933363584.

Jordan has a lower degree of decentralisation in revenues than in expenditures. The fact that governorates' institutional and fiscal arrangements make them more similar to deconcentrated units from the Ministry of the Interior than proper regions with autonomy on their policies, services and finances is preventing them from playing the role that the ongoing decentralisation discourse would like them to.

That means that in practical and financial terms, only the central government and municipalities can be considered for the moment as the key public economic and social actors. They represent a large share of public spending and have important spending responsibilities in key sectors. The share of staff expenditure in public staff expenditure and in local expenditure is above the OECD average (OECD-UCLG, 2016).

Table 3.1. Expenditure of Jordanian local governments

Expenditure	% GDP	% General Government (same expenditure category)	% local government
Total expenditure (2013)	2.1%	5.8%	100
Current expenditure	1.4%	-	47.4%
Staff expenditure	1.1%	15.8%	51.2%
Investment	0.7%	12.9%	32.4%

Source: OECD - UCLG (2016), Subnational Governments around the World, www.oecd.org/cfe/regional-policy/sngs-around-the-world.htm.

Similarly, municipalities are expected to prepare and execute plans to achieve sustainable development in co-operation with local communities. However, as mentioned before, the law limits their competencies and functions. Municipalities are financed from central government funds essentially from an 8% coming from petrol revenue (MoMA), which are complemented by their own revenues (local taxes, tariffs and fees) and borrowed funds. As a result Jordan's municipalities still exhibit a dependence on transfers from the central government, which generates a problem of vertical fiscal imbalance (Table 3.2).

Table 3.2. Central government transfers to municipalities in 2010 (in millions JD)

Description of funds	Amount		Percentage
	Budget	Actual	Actual
Government allocation to municipalities This subsidy replace the allocation resulting from the share (6 percent) of the Municipal Councils in the taxation of certain gasoline product that was stipulated in article 48 of 2007 ML and cancelled in 2009 by the temporary amendment of the Law No.29 for Sales Tax.	85	75	76%
40 percent share in the proceeds of the annual car registration fee	-	23.7	24%
Allocations issued by fines for traffic law violation	-		
Global transfers from Central Government to Municipalities	85	98.7	100%
Total expenditures in 2010	5.460	5.705	
Global transfers in percentage of Central Government expenditures			**1.7%**

Source: ACE (2011), Jordan: Repeat Public Financial Management, Assessment following the PEFA Methodology.

According to the 2011 Law of Municipalities, the budget of the municipalities, their end-of-year accounts, loans, staffing, purchase, rent and hire have to be approved by MoMA, and expenditure cannot exceed allocations in the budget (Articles 41-56), which results in a situation by which municipalities needs to heavily depend on or - in the best case scenario - collaborate with MoMA to define and implement their own development strategies. Since 2010, the Cities and Villages Development Bank (CVDB), attached to MoMA and created in 1985 to assist municipalities in providing public services and managing local and international funding, also participates in preparing municipality budgets. All municipalities must send their final accounts and balance sheets to MoMA and CVDB within four months of the end-of-year, and MoMA is responsible for their approval. A consolidated report on municipalities' budget execution is prepared by a committee integrated by MOMA and MoF within 18 months of the end of the fiscal year. The municipalities require the approval of MOMA to borrow from any entity. They also need the approval of the Cabinet when the loan is to be guaranteed by central government.

Most municipality debt (98%) is directly with the CVDB, and the balance with the commercial banks that generally require the guarantee of the CVDB. The total outstanding municipality debt was Jordanian Dinar (JD) 89 million at the end of April 2011 (Ababsa, 2013).

Table 3.3. Loans granted to municipalities by CVDB (by governorates) in 2010

Governorates	Number of loans	Amount (in M JOD)	%
Amman	2	0.12	0.6
Irbid	40	9.563	46.2
Kerak	13	0.567	2.7
Balqa	3	0.339	1.6
Ma'an	54	1.098	5.3
Zarqa	21	3.204	15.5
Mafraq	44	2.941	14.2
Tafilah	4	0.081	0.4
Madaba	20	1.672	8.1
Jerash	16	0.761	3.7
Ajloun	36	0.257	1.2
Aqaba	2	0.083	0.4
Total	**255**	**20.686**	**99.9**

Source: CVDB (2011), annual report, www.csb.gov.jo/csb/?lang=en-gb.

The 2015 ML lists their own resources (Article 6) to include: 1) municipal taxes and fees; 2) revenue from investment projects; 3) self-revenue; 4) grants and donations, conditioned with obtaining the approval of the Cabinet if the source is not Jordanian; 5) other taxes and fees stated in the law. However, resources at the local level are very limited, as revenue collection is very low in Jordan. On average, only about 32 US dollars

(JD 23) per capita was collected in 2009 (MoMA). Some municipalities do not collect their own revenues at all. This raises the question of whether local governments are willing to tax their citizens and whether these low returns from their own tax sources will at least cover collection costs (SOFRECO/European Commission (2010).

Weak tax administrative capacity also has a negative impact on tax collection. To foster the tax administrative capacity of subnational governments, some countries like Peru have created specific tax administrations agencies (Tax Administration Agencies - SATs) for the larger municipalities. These agencies enjoy a high degree of financial and administrative autonomy as they are financed by a share of collected taxes and fines. The main remaining challenge is the setup of a tax administration for medium and smaller municipalities, where tax collection is poor. Yet, implementing a specific structure to collecting taxes also requires significant investments in staff and implies high current expenditure (OECD, 2016a). In some countries with an important number of small municipalities like Spain, Provincial Councils (Diputaciones Provinciales) offers to manage and collect local taxes on behalf of small municipalities and inter-municipal associations of municipalities with limited capacity.

Current spending as a share of municipal budgets is high at 68%, on average. Some 45% of all municipalities are above average, with some municipalities achieving shares as high as 90% and more (Talal Al-Jadeda, Rabiet Al-Kura, Al-Qatraneh, Ma'adh bin Jabal, Al-Hassa). For this type of spending, the wage bill predominates. These figures indicate a dysfunctional municipal financial sector in Jordan, which is also in severe financial distress (SOFRECO/European Commission (2010). Moreover, there are big differences between the Great Municipality of Amman (GAM) with more own revenues and all of the other Jordanian municipalities.

In several interviews with the OECD delegation, mayors revealed that the financial situation can vary from one municipality to another based on the size of the municipality and the number of inhabitants. Whilst the budget allocated to GAM alone is roughly JD 350 million (i.e. approximately USD 494 million), the budget for all the other municipalities in Jordan collectively is about JD 200 million (i.e. approximately USD 282.5 million). Apart from GAM, the financial situation for the municipalities is critical, and many have difficulties in carrying out basic duties and tasks also because the municipal team lacks technical and financial skills. The majority of mayors indicated that their financial resources are insufficient to implement future plans or development projects.

Mayors confirmed that lack of financial support is one of the most important challenges affecting investment in municipalities. Overall, they agreed that the share allocated to municipalities from the national budget is not enough, and that the total municipal debt for the country exceeds USD 1.3 million.

Overall, Jordan’s municipalities represent a small percentage of general public spending (only roughly 3%, excluding the Greater Amman Municipality, GAM), which - together with the limited local public services they currently provide - gives an idea of the importance of promoting a greater degree of functional and financial decentralisation in order to better align the rhetoric of the ongoing reform with real changes in the architecture of the Jordanian public sector.

An ambitious reform with scarce new resources at governorate and municipal level

The DL acknowledges new competences to governorates in promoting development and project investment but, still as deconcentrated administrations, they still have very limited autonomy over their expenditure and investments. The new law also states that governorate elected councils should enjoy administrative and financial autonomy since they have democratic legitimacy, however, this autonomy does not exist in practice. The DL simply states that "a sufficient sum of money is devoted for the annual governorate budget, enough to sustain its work" but doesn't provide details on how and what kind of own resources, which keeps decisions subject to approval by the central authority.

Table 3.4 shows in broader terms, the budget allocated to governorates. Data only reflect the direct budget allocated by the MoI after governorates' proposals, and usually cover administrative and functional costs. Budgets are already deconcentrated through each line ministry. This implies that even though there may be consultative bodies in support of a governor's attempt to co-ordinate sectoral policies, they will have little impact on horizontal planning and development.

Table 3.4. Budget allocation of governorates

Governorate	Sums allocated for capital expenditures in the general budget of 2016 in JD	Percentage per Governorate from the general budget of 2016
Irbid	108 043 200	0.11
Mafraq	50 086 000	0.05
Jarash	46 372 000	0.05
Ajloun	49 498 100	0.05
Amman	178 407 100	0.18
Balqa	77 989 800	0.08
Zarqa	88 806 700	0.09
Madaba	46 305 000	0.05
Karak	61 802 400	0.06
Maan	110 257 300	0.11
Tafilah	49 729 700	0.05
Aqaba	119 522 200	0.12
Total	**986 819 500**	**1.00**

Source: Government of Jordan (2016), Background report of the OECD Strategic Assessment of Jordan, unpublished working paper.

This lack of financial autonomy together with the budget in silos linked to line ministries also raises a problem of transparency and accountability. The elected council approved the drafted budget but there is no follow-up on the execution

For the time being, Governorates still lack of real autonomy to elaborate their own budget since they don't have the possibility of direct revenues such as imposition of fees or taxes. They draft a budget proposal that will be submitted to the MoI and Ministry of

Finance (MoF) and for the moment get transfers from the central level as well as donations and grants from international donors that have to be approved by MoI.

The different features and territorial realities in Jordan call for more autonomy in the management of incomes, expenses and investments not only at municipal but also at governorate level, since the needs can vary throughout the country. Centralised investments can only respond in part to local needs and, therefore, strategic planning of key projects to be defined at governorate level can contribute to a better fiscal framework for an inclusive territorial development.

Strategic planning

Jordan 2025 sets the ambition of more equitable socio-economic development in the whole country. As mentioned in Chapter 2, MoPIC is in charge of leading and co-ordinating strategic planning at the central and subnational level. Under this vision, the Executive Development Programme (EDP) 2016-2018 outlines development projects across priority sectors that include health, local development, education, water, energy, and transport for the next three years. This represents the first phase of implementing Jordan 2025 in the whole country.

The EDP is also replicated at the governorate level by the Governorates Development Programmes (GDD) for 2016-2018. GDD is one of the top priorities in the government, and one of the main innovations in recent years to promote a bottom-up approach to strategic planning. Those programmes have been elaborated by MoPIC in close partnership with governorates, as well as through field visits and consultation meetings with key stakeholders at the local level to discuss development priorities in the governorates. Each programme includes data regarding the socio-economic situation in each governorate, as well as Key Performance Indicators (KPIs) for the performance budgeting exercise on poverty, unemployment, family income, education, health and the job market.

Figure 3.6 shows the current institutional arrangement of this mechanism of consultation and elaboration. GLDUs also play an active role in this process by collecting data of their territory.

The DL gives authority to the governorate council to propose the establishment of investment projects and to carry out common projects with other governorates, with the approval of the competent authorities. The Executive Council plays an essential role in preparing the proposals.

Figure 3.6. Institutional mechanism of consultation: Governorate development plans

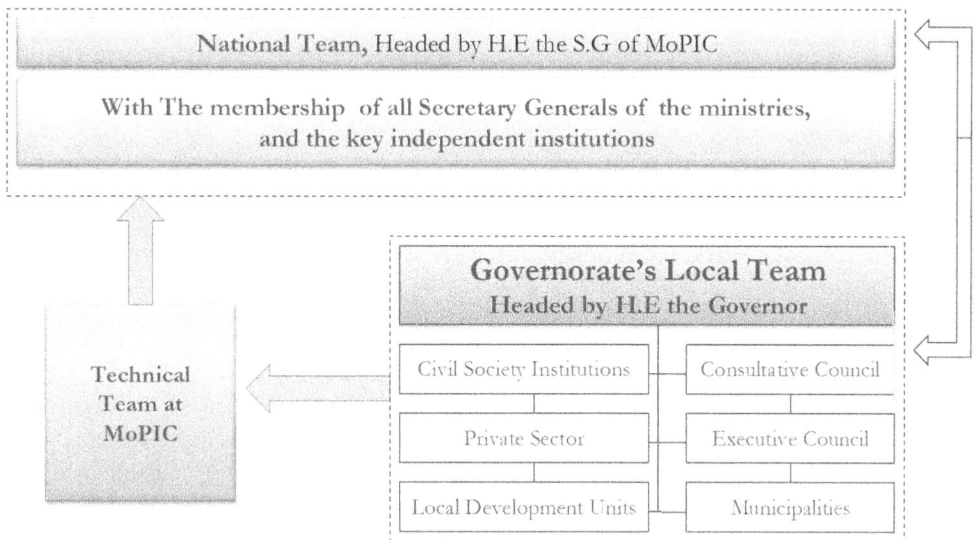

Source: Government of Jordan (2016), Background report of the OECD Strategic Assessment of Jordan, unpublished working paper.

Similarly, the ML gives more competencies for strategic planning at the municipal level, as it states that municipalities will adopt its budget project, as well as its strategic plan and the local needs' guide. GAM has already some experience on this topic with its own Development Strategy since 2002 that has specific objectives and programmes targeting a wide range of sectors, such as: institutional development, including improvement of the system of local revenue collection and management, and urban planning.

MoPIC is investing in a bottom-up approach to strategic planning, where local councils bring citizens' needs and submit them to the following level, the municipalities, who then forward them to governorates. This would encourage that all plans are linked and aligned at the different levels. While this is potentially the most relevant innovation introduced by the DL and ML in the way national development policies are drafted and implemented in Jordan, many aspects of these new mechanisms still need fine-tuning. Among them, it will be paramount that the Government ensures that governorate development plans and top priorities are taken into consideration by the municipalities and, vice versa, that municipalities' plans are fully represented in those elaborated by the Governorates. This will be a challenge in this new stage of participative strategic planning through a bottom-up approach.

Implementing Jordan 2025 and the Executive Programme (2016-2018) and Governorate Plans will also require more qualified expertise at subnational level. MoPIC has made important efforts in drafting the 12 Governorates programmes, some of the key challenges on strategic planning and institutional capacity are already identified such as:

- Weak connections between strategic and financial planning at government departments.

- Lack of accountability from government departments on levels of commitment to public sector development policies and programmes.
- The need to provide regular, larger and up-to-date data and indicators on development at governorate and local level.
- Lack of co-ordination between parties working in local development at the national level.
- The need to build the capabilities of human resources working in local administrations and local development planning.
- Providing sufficient funds to initiate real development in governorates.

In other to ensure the alignment of policies and a coherent strategic vision, some OECD countries have created deconcentrated structures at a regional level that focus on delivering integrated approaches to regional policies (OECD, 2015a). Regional Development Agencies (RDAs), and other deconcentrated agencies of different forms, are common in OECD countries. While regions may have the authority to initiate policies at their own discretion, the choice for central government action is nested in a set of alternatives, many of which may be used simultaneously (Box 3.3).

Box 3.3. Strategic planning at regional and local levels

A wide range of development agencies now exist in OECD member countries. Each makes a contribution to how the local economies perform and what they contribute to national economic performance. Development agencies can be at the regional, intermediate (such as Serra do Caldeirao in Portugal) or even local level in big cities.

Regional Development Agencies (RDAs) encourage a partnership-based approach to regional development, and mutually agreed contracts align budgeting across different levels of government towards shared outcomes.

Canada

RDAs across Canada help to address key economic challenges by providing regionally-tailored programmes, services, knowledge and expertise that: 1) build on regional and local economic assets and strengths; 2) support business growth, productivity and innovation; 3) help small and medium-sized enterprises (SMEs) effectively compete in the global marketplace; 4) provide adjustment assistance in response to economic downturns and crises; and 5) support communities.

RDAs, along with national innovation policy, continue to promote the importance of innovation and skills for regional development. For example:

- Western Economic Diversification Canada launched the Western Innovation Initiative (WINN), a Canadian Dollar (CAD) 100 million five-year federal initiative that offers repayable contributions for SMEs to move their new and innovative technologies from the later stages of research and development to the marketplace.
- The Federal Economic Development Agency for Southern Ontario's (FedDev Ontario) Southern Ontario prosperity initiatives focus on innovation, productivity and economic diversification. In addition, the agency's Advanced Manufacturing Fund is a USD 200 million fund to support product and process innovation in the manufacturing sector.
- The Atlantic Canada Opportunities Agency provides approximately CAD 90 million annually to support innovation and commercialisation under its current programmes, including the Atlantic Innovation Fund and the Business Development Program.

Box 3.3. Strategic planning at regional and local levels *(cont.)*

Serra do Caldeirão (Portugal)

The Serra do Caldeirão is a mountainous area located in the south of Portugal, between the coastal tourist zone of the Algarve and the agricultural plateau of the Alentejo. It is an area of small farm holders and craft workers with a population of approximately 74 000 persons spread over nearly 3 500 square kilometres. It has suffered from depopulation and the decline of forestry and agriculture, even though Portugal as a whole has witnessed rapid social and economic expansion.

The local development agency for the area, In Loco (www.in-loco.pt/), is one of the most highly regarded in Portugal. Some of its recent achievements are:

- Creation of jobs in new and small enterprises in the last 20 years, through training, soft support and investment grants, particularly in tourism agro-food and craft industries.
- Creation of new community facilities for childcare and telecentres.
- Demonstration of a successful local development approach to partners and other agencies, which has been adopted by others outside the area.

The Serra do Caldeirão experience also demonstrates a number of aspects of good practice and innovation in strategy, implementation methods and actions:

- Its strategy attempts to integrate the different constituents of development - economic, social, cultural, educational, and environmental - in each project. It starts from concrete problems on the ground and, through careful observation, identifies potential opportunities and approaches.
- Implementation rests on the active participation of local agencies, individuals and groups, and in particular women, at all the stages of the projects and development processes.
- A formal partnership has been negotiated and maintained with all institutional players, whether political or technical, in order to bring out the maximum co-operation. Every action seeks to balance the three strands of animation, training and organisation.
- All actions and assessments are combined in a permanent interaction.

Sources: OECD (2016a), *OECD Territorial Reviews: Peru 2016*, OECD Publishing, Paris, http://dx.doi.org/10.1787/9789264262904-en; OECD (2007a), *Linking Regions and Central Governments: Contracts for Regional Development*, OECD Publishing, Paris, http://dx.doi.org/10.1787/9789264008755-en; Clark, G., J. Huxley and D. Mountford (2010), *Organising Local Economic Development: The Role of Development Agencies and Companies*, OECD Publishing, Paris, http://dx.doi.org/10.1787/9789264083530-en.

Box 3.4. Turkey's new national regional development agency model

Background

The current network of RDAs in Turkey was established between 2007 and 2009. Among other factors, the alignment with European Union approaches to regional policy was an important factor to their establishment. The initial phases of the RDAs focused on establishing the institutions themselves and building institutional capacity at the subnational level. The Ministry of Development oversees the agencies, and the Higher Council of Regional Development approves the regional development plans the RDAs are tasked with developing.

The 26 agencies cover the country's 81 provinces, with coverage ranging from 1 to 6 provinces, depending on the region. The 26 regions correspond to the NUTS II level statistical unit principles used by the European Union. The National Development Plan (2014-2018) has a stated goal of strengthening connections across the RDA network.

Roles and responsibilities

These RDAs have three key functions; 1) planning, research and analysis; 2) conducting grant programmes for profit and not-for-profit institutions; 3) promoting and supporting investments and promoting their region. They also play capacity building and service delivery roles. Capacity building includes: technical support for local authority planning studies; capacity improvements for rural and local development; improving co-operation between the public, private and non-profit sectors; and ensuring research on the resources and opportunities of regions. Business support roles include the promotion of business and investment facilities, supporting the administrative process for investors in the regions, supporting SMEs and start-ups, and supporting other activities to ensure implementation of the regional plan.

Ministerial linkages

The State Planning Organisation is responsible for co-ordination of the agencies. They are under the line authority of the Ministry of Development for final approval of the regional development strategies and corresponding work programmes. In addition to the Ministry of Development, the RDAs are also increasingly taking on roles on behalf of other national ministries, such as the Ministry of Economy (for delivery of incentive programmes for selected industries, investment programmes, research and development incentives, etc.). There is tendency for RDAs to increasingly serve as a one-stop-shop for firms to access different national programmes.

Oversight and management

Agencies comprise a Development Council, as well as the RDA Administrative Board and General Secretariat. The Development Council is a public-private platform that includes (maximum of 100) local authorities, private sector representatives, NGOs, and universities. This body can make recommendations to the RDA in an advisory role via its feedback in meetings (at least twice per year). While some regions have tested ad hoc working groups within the Development Councils, in the future, some form of leadership group within the Development Councils may be established to facilitate an increasing role in RDA oversight. The Administrative Board is the decision-making body composed of the provincial governors, the mayors of metropolitan or provincial municipalities, Chairmen of the Provincial Councils and Chairmen of the Chambers of Commerce and/or Industry. The Administrative Board Chairman represents the agency and is always a provincial governor; rotating on an annual basis if the RDA covers more than one province. The Administrative Board is supported by a Secretary General and the Secretariat that implements decisions of the Administrative Board, and prepares the work plans, manages finances, supports projects and provides technical assistance.

Box 3.4. Turkey's new national regional development agency model *(cont.)*

Funding

Resources are grouped into a single pot. Funding includes mainly appropriations by the High Planning Council (based on population, level of development and performance of each agency), international funds (including the European Union), funds from own activities, 1% of yearly revenues of the special provincial administrations, 0.5% of yearly revenues of the municipalities and 1% of yearly revenues of the chambers of industry and commerce. Since 2008, central government has provided EUR 630 million (67%), and local institutions (municipalities, special provincial administrations, chambers of commerce and industry) provided EUR 310 million (33%) to RDAs.

Instruments

Within the context of national rules regarding requests for proposals, RDAs may adapt some of their programmes for local needs within a set of common instruments across the country. The variations may include the sectors for support or the types of organisations (in some cases this may be an NGO), etc. Any RDA action must be in compliance with national policy and international agreements, therefore support to certain sectors may be restricted. In addition to business support-related measures, RDAs also have an explicit technical assistance role (see description of mission above). Local institutions may apply for training, human resource development, or other capacity building needs. The RDA can either provide services directly or contract out those services. The RDA may also support certain infrastructure investments for innovation and business development. RDAs also provide the promotion of business and investment facilities, supporting the administrative process for investors through Investment Support Offices established in each province. Since 2008, RDAs have supported more than 12 000 projects, through all modalities, by allocating nearly EUR 770 million.

Performance monitoring

The original law does not specify any overarching performance targets/indicators of RDAs, but does require performance evaluation by the Ministry of Development and an evaluation/impact evaluation by RDAs of their own programmes after two years. The Turkish government is looking into the development of a performance evaluation system. To facilitate the evaluation of individual programmes, the national government has provided all RDAs with a standardised management information system. This harmonised tracking tool for all entities, supported by the RDAs and implemented across the country, facilitates evaluations of specific programmes and their impact on recipients. The system is recognised by the OECD Observatory of Public Sector Innovation (OPSI).

Source: OECD (2015b), *Multi-dimensional Review of Peru: Volume I. Initial Assessment*, OECD Development Pathways, OECD Publishing, Paris, http://dx.doi.org/10.1787/9789264243279-en.

As described earlier, the MoI's role within governorates is essentially related to the administrative and financial management and supervision of governorates. MoPIC can play an important role in developing Governorate capacity in socio-economic planning and development. Furthermore, the linkages to municipal socio-economic development remain to be established effectively in this complex institutional arrangement, where not only MoPIC but also MoMA and MoI still play a supervisory and monitoring role.

The Government of Jordan already has some interesting experiences on data collection and planning. Box 3.5 describes an innovative toolkit used for Jordanian Public Health services in the framework of a project by the United States Agency for International Development (USAID), which could be inspiration for data collection at the local level.

Box 3.5. TANMIA strategic toolkit

The TANMIA tool was designed in the context of the Jordan Health Communication Partnership (JHCP), implemented by Johns Hopkins Bloomberg School of Public Health - Center for Communication Program, and funded by USAID (2004-2013). Its aim is to support decision making at the local and national levels by providing the knowledge and information required through statistical and analytical reports, feedback systems, and a geographical information system. TANMIA also supports and documents the strategic planning process by providing the indicators that measure its accomplishment.

TANMIA helps decentralised Jordanian governorates organise the flow of information on developmental projects through population support systems, geographic maps, and smart analysis tools. TANMIA also serves as the supportive basis of the current planning process by linking goal indicators to measure their achievement through parallel work with the current planning process in a systematic and scientific manner.

TANMIA facilitates decision-making processes in all governorates of Jordan by providing them with information on health, education, agriculture, environment, and other various sectors. The overall long-term goal of TANMIA is to provide a system and guidelines for the eventual application of Geographic Information Systems (GIS) and business intelligence in support of plan formulation and project implementation at both the national and governorate levels across all sectors in Jordan. TANMIA makes it possible to go beyond a simple presentation of data as points on a map.

TANMIA's system organises project and population-related data in a shared platform for decision makers at the regional and national level. It develops clear, relevant and easy-to understand measures that are tied to goals. It gathers, monitors, and analyses programme data. It also evaluates the effectiveness of programmes.

Source: K4 Health (2017), TANMIA Strategic Planning Tool website, www.k4health.org/toolkits/jhcp/tanmia-strategic-planning-tool (accessed 14 February 2017).

Promoting inter-institutional dialogue

Challenges to be faced at subnational level are inter-independent and therefore require an integrated approach with the implication and participation of all key stakeholders are present. "OECD member and non-member countries are actively looking for ways to facilitate, and create innovative approaches to improve relationships and co-ordination among levels of government. These relationships lie between the central and subnational levels (vertical level), as well as at horizontal level (i.e., among ministries, across regions, between municipalities)" (Charbit and Michalun, 2009).

Multi-level governance

Institutional factors are critical to promote inclusive growth at subnational levels across the OECD. Formal and informal institutions that facilitate negotiation and dialogue among key actors in order to mobilise and integrate them into the development process are vital, as are those that enhance policy continuity. This co-operation is easier when citizens trust each other and expect reciprocity, and there is confidence in democratic institutions. (OECD, 2009a; 2012).

The relationship between and across levels of government in Jordan is characterised by mutual dependence with a predominance of the central level. The new reform aims to bring policies and services closer to citizens through a bottom-up approach and by introducing elected bodies at the lowest level that means that more attention will need to be paid to co-ordination mechanisms to ensure coherence and consistency of policies at each level.

In fact, the trend of allocating competences to lower levels of government across OECD countries has resulted in a dynamic relationship, "with constant movement along a continuum of decentralisation, as well as recentralisation activity" (Charbit and Michalun, 2009). Decentralisation requires though, effective co-ordination that goes between the same level of government (horizontal co-ordination through different ministries) and across different levels of government, the so-called vertical co-ordination. This vertical co-ordination is particularly important since different levels of government can have different kinds of competences on the same topic. For instance, in the case of social affairs this is usually a shared competence where national government decides the national strategy and the lowest levels either implement concrete services or give support to other administrations in their implementation. Co-ordination is hence essential to ensure a coherent approach. Co-ordination mechanisms not only affect administrations, they often also imply multiple actors and stakeholders from civil society and the private sector. (Charbit and Michalun, 2009). Thus, in order to manage the relational outcome of decentralisation policies, multi-level governance is key. The OECD seven gaps in multi-level governance are described in Box 3.6 and show the key challenges to pay attention to and to be faced.

Box 3.6. The seven gaps in multi-level governance

The relationship among levels of government resulting from decentralisation is characterised by mutual dependence, since it is impossible to have a complete separation of policy responsibilities and outcomes among levels of government. It is a complex relationship, simultaneously vertical, across different levels of government; horizontal, among the same level of government; and networked. Governments must therefore bridge a series of challenges or "gaps" between levels, both vertically and horizontally.

These gaps include, notably, the fiscal capacity of governments to meet obligations; information asymmetries between levels of government; gaps in administrative responsibility, with administrative borders not corresponding to functional economic and social areas at the subnational level; and gaps in policy design, when line ministries take purely vertical approaches to cross-sectoral regulation that may require co-design of implementation at the local level, and when there is often a lack of human or infrastructure resources to deliver services and design strategies. Countries may experience these gaps to a greater or lesser degree, but given the mutual dependence that arises from decentralisation and the network-like dynamics of multi-level governance, countries are likely to face them simultaneously.

The OECD approach of co-ordination and capacity "gaps" has to be considered as a diagnosis tool for identifying the main difficulties in implementing effective policies in decentralised contexts. It can also serve to assess the instruments used by governments to face these difficulties. The series of "gaps" does not just concern the current dimension of the

Box 3.6. The seven gaps in multi-level governance *(cont.)*

interdependence among public actors; it also engages their dynamic relationship and risk for future difficulties if the interaction between levels of government is not fructuous. The seven gaps are as follows:

- The **information gap** is characterised by information asymmetries between levels of government when designing, implementing and delivering public policies. Sometimes the information gap results from strategic behaviours of public actors who may prefer to not reveal too clearly their strengths and weaknesses, especially if allocation of responsibility is associated with conditional granting. However, information about territorial specificities is often not perceived by the central decision maker, and subnational actors may be ignorant about capital objectives and strategies. The **capacity challenge** arises when there is a lack of human, knowledge or infrastructural resources available to carry out tasks, regardless to the level of government (even if, in general, it is considered that Subnational Governments suffer more from such a difficulty than central government).
- The **fiscal gap** is represented by the difference between subnational revenues and the required expenditures for Subnational governments to meet their responsibilities and implement appropriate development strategies. In a more dynamic perspective, fiscal difficulties also include a mismatch between budget practices and policy needs. For example, in the absence of multi-annual budget practices, SNGs may face uncertainty in engaging appropriate spending, as well as the absence of flexibility in spending, which is very beneficial in an uncertain environment. An overly strict earmarking of grants may also impede appropriate fungibility of resources and limit the subnational ability to deliver adapted policies.
- The **policy challenge** results when line ministries take a purely vertical approach to be territorially implemented, while SNGs are best placed to customise complementarities between policy fields and concretise cross-sectoral approaches. Limited co-ordination among line ministries may provoke a heavy administrative burden, as well as different timing and agenda in managing correlated actions, etc. It can even lead to strong inconsistencies and readability concerns when the objectives of sectoral policy makers are contradictory.
- The **administrative gap** occurs when the administrative scale for policy making, in terms of spending and strategic planning, is not in line with functional relevant areas. A very common case concerns municipal fragmentation, which can lead jurisdictions to set ineffective public action by not benefitting from economies of scale. Some specific policies also request very specific, and often naturally fixed, boundaries.
- The **objective gap** refers to different rationalities from national and subnational policy makers, which create obstacles for adopting convergent strategies. A common example deals with political party membership, which may lead to opposing approaches. In such a case, divergences across levels of government can be "politically" used for cornering the debate instead of serving a common good. Even without any difference in political "colour" from the central government, a mayor may prefer serving his/her local constituency instead of aligning decisions to national broader objectives, which may be perceived as contradictory.
- The **accountability challenge** results from the difficulty of ensuring the transparency of practices across different constituencies and levels of government. It also concerns possible integrity challenges of policy makers involved in the management of public investment.

Box 3.6. The seven gaps in multi-level governance *(cont.)*

OECD member and non-member countries are increasingly developing and using a wide variety of mechanisms to help bridge these gaps and improve the coherence of multi-level policy making. These mechanisms may be "binding", such as legal mechanisms, or "soft", such as platforms for discussion, and they must be sufficiently flexible to allow for territorially specific policies. The involvement of subnational governments in policy making takes time, but medium to long-term benefits should outweigh the costs of co-ordination.

Sources: Charbit, C. (2011), "Governance of Public Policies in Decentralised Contexts: The Multi-level Approach", OECD Regional Development Working Papers, No. 2011/04, OECD Publishing, Paris, http://dx.doi.org/10.1787/5kg883pkxkhc-en; Charbit, C. and M. Michalun (2009), "Mind the Gaps: Managing Mutual Dependence in Relations among Levels of Government", OECD Working Papers on Public Governance, No. 14, OECD Publishing, Paris, http://dx.doi.org/10.1787/221253707200.

The seven gaps can apply to Jordan at different levels. For instance, the fiscal gap, should be implemented according to the responsibilities and competencies allocated. This would not mean fiscal decentralisation strictly speaking, especially in a deconcentrated model such as the one chosen by Jordan though it would definitely need the adequate resources for the new competencies and the objectives to be achieved following Jordan 2025. The information, capacity, policy (in particular, fragmentation and policy silos), administrative, objective and accountability gaps are challenges that Jordan still needs to overcome regarding multi-level governance.

In fact, and according to the information provided through the questionnaire to the OECD, the main co-ordination and dialogue channel between central and regional governments is via the direct informal dialogue of mayors and governors with the central government authorities. There's no official association of mayors or municipalities. Governorates have regular bilateral meetings with representatives of the MoI, although these are on demand rather than on an institutional basis. Other interactions occur on a case by case basis via the deconcentrated administrative bodies of the central government on the ground. Box 3.7 shows different examples of vertical and horizontal co-ordination mechanisms in OECD countries that could inspire Jordan to promote multi-level co-ordination.

Box 3.7. Main mechanisms for vertical and horizontal co-ordination in OECD countries

Vertical co-ordination mechanisms

Legal mechanisms (binding laws and legislation) are the strongest method for organising multi-level governance relations. This mechanism is often used with respect to fiscal resources and to allocate competencies.

Standard setting. Many OECD countries establish universal standard setting to ensure a similar level and quality of service provision across the country. In Sweden, for example, municipalities enjoy a high degree of autonomy in the provision of public services, but need to meet nationally set standards and regulations.

Contracts or agreements between national and subnational governments concerning their mutual obligations, i.e. assignment of powers of decision, distribution of contributions (including financial commitments) and contract enforcement mechanisms. These arrangements offers several advantages: they allow for customised management of interdependencies; they are useful tools for dialogue that can be used for clarifying responsibilities and making mutual commitments explicit; they open possibilities for judicial enforcement; and they can be used as learning mechanisms. In federal and decentralised countries, "contracts" are a particularly important tool for promoting co-operation, coherence and synergies among levels of government. Examples include "arrangements" in Canada; "joint tasks" in Germany; "accordi" in Italy; and "convenios" in Spain. Challenges with contracts that have been observed across OECD member countries include high transaction costs and a power bias towards higher education compliance by all parties.

Strategic co-ordinating committees and partnership groups. The interests and inputs of key actors from different levels are co-ordinated through joint representation on administrative bodies or working groups. These committees can serve as forums for improved communication and dialogue over subjects of common interest. They can also help align interests and timing, and set the basis for signing contracts and agreements among government levels. They can help disseminate good practices vertically between different levels of government, or, horizontally across regions. In some countries, co-ordination bodies are leading actors in fiscal capacity building by representing the interests of the local or regional level to national level decision makers. In Norway, for example, the Association of Local and Regional Authorities provides a forum to discuss the framework for distributing revenues in relation to the tasks carried out by local governments, the financial situation of local government, and efficiency measures.

In the Czech Republic, the Union of Municipalities and the Association of Regions have representatives on the national government's Board of Deputy Ministers for Regulatory Reform and Effective Public Administration, and represent the regions' interests in the Czech parliament, the Cabinet and in European institutions. In Spain, examples include the sectoral conferences and the Conference of the Presidents of Autonomous Communities.

Horizontal co-ordinating mechanisms

The governments of the German Länder (regions) co-operate through the Council of Prime Ministers and 19 subject-specific standing conferences of ministers. The council/standing conferences are not part of the German government and cannot pass legislation. Nevertheless, they play an important role in the federal system. Councils have two primary functions: in policy fields where legislative powers reside with the Länder, they are the main forum for policy co-ordination across the Länder; and in policy fields where the Länder have limited powers, council/conference resolutions articulate common interests of the Länder to other actors, such as the federal government or the European Commission. Co-operation in the council/conferences is consensus-based and most decisions are made unanimously. Formally, the Council of Prime Ministers and most other permanent conferences require the approval of 13 of the 16 German Länder to pass a resolution. Although resolutions are not legally binding, they have a strong symbolic power, and are almost always enacted by Länder governments.

Box 3.7. Main mechanisms for vertical and horizontal co-ordination in OECD countries *(cont.)*

Some permanent conferences also draft model laws and regulations to support state administrations and to further harmonise laws across states. The Council of Prime Ministers convenes four times a year. After the council meetings, prime ministers meet with the German Chancellor. Subject-specific permanent conferences have their own meeting schedule and tend to meet between one and four times a year. The federal minister in charge of the respective portfolio typically attends the meeting in an observing role. Several permanent conferences have established additional committees to discuss particular topics in more detail. The administrative structure of permanent conferences varies depending on their responsibilities. Some permanent conferences have their own permanent secretariats with sizable staff numbers, while others use the administration of the state that holds the rotating presidency of the permanent conference.

The Association of Regions of the Czech Republic (AK CR) was founded in 2001 to represent the collective voice of the Czech regions. It associates the Czech Republic's 13 regions and the capital Prague. The supreme body of the AK CR is the council composed of the president of each region and the Mayor of the capital, Prague. The association offers services ranging from representing regional interests in parliament, the Cabinet and European institutions, to drawing up various reports, standpoints and initiatives. The council elects a chairman and three vice chairmen, and decides on setting up commissions. Commissions serve as advisors to the council. Commissions include the Commission for Regional Development, the Commission for Public Administration, the Commission for Regional Financing, the Commission for Education, the Commission for Health Services, the Commission for the Environment and Agriculture, and the Commission for Transportation. Commission sessions serve for monitoring and issuing standpoints on major national and European issues in their area of competence.

The council meets once every six to eight weeks, on a rotating basis in one of the regions. External guests, from the central government administration, members of parliament, public organisations or international companies, may also be invited to the meetings. The association has a small secretariat and is financed through membership fees.

Source: OECD (2016a), *OECD Territorial Reviews: Peru 2016*, OECD Publishing, Paris, http://dx.doi.org/10.1787/9789264262904-en.

Most OECD countries have developed their own multilevel co-ordination based on their reality, needs and demands. Federal and unitary OECD countries have high level meetings between central government and their regions to discuss on the impact on national policies at subnational level. This is the case for a federal country like Australia (Council of Australian Governments) as well as for a unitary country like Italy with the State-Regions Conference (Conferenza Stato Regioni). Similarly, Poland has created a Committee for Co-ordination of the National Development Strategy with the participation of the regions to discuss on national policies with an impact at regional level whereas France has developed for many years the "Contrats-Plan", the state-region planning contracts have been adopted as important tools in regional development policy for planning, governance and co-ordination (OECD, 2016c).

These institutions can play a key role in the future in enhancing the effectiveness of much-needed co-ordination mechanisms, both vertically and horizontally. These organisations that are focused on regional and strategic development, and co-ordinated by a sectoral ministry like in Poland, could also serve as inspiration for Jordan on how to ensure integrated and co-ordinated development strategies from the bottom to the top.

Multi-level co-ordination is also particularly relevant for public investment. Whether in Federal countries or in unitary ones, subnational governments usually also have some prerogative in promoting public investment either at regional or at the local level. For instance, in unitary countries like Japan, Israel, Netherlands, France or Korea, investing is a key function of local government, accounting for more than 25% of their total budget, as compared to the OECD average of 11%[8].

Since DL has introduced new competencies to Governorates on strategic planning and on proposing new investment projects, the OECD recommendations developed to help governments to assess the strengths and gaps on their public investment capacity and to ensure a better co-ordination across levels of governments could also serve Jordan as an inspiration (Box 3.8).

Box 3.8. OECD Recommendation on Co-ordinating Public Investments across Levels of Government

The OECD Instrument groups 12 principles under three pillars: co-ordination, capacities and framework conditions.

- **Pillar 1: Co-ordinate across governments and policy areas**
  - Invest using an integrated strategy tailored to different places
  - Adopt effective co-ordination instruments across levels of government
  - Co-ordinate across subnational governments to invest at the relevant scale
- **Pillar 2: Strengthen capacities and promote policy learning across levels of government**
  - Assess upfront long term impacts and risks
  - Encourage stakeholder involvement throughout investment cycle
  - Mobilise private actors and financing institutions
  - Reinforce the expertise of public officials & institutions
  - Focus on results and promote learning
- **Pillar 3: Ensure sound framework conditions at all levels of government**
  - Develop a fiscal framework adapted to the objectives pursued
  - Require sound, transparent financial management
  - Promote transparency and strategic use of procurement
  - Strive for quality and consistency in regulatory systems across levels of government

A toolkit is also available to help government implement those principles: www.oecd.org/effective-public-investment-toolkit/.

Source: OECD (2014), Recommendation of the OECD Council on Effective Public Investment Across Levels of Government, www.oecd.org/regional/regional-policy/Principles-Public-Investment.pdf.

As for the relations between central governments and municipalities, information and policy co-ordination is also essential. Co-ordination mechanisms go beyond the privileged relation that municipalities can have with a specific ministry. In the case of Jordan, municipalities are under the umbrella of Ministry of Municipal Affairs. Yet, since they have financial and administrative autonomy, co-ordination and institutionalised system could help to get a regular overview of the needs and challenges they face. At the same time, co-ordination mechanisms between central government and municipalities also help to make consultations on key topics that may have a direct impact on them.

In practice, Jordan's municipalities have strong but informal links and relations with sectoral ministries, such as health and education. The Ministry of Municipal Affairs is responsible for the co-ordination of government measures concerning municipalities. It evaluates whether such measures are in accordance with general guidelines concerning the distribution of activities between different levels of administration. However, the majority of municipalities suffer from a lack of co-operation, co-ordination and communication with governmental authorities.

The importance and effects of informal dialogue should not be underestimated, particularly continuous and consolidated informal dialogue. However, this should go hand-in-hand with formalised agreements that other municipalities could benefit from. In some OECD countries, central state co-ordination with local governments is organised without the intermediation or participation of regional governments. Box 3.9 below describes the examples of Spain, Switzerland and Sweden where central government has consolidated co-ordination mechanisms with local governments essentially through representative national association of municipalities.

Box 3.9. Integrating lower levels of government in consultation procedures: The cases of Spain, Sweden and Switzerland

In **Spain**, the National Commission for Local Administrations (CNAL) is the standing body for collaboration between central and local governments. It is composed of an equal number of representatives of central and local governments and chaired by the Ministry of Finances and Public Administration. Local government representatives are designated by the National Association of Local Governments most present throughout the national territory; they are locally elected. The CNAL issues a report on state draft laws and regulations regarding local government and its administration. The other body of co-operation between central, regional and local governments is the Sectoral Conference for Local Affairs.

In **Sweden**, the process that precedes the development and passage of a new law includes setting-up committees of inquiry. The terms of reference of such committees are stipulated by the government and its members, who include special advisers and experts appointed by the lead minister concerned. Experts are often recruited from local and regional authorities and from the Swedish Association of Local Authorities and Regions (SALAR). Committees normally hold public meetings, and their results are extensively circulated for comments. Even if there are only limited formal consultation mechanisms, groups and citizens present their views through the normal work of local municipal councils and committees in the course of their normal public business. Informal consultation mechanisms also involve contacts with local enterprises and business organisations, municipalities, SALAR or other state agencies.

In **Switzerland**, extensive consultation procedures are used at cantonal level, and to integrate cantonal views at the federal level following Article 45 of the federal Constitution. Since cantons are in charge of the implementation of federal laws, the Confederation informs them in advance and in detail about future projects, and is obliged to involve them in the consultation procedure. The participation of the Association of Cantons in the consultation is important, but not the only way of participating. Cantons can also raise their voice through representatives in mixed working groups or institutionalised meetings. The commissions of the Council of States consult with cantons on the applicability of laws.

Note: For further information visit: Ministry of Finance and Civil Service, Government of Spain www.minhafp.gob.es/en-GB/Paginas/Home.aspx.

Sources: OECD (2007b), *Multi-level Regulatory Capacity in Sweden*, OECD Publishing, Paris, www.oecd.org/gov/regulatory-policy/38287547.pdf; OECD (2007c), *Government Capacity to Assure High Quality Regulation in Switzerland*, OECD Publishing, Paris, www.oecd.org/regreform/regulatory-policy/38286959.pdf; OECD (2016c), *OECD Public Governance Reviews: Peru: Integrated Governance for Inclusive Growth*, OECD Publishing, Paris, http://dx.doi.org/10.1787/9789264265172-en.

The relationship between the governorate and the municipal councils

The DL simply describes the relationship between governorates and municipal councils and highlights that one of the duties of the governor is to co-ordinate between the governorate council and the municipalities in the governorate, as well as with the ministries, the public departments and the public institutions (Article 3.3). It also states that the governorate council approves "development projects that benefit the governorate while taking into account the development projects proposed by municipal councils and departments and official institutions within the governorate and submitting them to the Governor to take action" (Article 8.6). One of the reasons behind the lack of clarity may be that municipalities and governorates are linked to different ministries, MoI and MoMA, and no clear mechanisms of co-ordination have been created to ensure clear channels and common procedures for submitting proposals. If the decentralisation reform and development objectives are to be achieved, efficient and effective mechanisms of co-ordination at the subnational level will have to be set in a short-term period.

Inter-municipal co-operation

The main objective of inter-municipal co-operation is the improvement of efficiency in public spending. Finding the optimal scale for the provision of public services is a complex issue that is being solved in different ways across OECD countries.

Some countries remain attached to the idea of reinforcing mergers by using one specific public service as the proxy for defining the size of the multi-service operators that municipalities are to become (OECD, 2005b). In Denmark, for instance, the policy concerning mergers relates to criteria based on the efficient size for providing education services, which is considered to be 30 000 people. However, most countries rely on voluntary decisions from municipalities rather than on hierarchical decisions (OECD, 2005a). This is the case for Finland, which also uses experimental approaches to identify the best adapted solutions (OECD, 2005b). Box 3.10 shows the experience of France with intercommunalités.

Box 3.10. Inter-municipal co-operation: France and the intercommunalité

France is characterised by voluntary co-operation at the local level. It has more than 36 000 communes (the basic unit of local governance). Although France has resisted municipal mergers, the need for local co-operation is clear. As such, the communes are united by approximately 19 000 inter-communal structures (which includes 2 525 public establishments for inter-communal co-operation, EPCI (établissement public de coopération intercommunale), and other forms of syndicates) aimed specifically at facilitating horizontal co-operation.

The current system of inter-communal structure was first established in 1992 and reformed in 1999. There are now three main types of supra-communal structure: 1) communities of communes (groupings of small rural communes); 2) "agglomeration" communities (groups of 50 000 inhabitants subject to a single business tax); and 3) the urban communities (groupings of 500 000 inhabitants or more). Single purpose inter-communal associations (syndicates) first established in 1890, and multi-purpose syndicates, which date back to 1959 are also still in existence. Each grouping of communes constitutes an EPCI, which assume limited, specialised, and exclusive powers transferred to them by member communes. Unlike the communes themselves, the EPCI is not governed by elected officials, but by delegates of municipal councils.

Box 3.10. Inter-municipal co-operation: France and the intercommunalité *(cont.)*

This essentially shifts power away from elected officials to civil servants in the areas of competence ceded by the municipalities. Although the EPCI are created by the communes directly, there are two notable roles for the central government. First, EPCIs must be approved by the State in order to exist legally. Second, to encourage municipalities to form an EPCI, the central government provides a basic grant plus an "inter-communality grant" to those communes that accept a single business tax, which is established to preclude competition on tax rates among participating municipalities in order to attract business. EPCIs draw on two sources of financial resources: budgetary contributions from member communes (for the syndicates), and/or their own tax revenue (for the EPCIs).

There are some indications that inter-communal co-operation has produced efficiency gains. For example, some outdated governance structures disappeared after the 1999 reforms and communes tend to collaborate in areas such as public works, which are likely to exhibit economies of scale. However, growth in inter-communal spending has not been accompanied by a decline in communal spending, transfers of personnel from communes to communities are associated with a rise in payroll costs and local tax increases, and the presence of communal and inter-communal governance structure results in overlaps and extra costs. Overall, however, measuring the efficiency and effectiveness of municipal co-operation is difficult in France, as there is no culture or institutional structure for the evaluation of public policies in this regard.

The New Territorial Organisation of the Republic Act – NOTRe (7 of August of 2015) boosted the merge of EPCIs and there has been a substantial decrease of the number of EPCI from 2600 in 2010 to 1266 in 2017.

Note: http://www.collectivites-locales.gouv.fr/files/files/statistiques/brochures/bis_113_0.pdf

Sources: Cour des Comptes (2005), "L'intercommunalité en France, rapport au Président de la République", novembre, www.ccomptes.fr/fr/publications/lintercommunalite-en-france ;
OECD (2016c), *OECD Public Governance Reviews: Peru: Integrated Governance for Inclusive Growth*, OECD Publishing, Paris, http://dx.doi.org/10.1787/9789264265172-en .

In Jordan, municipalities can engage in local economic development operations in partnership with one or more neighbouring municipalities through Joint Service Council (JSC) arrangements. JSCs were created to provide services (especially waste collection) for several groups of municipalities and villages (their number was reduced from 44 to 21 in 2001). This institution is not new, but has been specifically enshrined in the 2015 ML.

The establishment of a JSC can be a local initiative, however the ML states that it is "the Minister, as recommended by the governor [that] may establish joint services council (…) dissolve, or adding any village or town or population gathering to it". All JSC mechanisms are, by law, ruled by the Cabinet but the council has "no less than two thirds of the council members" coming from the municipal council. This is a minimum request for respecting local democracy. This is also a big difference to other countries, for example, in France, every member of the EPCI council needs to be member of the municipal council, and the composition of the EPCI council needs to reflect precisely the demographic balance between the Communes (in order to not advantage little towns or big cities[9]).

Inter-municipal co-operation is likely to be reinforced in sectoral and strategic areas, such as water. The experience of the Jordan Valley Authority, shown in Box 3.11, could serve as inspiration for promoting joint and co-ordinated actions among municipalities in the area.

Box 3.11. Jordan Valley Authority

The Jordan Valley Authority (JVA) was established in 1977 with a mandate for the integrated development of the Jordan Valley encompassing all aspects of life. In 1988, the JVA became part of the Ministry of Water and Irrigation (MWI).

The Jordan Valley Authority manages and protects water and land resources and their supporting infrastructure in the Jordan Valley in an environmentally and economically sound manner through creating partnerships with the private sector, where appropriate.

Empowered by its special law, the JVA represents the Jordanian Government in the valley with a broad spectrum of authority and administrative and financial autonomy. It performs its activities with more flexibility than other Jordanian public entities.

During the last 30 years, the JVA has completed numerous infrastructure projects, including electricity, communications, roads, schools, health centres, government and residential buildings, in addition to its core activities in land and water resources development.

Presently, the JVA is focusing its efforts on water and land resource development, management and protection, in addition to tourism development and promotion in the Jordan Valley.

In this context, the Jordan Valley Municipalities Union gathers nine municipalities of the Valley, headed by the Mayor of Deir Alla, to build common projects that are based on joint co-operation to serve the local community. An example of this is the container factory between the municipalities of Bereen and Al-Hachemia, as well as other projects between municipalities.

Source: JVA (2017), Jordan Valley Authority website, www.jva.gov.jo/sites/en-us/default.aspx (accessed 14 February 2017).

Building local capacities and human resource management at the subnational level

The existence of different levels of administration also implies the existence of subnational governments' own organisational structure in terms of human resources. Since decentralisation is intended to enable governments' to better respond to the local needs, a certain level of differentiation and nuances from the central level to the local are also expected when it comes to human resources management at the subnational level. For instance, some technical profiles such as engineers, architects may be more adapted to the local needs than to the central level. This does not preclude the fact that all employees can be equally expected to duly carry out their duties according to their position and be similarly paid for similar skills and capacities (OECD, 2008).

In Jordan, as in OECD countries, building sufficient capacity and professionalism in subnational governments is central to ensuring that they are able to meet their responsibilities and contribute to national economic growth. Subnational civil servants are a substantial portion of government workers around the world. Excluding health and education workers which can easily "monopolise" part of the data subnational employment is often over 50% of the total of public sector workforce not only in federal countries but also in some unitary countries.[10] Figure 3.7 shows that unitary countries' share of subnational governments employees can also be high like in Sweden (86%), Japan (80%), Hungary (70%) and France (50%).

Figure 3.7. Employment in government (general government) by level of government (2005)

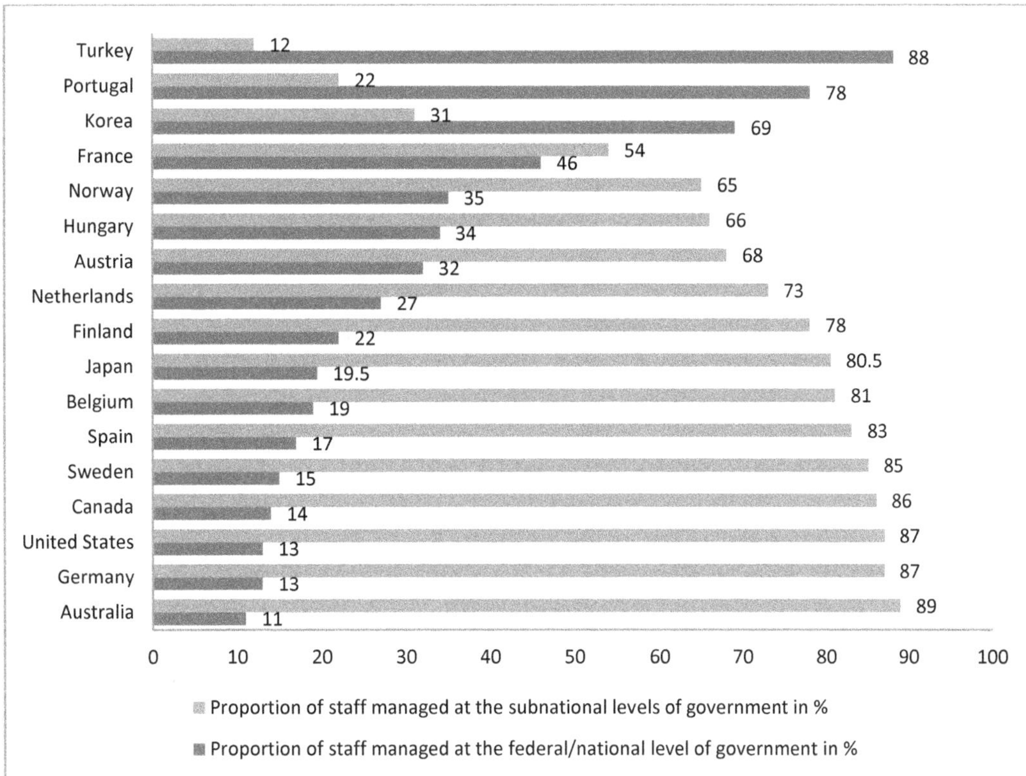

Source: OECD (2005c), Challenges of Human Resources Management for Multi-Level Government – Final Draft, www.oecd.org/officialdocuments/publicdisplaydocumentpdf/?cote=GOV/PGC/PEM(2008)6&docLanguage=En.

Public employment arrangements can also vary across OECD countries according not only to the State model but also on the administrative background and legal tradition. There is one spectrum from career-based to position-based systems, and another from uniform statutes to differentiated contracts (OECD, 2008). As shown in Table 3.5 the employment systems can also vary from one country to another with different systems for hiring public official (either through the civil service system or the dual that is combined with contractual system). In countries with a high level of decentralisation, the public employment system can also be decentralised to be more adapted to the competencies and particularities of the local level. This is the case of Germany, Denmark or Iceland where the public employment system is also managed at the subnational level.

Table 3.5. Employment systems in OECD countries

Country	Employment system
Chile	Civil service systems Initiated decentralisation of competences
Belgium, France, Spain	Dual systems, with dominating civil service systems Intends to modernise civil service system
Germany	Dual system Has initiated decentralisation of competences in the civil service system Full devolution in the public employment system
Denmark, Iceland	Dual systems, with dominating public employment system Full devolution in the public employment system

Source: OECD (2005c), Challenges of Human Resources Management for Multi-Level Government: Final Draft, www.oecd.org/officialdocuments/publicdisplaydocumentpdf/?cote=GOV/PGC/PEM(2008)6&docLanguage=En.

OECD experience demonstrates that developing and embedding strategic human resource management (HRM) requires an incremental approach to reform while maintaining impetus and political commitment, and that these reforms also must include the subnational level.

In the case of Jordan, decentralisation reform cannot be understood without taking into consideration the human factor. While there is no updated or precise quantification of subnational administrative staff, Jordan has a medium public sector workforce with approximately 227 805 public sector employees in 2014 (excluding the military),[11] both at the national and subnational levels; the OECD average is 1.16 million public servants. This situation is explained by the externalisation of certain functions, such as healthcare workers who are employed as private contractors, staff restrictions and fiscal pressures.

The Civil Service Bureau (CSB) is the one of the most relevant structures at the central level in charge of HRM for civil servants in Jordan (together with Ministry of Public Sector Development). According to the CSB in Jordan, over 46% of its employees are located at the subnational level (22% at regional level and 36% at municipal level), and approximately 42% at the national level. Table 3.6 shows a distribution of civil servants by governorates.

Table 3.6. Number of civil servants distributed by governorate

Governorate	Total	Ratio in %
Amman	69,490	32
Balqa	15,904	7.3
Zarqa	19,885	9.2
Madaba	7,110	3.3
Irbid	37,476	17.3
Mafraq	15,740	7.3
Jerash	7,276	3.4
Ajloun	6,157	2.8
Karak	15,379	7.1
Tafilah	6,063	2.8
Maán	9,115	4.2
Aqaba	7,494	3.5
	217,089	100

Source: Civil service Bureau (2014), annual report, Government of Jordan, www.csb.gov.jo/csb/.

At the subnational level, the two largest ministries, Health and Education, whose workforce represent 87% of total civil service employment, have institutionalised the principle of regional distribution of services and delegated most of the ministers' authorities to regional directors. In the same vein, the Civil Service Bylaw of 1998 transferred the central employment authority of the Civil Service Bureau to the governors in the districts. It provided the creation of personnel units in every district chaired by the governor, with the membership of the deputy governor, representatives of the concerned agency, a legal counsellor, and one of the directorate's employees in the district. The committee's role is to advertise, recruit and hire civil service employees in the districts.[12]

According to answers to the OECD questionnaire, Jordan's subnational governments appear to be facing largely similar or even more challenges and opportunities than the central government to enhance the capacity and capability of their internal workforce to enhance the design, provision and implementation of policies and services. At the same time, there is an unequal territorial distribution of civil servants among governorates. The central region (Amman, Balqa, Zarqa and Madaba) represents about 52% of employees, followed by the northern region (Irbid, Mafraq, Jerash and Ajloun) with 30.7% of total employees, and finally the southern region (Karak, Tafilah, Ma'an and Aqaba) with 17.5% of total employees.[13] This also reflects the diversity and unequal distribution of population in the different governorates (Figure 3.8).

Figure 3.8. The distribution of civil service employees by governorates, 2014

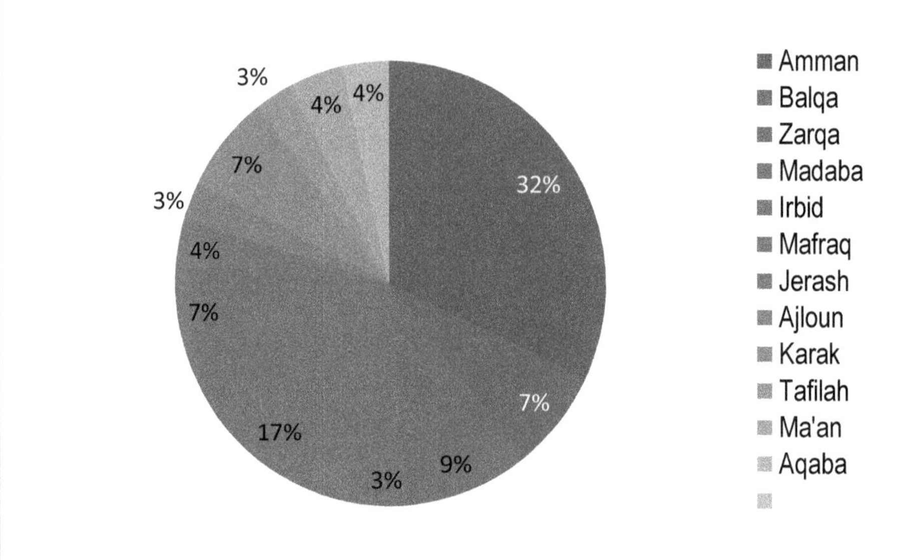

Source: Civil service Bureau (2014), annual report, Government of Jordan, www.csb.gov.jo/csb/.

According to the MoI and MoMA, there is currently no evidence of a training strategy that links the training of individuals to organisational objectives, and there does not seem to be sufficient investment in training on the part of local authorities. While the Institute of Public Administration (JIPA) conducts a wide variety of training courses, including top management courses considered as a prerequisite for promoting civil servants into the highest category (middle-management courses, general training courses, specially tailored courses to meet departmental training needs, and short seminars and symposia on specific subjects for high-ranking officials), there is no specific training for the governorate or civil servants at the local level.

Box 3.12 shows an example of training for civil servants at subnational levels in Morocco that could serve as inspiration for Jordan.

Box 3.12. Maison de l'élu - Morocco

The "Maison de l'élu" foundation in Marrakech is a pilot project in Morocco. It provides support to municipalities in management tasks. Created in 2011, the foundation's main role is to train and support civil servants at the regional level and to prepare them for a proper performance of their political or administrative duties within the municipalities.

The training programs, led by experienced academics and high official the State decentralised services, as well as by experts in territorial management and sustainable development, focus on financial and administrative management, urban planning, land use planning , Sustainable development, planning, good territorial governance, communication and decentralised co-operation.

As part of the opening on the continent, the House of the Elect has concluded co-operation agreements with elected regional bodies in Mali and Côte d'Ivoire on training in municipal management and decentralisation, proving Hence, this decentralised co-operation is also likely to develop South-South co-operation, which has been strategically chosen by.

Source: Menara (n.d.), www.menara.ma/fr/2014/12/25/1519679-la-maison-de-l%E2%80%99%C3%A9lu-de-marrakech-des-programmes-de-renforcement-des-comp%C3%A9tences-au-profit-de-plus-de-4000-%C3%A9lus-et-cadres-locaux.html.

According to the answers to the OECD questionnaire, MoMA organised "several technical, administrative and financial programmes for employees within the municipalities in compliance with national targets", however, those efforts are considered insufficient to the municipalities. In the case of employees of governorates, there is also room for improvement.

A restricted workforce, high staff turnover and low salaries limit capacity building at the local level. Boxes 3.13 and 3.14 show different examples of recruitment systems of civil servants in OECD countries, as well as different modalities to promote training and capacity building for civil servants at the subnational level.

Box 3.13. Local government officials with a national qualification: Spain

Local government officials with national qualifications (*Funcionarios de administración local con habilitación de carácter nacional* in Spanish) are configured as one of the key pieces of the bureaucratic-administrative structure of Spanish local governments, due to the impartiality and independence in the exercise of their assigned functions. They are selected on their qualifications and merit. The national qualification is reserved for officials with core functions within the municipality, such as Secretary General (attestation and mandatory legal advice) and economic-budgetary management control.

The selection of this group of officials is carried out by the central government's National Institute of Public Administration through a selective process regulated by a call, bases and programmes that are approved in a bylaw.

The essential characteristic of these officials is their dual organic and functional dependence: they are selected by the central government so that the Ministry of Finance and Civil Service has the administrative management of these officials, including disciplinary power, however they provide services in local governments, from which they receive their salaries.

Source: Orduña, E. (n.d.), Annex 2, www.famp.es/famp/programas/seminarios_cursos_jornadas/14_AdmonLoc/informe.pdf.

The complexity and difficulties of attracting qualified workforce at governorate and municipal levels is also a challenge. Box 3.14 shows the specific recruitment for French civil servants at the subnational level in France.

Box 3.14. Civil service recruitment at subnational levels of government in France

Civil service recruitment for French subnational governments is done through a national competitive examination, which is similar to the exam for national civil service recruitment. The national government retains responsibility for managing subnational civil service competencies. Civil servants who have successfully passed the exam for subnational governments can pursue a career at different levels (region, department and municipality).

There are three types of entrance examination to the civil service: external competitions open to candidates with a given qualification; internal competitions open to civil servants meeting certain conditions in terms of length of service; and a third competition that is open to elected officials, managers of associations and the private sector.

Unlike the national civil service, successful candidates for the subnational civil service are not automatically assigned a post, but allowed to conduct a job search for posts that may be located anywhere in France. A civil servant at the subnational level may perform different duties during their professional career and advance to higher-level jobs through internal competition, promotion, a professional examination or according to seniority.

Box 3.14. Civil service recruitment at subnational levels of government in France *(cont.)*

Employment conditions at subnational levels are strongly regulated, with employment frameworks being similar to those at the national level and across different governments at the same level. This allows a level of fluidity in the public sector labour market to be maintained, and builds on existing capacities in managing human resources. In some cases, when specific skills and qualified workers are required, local administrations may also employ under private contract.

Source: OECD (2009), *OECD Rural Policy Reviews: China 2009*, OECD Publishing, Paris, http://dx.doi.org/10.1787/9789264059573-en.

Assessment and recommendations

Jordan has developed an ambitious discourse on decentralisation that does not seem to be fully aligned with the current arrangements on the ground. Several challenges inhibit Jordan's ability to ensure policymaking and service delivery at the local level from a bottom-up perspective, including: a mismatch between municipal and governorates' fiscal capacities and allocation of competences; fragmentation and low levels of co-ordination and co-operation both vertically among levels of government and horizontally within the two subnational levels.

For the decentralisation reform to be effective and for subnational governments to be able to deliver public services, Jordan needs to strengthen existing structures and institutional co-ordination mechanisms to ensure effective and efficient administrative management. In this sense, the decentralisation reform is at a delicate stage. On the one hand, newly elected bodies maybe with no previous experience on local politics will start working while, on the other hand, the administrative machinery to support decentralisation needs to be reinforced to comply with the new competences and achieve the established objectives. Decentralisation reform is much more than an objective in itself as it is a mean to get services and policies more adapted to citizens' and businesses 'needs and should be gradually implemented and adapted to the country's reality[14].

Successful implementation of the reform also requires clear leadership, a roadmap and a regular follow-up and monitoring performance of the expected outcomes from the central level. In so doing, Jordan needs to reinforce a multi-sectoral and multi-stakeholder dialogue approach where the central government- not only the leading ministries MoI and MoMA but also line ministries on the ground- co-ordinate with the governorate and the municipal level so that a constructive dialogue can take place between key stakeholders

In this context, the local development units at the governorate and local levels can become key actors. Nevertheless, all of the actors involved in decentralisation, including communities, local governments, the central government and international donors, should make an effort to learn from experiences to date. The Jordanian central government needs to be aware of the importance of seizing the "momentum" that is conducive to good governance and that supports lower levels of government and civil society as they move forward with the reform. At the same time, governorates and municipalities need to realise that they can take important actions autonomously to improve local governance. While subnational levels of government do not have to stand by until the centre moves forward, they nevertheless need to ensure they work with an accurately represent communities. Donors also need to be aware that decentralisation is a long-term process and requires a great deal of national consensus building. All actors should recognise that they must work together in creative and mutually supportive ways to make local governments more effective.

To address these issues, the Government of Jordan could consider the following recommendations:

Reinforcing institutional arrangements to deliver effective decentralised governance

The framework for service delivery: Local Development Units

- **Local Development Units, in municipalities and governorates, should be enhanced by more clearly delineating their roles and activities**. In addition to their development and data collection role, they have the potential to play a horizontal co-ordination function as the interface between the technical administration and the elected institutions both in Governorates and Municipalities. This would go hand in hand with a direct line of co-operation between LDUs in municipalities and governorates.
- **Promote a closer relationship between MoI and MoMa on decentralisation matters.** Better communication from the top could then easier be reflected across levels of government. A first step could be to establish common administrative procedures and a common system for data collection for LDUs at the governorate and municipal levels (such a focus could include shared IT tools, etc.).
- **Consider reinforcing capacity in the administrative unit(s) supporting the governor to enable functions to be carried out effectively in governorates**, and reinforce interface capacity within governorates to engage effectively with local and central administrations.
- **Ensure that governorates and municipalities can contribute substantially to national strategy setting** and implementation through effective multi-level governance.
- **Implement an outcomes-based performance monitoring system for decentralisation and subnational management and administration.** This system should be aligned with an integrated centre of government (CoG) monitoring and evaluation system. Budgetary programmes should be aligned at the three levels of government.

An ambitious reform with scarce new resources at governorate and municipal level

- **Adapt and strengthen the financial arrangement of governorates according to their new competencies.** It will be essential to build up expertise to deal with budgeting and financial responsibilities, taking into consideration the governorate's situation regarding: population, area, poverty, geographical situation, and other vital indicators. Hiring professional staff and capacity building should also be considered.
- **Governorates could promote and support the creation of Joint Council Services** once needs are identified.

- **Strengthen the working relationship on decentralisation with the MoF to ensure that performance budgeting is implemented at the subnational level**, and that subnational expenditure performance information is fed back into biannual development programme planning.
- Over time, **consider creating a specific unit within the governorate that is dedicated to strategic planning**. This unit could count on MoPIC's expertise (and could even include officials from MoPIC) with operational responsibility to work with governorate and local governments to implement decentralisation in each governorate. This could include managing intergovernmental arrangements (such as contracts, see below) to deliver co-ordinated fiscal resources to subnational governments, and helping to monitor expenditure performance against the achievement of results for regional development, regional disparity reduction and improved outcomes for people in each governorate. The cases of Morocco or Turkey with regional development agencies could serve as inspiration for Jordan.
- **Mandate the MoF and MoMA to strengthen municipal government fiscal capacity and administrative capacity for fiscal management and collecting local taxes.** Local governments could also raise citizens' awareness for paying taxes on time so as to deliver better basic public services.
- **Improve municipal budgeting and accounting processes**.
- **Promote accountability through improved management of municipal financial information**

Strategic planning

- **Strengthen the partnership between the municipal and district councils, the private sector and international donors in order to enhance the role of municipal and district councils in approving and implementing development projects in local communities.** Municipal and district councils should have a key role in the partnership by providing the appropriate environment to stimulate investment, especially regarding the simplification of procedures and the provision of appropriate infrastructure.
- **MoPIC could play a greater role in providing support to Governorates and in particular to the GLDUs in the Executive Development Programme** and implementation of governorate strategic plan. Specific training and capacity-building could also be addressed.
- Once the strategic unit within the GLDUs is created, **MoPIC could second qualified staff at the governorate level** that would support the strategic unit within the GLDUs.

Promoting inter-institutional dialogue

- Institutionalise mechanisms for the inter-governmental co-ordination of the decentralisation process by implementing a more flexible and adapted structure and ensuring that it is fully supported by centre of government structures and line ministries. This could include:
  - Effective **interministerial co-ordination**. National ministers responsible for key policies will need to work together more effectively. There is a large variation in economic conditions and governance capability across the country, and a need to better integrate national policies at the regional level. Vertical co-ordination occurs within a complex governance system. The national government therefore needs to co-ordinate more effectively and in a way that accounts for the diversity and differences in capability across the governorates.
  - Establish a **co-ordination council** between governorates to share experiences, information and tackle challenges. This would also allow governorates to share experiences on decentralisation implementation and strategic planning, together with the designing and implementing of a basic single framework for subnational management that is linked to performance-based management. This co-ordination council could be composed of the CoG at the central level and representatives of each governorate (political, governor and a technical manager).
- **Ensure that the leading role given to governorates in strategic planning through a bottom-up approach effectively integrates the lowest levels of the administration**, as well as civil society and the private sector.
- **Municipalities, and in particular mayors, could also gather in a national association** to promote the role of municipalities in strengthening decentralisation reform and local development.

Capacity building and human resource management at the subnational level

- **Identify the needs of civil servants at the governorate and local level** in the context of the decentralisation reform, and provide capacity building and training at the subnational level to ensure a well-prepared, competent and efficient civil service.
- **Develop and extend the national Law on Civil Service Reform** and the tasks attributed to the Civil Service Bureau to the governorate and municipal levels.
- **All levels of government should be encouraged to define and plan for the types of workers they will need in order to carry out new responsibilities**. Training should contribute to the formation of new working relationships. In addition to building local capacity, training can be a tool for creating personal networks among various levels of government, regions, or types of government workers. One recommendation, for example, might be to train career civil servants and local politicians together to insure that they better understand what is expected of them and what they can expect from each other.
- **Create a network of community agents to provide local government with capacity building especially to the LDUs.** A national federation/association of

municipalities (once created) may also be involved to connect local experiences and identify good policy practices across municipalities. Councils should involve citizens and non-governmental organisations in the identification of key local assets and economic drivers, which should be taken into account in local development strategies.

- **Greater flexibility in managing the workforce at the local level is required**. Subnational governments need to develop competency-management systems so that they can ensure they have a well-selected, trained and evaluated public workforce.
- This regime should be **co-ordinated by key ministries such the Civil Service Bureau (together with the Ministry of the Public Sector), MoI and MoMA.**

Notes

1. www.vng-international.nl/wp-content/uploads/2015/06/Service_Delivery_challenge_local_goverments.pdf.
2. One of the most important is a MoI regulation describing GLDUs' functions in 2006.
3. www.arabstates.undp.org/content/dam/rbas/doc/syriaresponse/jordan%20needs%20assessment%20-%20november%202013.pdf.
4. UNDP project in Zarqa, Aecid's inititiave in Mafraq and VNG's project in Irbid.
5. Answers to the OECD questionnaire.
6. EU-supported PAMB, PALD and Baladyat projects, UNDP and USAID, VNG, among others.
7. Evidence gathered in UNDP, USAID, EU, AECID, VNG's projects at governorate and local level in Jordan.
8. http://cor.europa.eu/en/documentation/brochures/documents/results%20of%20the%20oecd-cor%20consultation%20of%20sub-national%20governments/2794-brochurelr.pdf.
9. Décision n°2014-405 QPC du 20 juin 2014, commune de Salbris, Conseil constitutionnel (French supreme court).
10. http://siteresources.worldbank.org/publicsectorandgovernance/resources/285741-1345485407865/subnationalgovernmentadministrativetradition.pdf.
11. www.csb.gov.jo/csb/SocialRole/Number-of-jobs.
12. http://unpan1.un.org/intradoc/groups/public/documents/un/unpan023177.pdf.
13. 2014 Civil Service Bureau Annual Report www.csb.gov.jo/csb/.
14. http://unpan1.un.org/intradoc/groups/public/documents/un/unpan006230.pdf.

References

Ababsa, M. (2015), "Decentralization in the Mashrek Region: Challenges and Opportunities", Platforma, SKL international, www.commed-cglu.org/wp-content/uploads/2014/04/Mashrek-Decentralisation-in-the-Mashrek-region.pdf.

Ababsa, M. (2013), *Atlas on Jordan*, http://books.openedition.org/ifpo/5021?lang=en.

ACE (2011), Jordan: Repeat Public Financial Management, Assessment following the PEFA Methodology.

Bergh, S. (2010), *Decentralisation and Local Governance in the MENA Region*, Medyear, Iemed, Barcelona.

Charbit, C. (2011), "Governance of Public Policies in Decentralised Contexts: The Multi-level Approach", *OECD Regional Development Working Papers*, No. 2011/04, OECD Publishing, Paris, http://dx.doi.org/10.1787/5kg883pkxkhc-en.

Charbit, C. and M. Michalun (2009), "Mind the Gaps: Managing Mutual Dependence in Relations among Levels of Government", *OECD Working Papers on Public Governance*, No. 14, OECD Publishing, Paris, http://dx.doi.org/10.1787/221253707200.

Civil Service Bureau (2014), Annual report, Government of Jordan, http://www.csb.gov.jo/csb/.

CIPFA (2017), Aligning local public services, www.cipfa.org/cipfa-thinks/aligning-local-public-services (accessed 14 February 2017).

CVDB (2011), annual report, www.csb.gov.jo/csb/?lang=en-gb.

Clark, G., J. Huxley and D. Mountford (2010), *Organising Local Economic Development: The Role of Development Agencies and Companies*, OECD Publishing, Paris, http://dx.doi.org/10.1787/9789264083530-en.

DCLG (2017), Department for Communities and Local Government Website, www.gov.uk/government/organisations/department-for-communities-and-local-government (accessed 14 February 2017).

Government of Jordan (2016), Background report of the OECD Strategic Assessment of Jordan, unpublished working paper.

JVA (2017), Jordan Valley Authority, www.jva.gov.jo/sites/en-us/default.aspx (accessed 14 February 2014).

K4 Health (2017), TANMIA Strategic Planning Tool, www.k4health.org/toolkits/jhcp/tanmia-strategic-planning-tool (accessed 14 February 2017).

Law on Municipalities (2015), Law No 41 of 2015, www.iec.jo/sites/default/files/2015%20Municipalities%20Law%20EN.pdf.

Law on Decentralisation (2015), Law No 49 of 2015, www.iec.jo/sites/default/files/2015%20Decentralisation%20Law%20EN.pdf.

LOGOReP Component Three: Consultancy Mission (Local Economic Development Units – LDU) (n.d.), Analyzing Local Development Units - Mafraq Governorate Case Study, Local Governance Resilience Programme for the Middle East and North Africa.

Mango, T. and A. Shabaneh (2016), *Service delivery, legitimacy, stability and social cohesion in Jordan. An analytical literature review*, Leading Point Services, http://publications.dlprog.org/JordanAnalyticalLiteratureReview.pdf.

OECD (2016a), *OECD Territorial Reviews: Peru 2016*, OECD Publishing, Paris, http://dx.doi.org/10.1787/9789264262904-en.

OECD (2016b), *Regional Outlook 2016: Productive Regions for Inclusive Societies*, OECD Publishing, Paris, http://dx.doi.org/10.1787/9789264260245-en.

OECD (2016c), *OECD Public Governance Reviews: Peru: Integrated Governance for Inclusive Growth*, OECD Publishing, Paris, http://dx.doi.org/10.1787/9789264265172-en.

OECD (2016d), OECD Subnational government Structure and Finance (database), http://dx.doi.org/10.1787/888933363584.

OECD (2015a), *Regional Development Agencies (RDA): a tool for regional development*, Paper for the 33rd Session of the regional Development Policy Committee.

OECD (2015b), *Multi-dimensional Review of Peru: Volume I. Initial Assessment*, OECD Development Pathways, OECD Publishing, Paris, http://dx.doi.org/10.1787/9789264243279-en.

OECD (2015c), *Costa Rica: Good Governance, from Process to Results, OECD Public Governance Reviews,* OECD Publishing, Paris, http://dx.doi.org/10.1787/9789264246997-en

OECD (2014d), Recommendation of the OECD Council on Effective Public Investment Across Levels of Government, www.oecd.org/regional/regional-policy/Principles-Public-Investment.pdf.

OECD (2013), *Fiscal Federalism 2014: Making Decentralisation Work*, OECD Publishing, Paris, http://dx.doi.org/10.1787/9789264204577-en.

OECD (2012), *Promoting Growth in All Regions*, OECD Publishing, Paris, http://dx.doi.org/10.1787/9789264174634-en.

OECD (2011), *Estonia: Towards a Single Government Approach*, OECD Public Governance Reviews, OECD Publishing, Paris, http://dx.doi.org/10.1787/9789264104860-en.

OECD (2009a), *How Regions Grow: Trends and Analysis*, OECD Publishing, Paris, http://dx.doi.org/10.1787/9789264039469-en.

OECD (2009b), *OECD Rural Policy Reviews: China 2009*, OECD Publishing, Paris, http://dx.doi.org/10.1787/9789264059573-en.

OECD (2008), *Challenges of human resources management for multi-level government – final draft*, GOV/PGC/PEM(2008)6,OECD, Paris, www.oecd.org/officialdocuments/publicdisplaydocumentpdf/?cote=GOV/PGC/PEM(2008)6&docLanguage=En.

OECD (2007a), *Linking Regions and Central Governments: Contracts for Regional Development*, OECD Publishing, Paris, http://dx.doi.org/10.1787/9789264008755-en.

OECD (2007b), *Multi-level Regulatory Capacity in Sweden*, OECD Publishing, Paris, www.oecd.org/gov/regulatory-policy/38287547.pdf.

OECD (2007c), *Government Capacity to Assure High Quality Regulation in Switzerland*, OECD Publishing, Paris, www.oecd.org/regreform/regulatory-policy/38286959.pdf.

OECD (2005a), Building Competitive Regions: Strategies and Governance, OECD Publishing, Paris, http://dx.doi.org/10.1787/9789264009479-en.

OECD (2005b), *OECD Territorial Reviews: Finland 2005*, OECD Publishing, Paris, http://dx.doi.org/10.1787/9789264012783-en.

OECD (2005c), Challenges of Human Resources Management for Multi-Level Government: Final Draft, www.oecd.org/officialdocuments/publicdisplaydocumentpdf/?cote=GOV/PGC/PEM(2008)6&docLanguage=En.

OECD - UCLG (2016), Subnational Governments around the World, www.oecd.org/cfe/regional-policy/sngs-around-the-world.htm.

Orduña, E. (n.d.), Annex 2, www.famp.es/famp/programas/seminarios_cursos_jornadas/14_AdmonLoc/informe.pdf.

Reach (2015), *Social Cohesion in Host Communities in Northern Jordan - Assessment Report*, www.alnap.org/resource/20803.aspx.

Smoke, P. (2015), "Accountability and service delivery in decentralising environments: Understanding context and strategically advancing reform", in Whaites et al. (2015), *A governance practitioner's notebook: alternative ideas and approaches*. OECD, Paris, pp. 219-232, www.oecd.org/dac/governance-peace/governance/docs/Governance%20Notebook.pdf.

SOFRECO/European Commission (2010), Building development capacities of Jordanian municipalities – Baladiaty, The Quest for Decentralizing Government in the Hashemite Kingdom of Jordan: Some Preliminary Findings of a Situation Analysis, Europe Aid.

UNDP (2010), *Capacity Building for Decentralization, Jordan: Focus on Governorate LDU*, Draft Final Report prepared for UNDP and MoPIC, internal document.

UNDP (2014), Municipal Needs Assessment Report. Mitigating the Impact of the Syrian Refugee Crisis on Jordanian Vulnerable Host Communities, United Nations Development Programme, New York, www.undp.org/content/dam/jordan/docs/Poverty/needs%20assessment%20report.pdf.

Work, R. (2012), Overview of Decentralisation Worldwide: A Stepping Stone to Improved Governance and Human Development. UNDP, New York http://biblioteca.unmsm.edu.pe/redlieds/Recursos/archivos/gestionestado/overview-decentralisation-worldwide-paper.pdf.

Work, R. (n.d.), The Role of Participation and Partnership in Decentralised Governance: A Brief Synthesis of Policy Lessons and Recommendations of Nine Country Case Studies on Service Delivery for the Poor, http://biblioteca.unmsm.edu.pe/redlieds/Recursos/archivos/gestionestado/participationandpartnership.pdf.

Chapter 4.

Openness and participation in Jordan: The expected impact of decentralisation reform

The 2015 Decentralisation Law and Municipality Law are giving impetus to enhancing local democratic governance and bear the potential of strengthening popular participation in the national planning and development process. The creation of elected councils has raised hopes to encourage citizen-driven initiatives and foster greater transparency and accountability. On the basis of an assessment of the current legal, institutional and policy framework for open government (e.g. access to information, public consultation, integrity system, CSO activity, political participation), this chapter discusses the expected impact of the decentralisation reform and its potential to bring about the emergence of a new administrative culture of more open and participatory governance at the level of the governorates and municipalities.

By passing the Decentralisation Law and Municipality Law in late 2015, Jordan has revamped its legal and institutional framework and given new impetus to enhancing local governance and strengthening citizen participation in the national planning and development process. The creation of elected councils at the governorate and local level will bring local authorities closer to citizens and has raised hopes of encouraging citizen-driven (bottom-up) initiatives, greater transparency and accountability.

Evidence from the survey conducted by the OECD Secretariat[1] shows that citizens and government officials take a positive attitude towards the reform process. Based on a more decentralised identification of service needs and policy priorities, decentralisation reform is expected to allow for more open and participatory policy making, and ultimately result in a more responsive delivery of public services and more balanced development across the territory. However, this chapter will show that the challenges for a new culture of open and participatory governance across the different layers of government should be tackled decisively.

Defining open government at the central and local level

The OECD defines open government as "a culture of governance based on innovative and sustainable policies and practices inspired by the principles of transparency, accountability, and participation that fosters democracy and inclusive growth" (OECD, 2016a).

Open government initiatives aim to strengthen the inclusive institutions that embrace transparency in practice. There are various forms and channels through which non-governmental stakeholders, including under-served groups, can express their needs and preferences, such as through stakeholder consultation, participation and engagement at different stages of the policy-making cycle (OECD, 2016a). Open government initiatives value pluralism and reinforce a system of checks and balances to prevent nepotism, clientelism, or any other form of misuse of power that risks undermining the cohesion of society.

The overview of the potential benefit of open government in Box 4.1 highlights the twofold target of any open government initiative:

- Improving the performance of government and the public administration (i.e. efficiency and effectiveness) in the delivery of (more responsive and better tailored) public services (intermediate goal).
- Strengthen the quality of democracy and rule of law based on more open and inclusive policy making that will ultimately foster citizen trust in government and more inclusive growth (long-term goal).

Box 4.1. Potential benefits of open government

Establishing greater trust in government. Trust is an outcome of open government that can reinforce government performance in other aspects. In addition, if citizens trust the government or specific government policies, then they may be more willing to pay (fees, contributions, taxes) to support these policies.

Ensuring better outcomes at less cost. The co-design and delivery of policies, programmes and services with citizens, businesses and civil society offer the potential to tap a broader reservoir of ideas and resources.

Raising compliance levels. Having people participate in the process helps them understand the stakes of reform and can help ensure that the decisions reached are perceived as legitimate.

Ensuring equity of access to public policy making by lowering the threshold for access to policy making processes for people facing barriers to participation.

Fostering innovation and new economic activity. Public engagement and open government are increasingly recognised as drivers of innovation and value creation in both the private and public sectors.

Enhancing effectiveness by leveraging the knowledge and resources of citizens who otherwise face barriers to participation. Public engagement can ensure that policies are better targeted and address the needs of citizens, eliminating potential waste.

Source: OECD (2010), "Background document for session 1 OECD Guiding Principles for Open and Inclusive Policy Making", expert meeting on Building an open and innovative government for better policies and service delivery, OECD, Paris, 8-9 June, www.oecd.org/gov/46560128.pdf.

To achieve these goals the central government is tasked with identifying a strategic approach to fostering open government across the whole of government (e.g. the National Open Government Strategy), securing the commitment of the political leadership, and initiating a national dialogue around objectives and programmes. The subnational level is a rich source of hands-on practice. It provides the space for turning open government principles and commitments into tangible improvements for the life of community members (OECD, 2016a).

In OECD countries, a new impetus for involving citizens in policy making emerged when a number of countries initiated decentralisation efforts in the 1970s. The reforms resulted in a transfer of authority, responsibility and resources from the national government to lower levels of government in an attempt to better respond to citizens' needs and demands (OECD, 2016a). The 2015 Decentralisation Law and Municipality Law do not stipulate a significant transfer of competencies away from the central level to the governorates or to the municipalities. However, seeing as the needs and priorities of each community will be identified in collaboration with non-governmental stakeholders before being transferred to the next higher layer, decentralisation reform offers a unique momentum to boost the open government agenda from the bottom. There are good reasons for the increasing shift of attention among open government advocates and practitioners towards the local level. When the physical distance between citizens and government is small, open government theory and principles turn into concrete practices and, if successful, generate a positive impact on the lives of community members. At the local level:

- **Transparency**: is critical for assessing the performance of governorates and municipalities to deliver public services and allocate scarce public resources to effective use. The "passive" access to relevant, accurate and easy-to-use information (e.g. public records) and the proactive disclosure and dissemination of information are of critical importance in this regard.
- **Participation**: The subnational level provides the space for innovative forms of governance to emerge, get tested in practice and inspire similar practices elsewhere. By virtue of its size and focus on the daily needs of the local population, subnational governments are requested to respond to the specific demands from society. Citizen participation can take the form of consultation (local governments define the agenda, set the questions and manage the process while citizens are invited to contribute their views and opinions, such as through public opinion surveys or local hearings) or active participation (citizens engage in defining the process and content of policy making/service design and have an equal standing in proposing policy options and shaping the dialogue, although the responsibility for the final decision rests with the government, e.g. consensus conferences). Formats such as local gatherings, hearings, community councils or participatory budgeting can take either form.
- **Accountability**: Given the proximity and direct exposure to government action, citizens at the local level can more easily monitor local policies and the quality of public service delivery (e.g. public expenditures for schools). This can put "elected representatives in a situation of enhanced accountability" (OECD, 2016a).

This chapter is divided into two parts. It will analyse the current environment for open government in Jordan and the expected impact of the decentralisation reform on the interaction between government and civil servants, and civil society and citizens. The first part of the chapter will assess the current legal, institutional and policy frameworks and contrast the findings with actual practices at the central and subnational level. The current state of play will provide the basis to discuss, in the second part, the potential of the reform to encourage the emergence of a new culture of open, inclusive, participatory, and accountable governance at the governorate and municipal level.

Improve the state of play for open government in Jordan

Turning commitments into results: The process towards a culture of open and inclusive governance

Jordan's membership in the Open Government Partnership

Despite the challenging political, economic and security context in the neighbouring region, Jordan has been engaged in a gradual democratisation process for more than a decade. While considerations to safeguard stability have always been dominant in the political agenda, the country was the first in the Arab world to join the Open Government Partnership (OGP) and pass an access to information law. The objective to increase popular participation and strengthen transparency and accountability mechanisms can build on a strong link to Jordan 2025 and previous achievements, in particular the progress made as a member to the Open Government Partnership.

Jordan 2025 does not include a direct commitment to fostering open government, but it seeks to advance key principles, including participation, transparency and accountability. In line with the recommendations of the National Integrity Strategy, Jordan 2025 states that the transparency and accessibility of government information shall be reinforced, and that public consultation mechanisms shall be institutionalised. It also acknowledges the need to improve the communication of government decisions and regulatory changes, and to address prevailing practices based on engrained attitudes, such as wasta and favouritism towards equal opportunities and merit-based decisions. As outlined in Chapter 1, strategy places citizens at the heart of the development process and lists concrete deliverables that should be implemented (e.g. platforms to facilitate citizen engagement with government; National Honours Programme to reward Jordanians for their contribution to society; civics component in the school curriculum). The vision underlines the need to institutionalise mechanisms for public consultation in the development of future plans and strategies across the government.

Jordan 2025 resonates with Jordan's commitment to foster more open, transparent and accountable governance through the Open Government Partnership. The validation of the third National Action Plan 2016-2018 coincides with the approval of a series of strategic policy documents and milestones in Jordan's democratisation process. In parallel to the beginning of the implementation phase of Jordan 2025, the plan draws on key recommendations developed in the Comprehensive National Human Rights Plan 2016-2025, and seeks to integrate the United Nations (UN) Sustainable Development Goals, in particular goal 16. The approval follows the 18th Parliamentary elections, in which candidates ran under a new Elections Law and the scrutiny of the Independent Elections Commission.

The National Action Plan is placed in the context of the decentralisation process and the government's commitment to expand the process of popular participation by allowing "citizens to identify their needs and priorities and to develop their areas and communities, thus enlarging popular participation in the decision making process". Commitment five binds the government to issue the required regulations and instructions to implement the Decentralisation Law and hold governorate council elections in 2017.

In the preparation of the National Action Plan, a working group was established with representatives from: government (Ministries of Planning and International Co-operation [MoPIC], Political and Parliamentary Affairs [MoPPA], Public Sector Development [MoPSD], Foreign Affairs and Expatriates, General Budget Department), the Anti-Corruption and Integrity Commission, civil society (i.e. Hemam, National Center for Human Rights), women (i.e. Jordanian National Committee) and youth organisations (We are all Jordan Youth Commission), and the Jordanian Businessmen Association. The increasing involvement of non-governmental stakeholders in the preparation of the plan was ensured by dissemination activities (e.g. publication of the draft plan on MoPIC's website and advertisements in daily newspapers), an electronic questionnaire and two consultation meetings with civil society organisations (CSOs) on 25 September and 16 October 2016.[2] In the plan, the Government of Jordan commits to work jointly with CSOs in the implementation of its commitments through a "systematic approach based on transparency, disclosure and open dialogue."

Box 4.2 presents the commitments of the third action plan. The National Action Plan presents a qualitative improvement on the two previous strategies as it defines a lead implementing agency, others actors involved and milestones to track progress, as well as additional information (status quo, objective, description, relevance and ambition) for each commitment.

Box 4.2. Jordan's third National Action Plan for the Open Government Partnership

- Commitment 1: Strengthen the legislative framework governing access to information.
- Commitment 2: Strengthen the facilities available for persons with disabilities to access the justice system.
- Commitment 3: Strengthen the framework governing the freedom of the media.
- Commitment 4: Launch and enhance the complaints registration system and follow-up mechanisms to deal with complaints in a serious manner and to refer them to the judiciary:
  - Complaints and grievances related to violations committed against citizen.
  - Complaints related to governmental services and the surrounding environment of its provision.
- Commitment 5: Issue the requisite regulations and instructions to implement the Decentralisation Law and hold governorate council elections in 2017.
- Commitment 6: Develop healthcare services and automate the healthcare sector through electronic linkages.
- Commitment 7: Develop an interactive observatory forum for citizens to monitor the implementation of the government's plans and progress.
- Commitment 8: Adopt the principle of budget disclosure in accordance with international standards and promote transparency and financial disclosure.
- Commitment 9: Develop transparent and participatory policies regarding climate change challenges.
- Commitment 10: Implement an open data sources policy.

Source: MoPIC (2016), *Jordan's Third National Action Plan 2016-2018 under the Open Government Partnership Initiative*, Ministry of Planning and International Co-operation, www.opengovpartnership.org/country/jordan/action-plan.

Table 4.1 provides a comparison of key features of the open government agenda in Jordan, Tunisia and Morocco and OECD member countries. It illustrates that Jordan shares many of the common features for implementing open government commitments in practice. Recently, OECD and OGP member countries have extended the scope of their open government agenda and activities to other (non-executive) actors and the subnational layers of government. For instance, Costa Rica is moving towards an "open state" by including the legislature, judiciary, independent state institutions and subnational governments in the national open government agenda (OECD, 2016a). Almost half of all OECD member countries have consolidated scattered initiatives aimed at increasing transparency, citizen participation and accountability into a single national open government strategy to strengthen coherence and impact.

Table 4.1. Tools and mechanisms used to implement the open government agenda in Jordan, selected Middle East and North Africa (MENA) countries and the OECD

Item	Jordan	Tunisia/Morocco	OECD
Access to information law	Yes	TUN: Yes, MOR: No	97%
National document for citizen engagement	No	TUN: No, MOR: Yes	46%
Office in charge of horizontal co-ordination of open government	American Relations Division (MoPIC)	TUN: Yes (E-Government Unit), MOR: Yes (Open Government Secretariat)	77%
Open government national strategy	No	TUN: Yes, MOR: No	49%
Funding mechanism of open government initiatives	Yes (Allocated by a single central institution)	TUN: Yes, MOR: Yes (both: allocated by institutions responsible for implementing each project)	89%
Monitoring of open government initiatives	Yes (ad hoc)	TUN: Yes (National Committee), MOR: Yes (Steering Committee)	86%
Evaluation of the impact of open government initiatives	Yes (through OGP self-assessment/IRM)	TUN: Yes (through OGP self-assessment/IRM and independent CSO assessment, MOR: No	56%

Source: Based on the answers provided to the OECD survey conducted for OECD (2016a), *Open Government: The Global Context and the Way Forward*, OECD Publishing, Paris, http://dx.doi.org/10.1787/9789264268104-en.

The decentralisation reform provides an opportune moment to reflect about what contribution government and local non-governmental stakeholders can make to achieve the commitments stipulated in the 2016-18 National Action Plan. An analysis of the two previous National Action Plans reveals that open government commitments have almost exclusively been dedicated to the national level so far. In Colombia, open government reforms have been extended to the subnational level, in particular in the province of Antioquia. The province holds accountability hearings in all 125 municipalities, with the large-scale participation of citizens (see Box 4.3).

Box 4.3. Open government at the local level in Colombia's second OGP Action Plan

In 2015, Colombia presented its second OGP Action Plan for the period 2015-17. The plan entails 18 commitments and provides 2 new aspects. The country has worked towards enhancing transparency and accountability in the judiciary, and it is also extending open government reforms to the subnational level. As laid down in Commitment 9, the province of Antioquia commits itself to developing a transparent and responsible government. The department (*departamento*) already leads in the Transparency Index of "Transparency for Colombia", and the Governor of Antioquia promised to further advance the open government agenda in his department. The department aims to adhere to the principles of the OGP by holding accountability hearings in all 125 municipalities of Antioquia. In these hearings, in which a total of 12 000 citizens shall participate throughout the two years, the municipalities will report on the compliance with the departmental development plan, the results of the Transparency Fairs on contracting, as well as the results of Public Agreements signed by the mayors of the municipalities of Antioquia.

Source: OECD (2016a), *Open Government: The Global Context and the Way Forward*, OECD Publishing, Paris, http://dx.doi.org/10.1787/9789264268104-en.

The two previous National Action Plans submitted by Jordan to the OGP have provoked mixed reactions from civil society and other non-governmental stakeholders, partly because of their exclusive focus on the central level, but also regarding their impact. Despite some notable achievements, the implementation of some previous commitments has been delayed or has not materialised. For instance, the third National Action Plan stresses that 7 of 14 commitments from the second plan were fully accomplished, while further work was necessary to complete the remaining 7. Evaluations are undertaken through the self-assessment and independent reporting mechanism (IRM) assessment, and the results are publicly available, as required for any OGP member. However, no independent monitoring or evaluation mechanism exists.

In Tunisia, civil society organisations play a significant role in the elaboration of the action plan, and they also assume a critical role in exercising scrutiny over the implementation progress, supported by an institutionalised mechanism (see Box 4.4).

Box 4.4. How to institutionalise non-governmental organisation (NGO) participation in the open government agenda: The example of Tunisia

Tunisia joined the Open Government Partnership as the second MENA country in 2014. In the process of formulating the first National Action Plan, a steering committee was established featuring an equal share of government representatives and non-governmental actors.

In addition to five officials from the Ministry of Finance, the Ministry of the Interior, the General Direction of Administrative Reform and Future Studies, the E-government unit, Legal Counsel of the government; the committee is composed of three CSO representatives (OpenGov.tn, Association Tuensa, Association Al Bawsala) and one representative from the private sector (Arab Institute of Business Leaders) and academia. The committee jointly drafts the plan and meets every month to follow up on the implementation of its commitments. The committee was enlarged for the elaboration of the second National Action Plan, but still features an equal number of government and non-government representatives.

This institutionalised mechanism for the formulation and follow-up on open government commitments has increased the legitimacy of the process and the quality of its outcomes.

Source: Based on the answers provided to the OECD survey conducted for OECD (2016a), *Open Government: The Global Context and the Way Forward*, OECD Publishing, Paris, http://dx.doi.org/10.1787/9789264268104-en.

Jordan's 2012-13 and 2014-16 OGP National Action Plans were linked to the broader democratisation agenda. The 2012-13 Action Plan lists 32 commitments in three areas (improving public services, increasing public integrity and the efficiency of managing public resources), and states the objective "to further strengthen the foundations for political inclusion, social stability, good governance, efficient public sector, improved service delivery, as well as the rule of law" (Government of Jordan, 2012). The plan points out that government initiatives to foster transparency, citizen participation and accountability preceded the country's membership of the OGP (Box 4.5).

Box 4.5. Selection of open government achievements prior to Jordan's OGP membership (2012)

Improving public services

- Creation of a centralised mechanism to administer citizens' complaints.
- Launching of a programme to simplify procedures at governorate/district levels (2011-13).
- Automation of departments and procedures (e.g. courts, Greater Amman Municipality [GAM], customs procedures).

Increasing public integrity

- Fighting corruption, good governance and promoting greater accountability.
- Enactment of the Financial Disclosure Law, the Anti-Money Laundering Law and the Anti-Corruption Commission Law (2006); amendment of the Associations Law (2009).
- Formulation of the National Anti-Corruption Strategy (2008-2012).
- Code of conduct and ethics for cabinet ministers and government employees.
- Establishment of the National Center for Human Rights (2006), Ombudsman Bureau (2009).

Promoting transparency and access to information

- Enactment of the law on the Access to Information (2007).
- Creation of an electronic portal on the Prime Ministry's website for the periodic monitoring and evaluation of the action plans of individual ministries, within the context of the implementation of the Executive Development Programme (2011-2013)
- Anti-Corruption Commission publishes annual reports since 2011, Audit Bureau published its annual report for the first time.

Enhancing citizen participation in decision making, and citizen feedback on governance

- Enactment of Public Gatherings Law (2011).
- Creation of a National Dialogue Committee to draft laws for parliamentary elections and political parties.
- Forming a Royal Committee on Reviewing the Constitution to review constitutional reform and propose amendments (creation of Independent Commission for Elections, 2011).
- Website at the Legislative and Opinion Bureau/Prime Ministry for the public to express views on pending legislation, regulations, and policy issues.

More effectively managing public resources

- Publication of a "Citizen's Guide to the Budget", and "Budget in Brief".

Source: Government of Jordan (2012), *The Open Government Partnership - Jordan: National Action Plan*, www.opengovpartnership.org/sites/default/files/legacy_files/country_action_plans/OGP%20Action%20Plan-Jordan-Final-April%202012_0.docx.

The 2014-16 National Action Plan was dedicated to support the Royal Committee for Enhancing the National Integrity System. Headed by the Prime Minister, the committee elaborated a National Charter to strengthen the integrity system, transparency, the rule of law, accountability, justice and equal opportunities.

As a member of the OGP, Jordan has made significant progress in turning commitments to foster open government principles into practice. By involving other state and non-governmental stakeholders from all layers of government in the process (including governorates and municipalities), Jordan could take a big step forward in promoting cultural change in the public administration, and hence contribute to delivering on the promises of the decentralisation reform. Stronger follow-up and accountability mechanisms will be as necessary as providing for adequate resources and awareness raising activities for public officials, civil servants and non-governmental stakeholders (OECD, 2016a). The results from the OECD survey for the members of the Civil Society Network bring further challenges to light: it finds that only 5 out of 17 CSOs are aware of Jordan's open government policy. The comments received suggest that even among the more "knowledgeable" CSOs, a sound understanding of the concept and its implications is lacking (e.g. only "partially" understood; "not defined and not clear"; missing clarity "of executive procedures in the rules and regulations").

The OGP National Action Plan is a strategic document that can facilitate the mainstreaming of open government principles across existing legal frameworks, guide institutions in their daily operations, and inspire innovative participatory approaches in practice. The subsequent sections will discuss to what degree the defining features of an open government agenda are in line with OECD standards and good practices in each area.

Access to information

Providing citizens access to complete, objective, clear and reliable government data and information is a cornerstone of open government. In fact, having an access to information law in place or constitutional provisions that guarantee access to information is an eligibility criterion for countries to become a member of the Open Government Partnership (Open Government Partnership, n.d.). More than 100 countries worldwide, including 65% of countries in the Latin America and Caribbean (LAC) region and all OECD countries have passed access to information (ATI) or freedom of information (FOI) laws (OECD, 2016a). At the local level, access to government information is a crucial condition for civil society organisations and citizens for holding local authorities to account for the delivery of basic needs and services and take an active stance in the development of their communities. Access to information is of particular concern for marginalised groups in society such as the poor, women, youth, disabled, and ethnic minorities.

Jordan was the first country in the MENA region to enact an access to information law in 2007 (Law of Access to Information No. 47/2007) and has signed various international conventions that prompt the country to make available government information to the public. The 2007 law obliges public officials to facilitate access to information and guarantee the disclosure within 30 days as of the date following the date of request submission (Law of Access to Information No. 47/2007).

When filing a request, each requestor is required to stress his/her name, domicile, profession and any other data that the board may deem necessary (Article 9). The lack of the opportunity to submit information demands anonymously can discourage the effective use of the law in practice, in particular when the requestor must fear any form of retaliation from the request. Another provision that may limit its full impact is that, if the request is not answered by the authorities within the time frame foreseen by the law, it shall be deemed rejected (Article 9). The requester shall bear the cost emerging from the photocopy of the requested information (Article 11). Finally, despite Jordan's pioneering role in adopting an ATI law in the region, Article 7 of the law has caused criticism as it places the burden on the shoulder of the information seeker Al-Dabbas (2008). It states that every Jordanian has the right to obtain information if the requestor has a lawful interest or a legitimate reason. In all OECD countries, the principle of maximum disclosure applies where exceptions are based on the class test (e.g. national security, international relations, personal data, commercial confidentiality, public order) or the harm test (e.g. persons, defence of state, commercial competitiveness) (OECD, 2011).

An amendment to the law in 2012 granted non-Jordanians access to information and enlarged civil society representation in the Information Council which is in charge of validating and adopting information requests, considering complaints, and approving annual reports. The amendment stipulates that the annual report on the implementation of the law shall be reported to the Prime Minister and both chambers of the Parliament. The response time to information requests and appeals was reduced from 30 to 15 days in order to meet international standards (usually within 20 working days or less in OECD countries) (OECD, 2016a).

Despite the improvements that the amendments introduced in the law, major impediments continue to hamper its effective use in practice:

- Existence of restrictive legislation,[3] in particular the provisions in the Protection of the State's Secrets and Documents Law No. 50 (1971), which can supersede the law.
- In 72% of OECD countries (in 2010), proactive disclosure is required by ATI laws for certain categories of information. However, no such clause exists in Jordan. The law protects all information that is "classified", "secret" or "protected by other legislation" (Article 13). The lack of a clearly defined set of circumstances has made it more difficult for citizens to exercise their right to information in practice.

The law does not identify a body in charge of classifying information and documents nor an independent agency to verify and review the classification system. Reportedly, different standards have been used by different public entities.

In 2010, 25 out of 31 OECD countries apply their ATI or FOI laws at the subnational level (see Table 4.2), acknowledging the importance of granting citizens the right to request information from local authorities. In Jordan, the scope of the ATI law does not cover actors at the subnational level. As it presents the space where policies and people meet, access to reliable government data and information is of critical importance at the local level. It is a precondition for the media, CSOs and independent state institutions to exercise scrutiny over the delivery of public services and ensure that public resources are spent for their intended purpose. In the process of aligning existing regulatory frameworks with the decentralisation laws, Jordan could consider amending the law to extend its scope to the subnational level and address the obstacles to its effective use in practice.

Table 4.2. OECD countries: Breadth of central government freedom of information laws (2010)

Level of government	
Central 31	Australia, Austria, Belgium, Canada, Chile, Czech Republic, Denmark, Estonia, Finland, France, Hungary, Iceland, Ireland, Israel, Italy, Japan, Korea, Mexico, Netherlands, New Zealand, Norway, Poland, Portugal, Russian Federation, Slovak Republic, Slovenia, Spain, Sweden, Switzerland, Turkey, United Kingdom and United States.
Subnational 25	Austria, Belgium, Canada (provincial/territorial legislation), Chile, Czech Republic, Denmark, Estonia, Finland, France, Hungary, Iceland, Ireland, Israel, Italy, Korea, Netherlands, New Zealand, Norway, Poland, Portugal, Russian Federation, Slovak Republic, Slovenia, Spain, Sweden, Turkey and United Kingdom.

Source: OECD (2011), *Government at a Glance 2011*, OECD Publishing, Paris, http://dx.doi.org/10.1787/gov_glance-2011-en.

In the process of extending the right to access information to the subnational level, activities to raise awareness could take new and innovative forms. For a community of practice emerge, a broad alliance of elected local authorities, media outlets, CSOs and community associations and members could be integrated in activities which could take the form of a film projection as recently organised in four universities around Jordan with the support of the United Nations Educational Scientific and Cultural Organisation (UNESCO, n.d.). Moreover, the Information Right Now! campaign (2012), launched by the European Youth Information and Counselling Agency (ERYICA) and the Council of Europe, has proven that creative approaches can be successful in involving different groups in society, including youth. The campaign involved youth and youth workers in meetings with the presidents of the municipality councils in the former Yugoslav Republic of Macedonia, information fairs in Croatia, and street art festivals in Sweden (OECD, 2016b).

Freedom of media and freedom of expression

The freedom of expression, press and assembly are cornerstones of democracy. Safeguarding these rights and liberties is an implicit requirement for any open government agenda to be successful. Independent national media plays a vital role in stimulating debate and dialogue and acting as a watchdog of government performance. Reliable local media outlets (e.g. newspapers, TV/radio broadcasters, online/social media) are critical for informing the electorate, empowering local communities, encouraging democratic participation and exercising scrutiny over local power holders.

The freedom of the media and expression are anchored solidly in the Jordanian Constitution. Article 15 stresses that every Jordanian shall be free to express his opinion and that the freedom of the press and publications shall be ensured within the limits of the law. The law stipulates that newspaper permits may be revoked in accordance with the provisions of the law. A limited censorship on newspapers, publications, books and broadcasts affecting public safety and national defence can be imposed in the event of the declaration of martial law or a state of emergency.

The Press and Publications Law No. 8 of 1998 (amended by Law No. 2 of 2012) reaffirms that journalists have “the right to access information, news and statistics of interest to the citizens from various sources” (Article 6c), and that “official authorities and public agencies shall facilitate their task and allow them to view their programmes, projects and plans” (Article 8). The law prohibits the imposition of any restrictions on the freedom of the press in fulfilling the provision of information to citizens, including procedures that would hinder the exercise of such right (WIPO).

Concerns about the tightening of the freedom of press and expression have increased in Jordan, which is attested by international assessments, such as the 2016 World Press Freedom Index of Reporters Without Borders (Jordan ranks 135th out of 180 countries), and the Freedom of the Press Index by Freedom House (Jordan is ranked "not free" with a score of 66/100, 100 being the worst). The World Report 2016 by Human Rights Watch finds that the following present an elevated risk to the freedom of expression: criminalisation of speech deemed critical of the King, foreign countries, government officials and institutions, as well as Islam and speech considered to defame others; the broad application of the counter-terrorism law.

The debate about an increasingly loose definition and implementation of freedom of expression and the media are not unique to Jordan, but have caused an intense debate in other Arab states and elsewhere (Khouri, 2016). The leeway of governments to interpret the work of journalists risks suppressing citizens' ability to speak out freely in public. Despite the increase in the number of regional outlets of private radio stations, many of which broadcast for specific groups (e.g. women and students), recent developments suggest that the operational freedom for the press has decreased in Jordan. Cases of self-censorship among journalists to avoid interference from state actors point to a number of challenges:

- Recent amendments and new regulations that risk tightening the freedom of journalists to report, including: the 2015 counter-terrorism law (Middle East Eye, 2016); the 2011 amendment to the anti-corruption law, which criminalises reporting on news that defames someone or "impacts his dignity"; and the 2012 amendment to the Press and Publications Law, which imposes restrictions on online news content, requires new websites to obtain licenses to operate and prescribes penalties of almost USD 40 000 for speech that denigrates the government or religion. Another source of concern is the decision of October 2015 that defamation charges against journalists and media outlets are no longer brought under the country's press law, but the cybercrimes law, under which journalists can be imprisoned for press violations (Freedom House, 2016).
- Media bans on news considered sensitive and addressing controversial topics (e.g. detainment of terror suspects).
- Registration requirements for print media and online outlets with the Ministry of Commerce and Industry, and the need to obtain a license from the Media Commission to work legally. The Media Commission can issue orders without a court ruling to block foreign and domestic websites that fail to comply with the law.
- Lack of diversity of media outlets: a study by the Jordan Media Institute found that over 60% of news stories published in the newspapers were from the Petra News Agency and other press statements issued by government entities, CSOs and the private sector (Ghazal, 2014).

Independent journalism is a crucial building block of any democracy, and instrumental for bringing potential threats to the attention of a large audience. In the process of reviewing potentially conflicting legislation with the decentralisation framework and the broader democratisation agenda, the government should consider revising the legal and regulatory obstacles to the work of journalists.

The need for a broad alliance of watchdogs over central and local political affairs

Transparency and openness are the conditions to secure the buy-in and participation of society at large for successful government reform, and are essential for holding decision makers to account. Translating transparency and accountability into practice is a critical element in any open government initiative. Fighting wasta, nepotism and corruption is critical for ensuring that scarce resources are spent for the intended objective, and to restore citizens' trust in government and public officials. CSOs and citizens can play a constructive role in this regard.

In the 2015 Corruption Perceptions Index by Transparency International, Jordan ranked 45, only surpassed by Qatar and the United Arab Emirates and ahead of Bahrain, Saudi Arabia, Kuwait, Oman and countries in North Africa (Transparency International, 2015). However, over the following year, 75% of the respondents believe that corruption has worsened – a serious degradation only outstripped by Lebanon (92%) and Yemen (84%) (Transparency International, 2016). In the 2016 edition, Jordan accordingly lost 12 places due to perceptions of increasing requests for bribes and petty corruption (Transparency International, 2016).

In the Royal Letter from 8 December 2012, which precedes the 2012 National Integrity Charter, King Abdullah II calls to secure the practice of access to information and consolidating transparency, justice and accountability within government institutions, the private sector and civil society. The Charter acknowledges that "there have been some loopholes in the integrity system that need to be addressed" and stresses that "it is a must to fight all forms of corruption: bribery, embezzlement, fraud, misuse of power, money laundering, conflict of interest, dishonest use of information to make personal gains, wasta, nepotism, and others." The Charter stipulates the need to uphold transparency in all operations of the public administration and to reinforce the link between responsibility and accountability.

For the executive branch, the Charter lists four priority areas that can be linked to Jordan's open government agenda:

- Establishing institutional mechanisms that enhance citizens' participation in the making of policies and decisions, and increase citizens′ awareness of government action.
- Promoting budget transparency.
- Ensuring transparency in government tender referrals and procurement.
- Empowering oversight agencies.

The Executive Plan to Enhance the National Integrity System (2012) takes up some of these priorities, stipulating that the government shall:

- Enhance the principles and practices of good governance in the public and private sector and civil society institutions.
- Entrench a culture of transparency in public work, among others, by adopting the principle of disclosure of budgets in line with international criteria.
- Strengthen civil integrity and oversight agencies, among others, by focusing on the role of the media in combating corruption, enforcing access to information, and activing the developmental and oversight role of civil society.

The decentralisation reform sheds light on the need to reinforce the integrity system and close existing loopholes, both at the central and subnational levels. As outlined in the previous chapters, many municipalities lack resources, face debt and suffer from overemployment and little productivity. In the absence of effective local oversight and control mechanisms to hold local power holders to account, elected local councils may risk perpetuating a status quo in which elected officials tend to secure family or tribal interests, in particular outside of the major cities (OECD, forthcoming). Therefore, remaining obstacles to the operation of local media outlets, civil society and independent institutions should be removed decisively to encourage the creation of a broad alliance of watchdogs over local political affairs.

Budget transparency

In the 2015 Open Budget Index by the International Budget Partnership, Jordan scores 55 of 100 points, which places it ahead of any other country in the MENA region covered by the Index. The survey examines 102 countries and measures how governments are managing public finances regarding the level of budget transparency, participation, and oversight. As of 30 April 2016, and in line with good practices in OECD countries, Jordan had made seven out of eight key budget documents available to the public in due time, the exception was the mid-year review. However, the survey finds that budget transparency could be improved by presenting more details (e.g. details on macroeconomic forecasts in the Executive Budget Proposal and a planned versus actual performance in the Year-End Report). A significant lack of transparency characterises the grants allocated by members of parliament at the subnational level, which can sometimes exceed the budget of municipalities (Ababsa, 2013). In France, for instance, this area used to be opaque until the database "Parliamentary Appropriation" (*dotation d'action parlementaire*)[4] was created. This database allows everyone to access the grants proposed by the senators for parliamentary action, and lists information about the beneficiary, the amount and the budget allocation programme (*programme budgétaire d'imputation*) for each grant.

Jordan has undertaken efforts to involve citizens in the budget process. A Citizen Guide to the Budget in Arabic has been published on the website of the General Budget Department each year since 2011,[5] and awareness seminars were organised in co-operation with Partners Jordan Centre, a civil society organisation, in Naur, Jerash and Kerak in 2015. Moreover, with the objective of allocating a share of the national budget to secure the needs and rights of the child, the National Council for Family Affairs and the United Nations International Children's Fund (UNICEF) have conducted a series of child budget analysis in 2009 (Ministry of Health, Ministry of Education, Ministry of Social Development, Ministry of Labour), 2013 (Ministry of Awqaf and Islamic Affairs, Ministry of Justice) and 2015 (Ministry of Public Works and Housing, Higher Council of Youth). Despite these positive examples, CSOs and citizens have few opportunities to engage in the budget process, as no formal mechanisms exist to relay their perspectives on spending priorities (International Budget Partnership, n.d.).

Efforts to formalise, including the perspective of the public on budget matters, could be accompanied by actions to strengthen budget oversight. In this respect, there is a need to reinforce the role of the parliament (e.g. submission of the Executive Budget Proposal at least three months before the start of the budget year) to clarify the roles and responsibilities of the three main oversight agencies, the Audit Bureau, the Anti-Corruption Commission and the Ombudsman Bureau; and to seek new partnerships with parliament, the media and CSOs to educate the public against the hazards of corruption (Executive Plan to Enhance the National Integrity System, 2012).

Legal status and operational freedom of civil society

The Jordanian Constitution grants the freedom of association in Article 16. There are 127 international non-governmental organisations and 4 500 local organisations operating in the civil society sector, in addition to numerous initiatives and platforms for volunteering (Inform, 2015). Recent data from the Ministry of Social Development for 2016 estimates that 5 108 civil society organisations are active in Jordan.

International indexes take a critical stance towards the level of freedom for CSOs to operate in Jordan. Although Jordan's status improved from "not free" to "partly free" in the 2017 Freedom in the World report, thanks to the approval of the 2015 Election Law, Freedom House stresses that the exercise of political rights (score: 5/7, 7 being the worst) and civil liberties (5/7, 7 being worst) continues to be challenging. The Transformation Index of the Bertelsmann Foundation (2016) ranks Jordan 88 out of 129 developing and transition countries in the political transformation sub-index ("moderate autocracy"), and 75 in good governance ("weak transformation management").

In OECD countries, civil society organisations fulfil many different roles. They act as watchdogs of government's activities, exercise public scrutiny over budget allocations, and provide a space for the collective action of less organised groups in society, including women, youth, disabled and minorities. In this sense, CSOs are a fundamental actor to preserve and strengthen democratic governance and defend civil rights and liberties.

There are significant differences regarding the organisation and work of CSOs in Jordan and most OECD countries. In Jordan, CSO activity is often rooted within the tribal system and has a long tradition of providing charity and welfare services alongside the activities of the government and the Royal Court. Jordanian CSOs with an agenda to defend fundamental rights and freedoms only started to emerge after the Kingdom acceded to international conventions (International Center for Not-for-Profit Law). Some CSOs in the area of service provision, Royal NGOs (RONGOs) and Government NGOs (GONGOs), benefit from the financial support and operational freedom granted by the authorities. The organisation of CSOs along tribal affiliations and their financial dependency on the government or the Royal Court have raised the question as to whether they can be considered CSOs in the first place (Identity Centre, n.d.).

The rights and responsibilities of civil society organisations in Jordan are regulated by the Law of Societies (No. 51 of 2008) as amended by Law No. 22 of 2009 (International Center for Not-for-Profit Law, ICNL). The law stipulates that for any CSO to be able to operate legally, it must be registered with the National Registry of Societies of the Ministry of Social Development, which is considered an independent entity. The Registration Management Council is responsible for its management and supervision. Despite the simplification of registration procedures in recent years, the Council still has the right to reject any application without stating a justification. Potential barriers to the entry and operation of foreign societies prevail as neither the main office nor any of its branches are allowed to have political or religious goals – a clause which can potentially limit their autonomy. Foreign donations to any Jordanian society are subject to the approval of the Council of Ministers.

On 17 March 2016, the Ministry of Social Development announced a series of draft amendments to the 2008 Law No. 51 on Society. The move sparked an intense debate about the future ability of CSOs in Jordan to fulfil the diversity of roles as outlined above.

If the amendments pass in their current form[6]:

- A minimum of 50 people would be required to form a society. This condition risks undermining the emergence of small-scale CSOs, which, given their diversity, have traditionally played an important role in providing services for neglected groups in society and strengthening accountability mechanisms.
- The government would have broad discretion to prohibit the establishment of organisations on the grounds of violating "national security, public safety, public order, public morals, or the rights and freedoms of others".
- Branch offices of international organisations would face additional layers of approval for inter-organisational transfers of funds, while the government would determine the duration of the branch office's registration.
- Jordanian CSOs would be subject to new requirements and restrictions regarding their ability to secure funding from outside of Jordan (International Center for Not-for-Profit Law, 2017).

2016 Election law

The 2016 Election Law was endorsed by King Abdullah II on 13 March 2016 after Parliament passed the bill. The Election Law introduces a major change in that the traditional "one person one vote" (single non-transferable vote, SNTV) system was abandoned in favour of an open proportional list at the level of governorates and constituencies.[7] Whereas the one person one vote system resulted in the dominance of tribal elites and other groups loyal to the King in the parliament at the expense of the electorate in big cities and Palestinians living in Jordan,[8] the new Election Law is expected to encourage the creation of political parties (Freedom House, 2016). Under the new system, each voter has a number of votes equal to the number of seats allocated to the district. Each voter can only pick one list, which must be composed of three to ten candidates, and vote for individual candidates on that list. The 2015 Election Law replaces the 2012 Election Law, which granted voters one ballot for a party list (27 seats, proportional representation in a nationwide constituency) and one ballot to select a candidate through the SNTV (108 seats, based on local electoral districts).

The bill divides the Kingdom into 23 electoral districts, one for each of the 12 governorates, with the exception of Amman (five districts), Irbid (four districts) and Zarqa (two districts). The law maintains 15 parliamentary seats for women (one per governorate and one for each of the three Badia districts). It also preserves nine seats for Christians and three for the Circassian/Chechen minority. The total number of seats in the lower house was reduced from 150 to 130.

The new system is expected to increase the participation of citizens in the elections, in particular at the local level, which is a matter of urgency given that voter turnout was as low as 11% in the local elections in Amman in 2013 (Bertelsmann, 2016). The OECD survey among the members of the CSO Network finds that 11 out of 17 organisations expect that the 2015 Law will encourage the participation of citizens in the elections, and hence contribute to improving local democracy; four NGOs disagree. While the new law is expected to foster the creation of political parties, public awareness is yet to be built among the wider public to increase voter turnout.

In the parliamentary elections held on 20 September 2016, 37% of the electorate went to the ballot box. Voter turnout varied significantly across the territory, with the highest turnout registered in the Southern Badia district (83%) compared to only 23.5% in Amman (Al Hayat Center for Civil Society Development, 2016). The RASED programme of the Al Hayat Center for Civil Society Development reported a total of 952 incidents throughout Election Day, including public voting, violence and attempts to influence voters or prevent them from voting. The Integrity Coalition for Election Observation, led by the Identity Center, an independent Jordanian NGO, identified the circulation of results by candidates and their supporters ahead of the official announcement by the Independent Election Commission (Identity Center, 2016).

Despite these irregularities, the parliamentary elections were overall perceived as successful (European Union, 2016). In addition to the 15 seats reserved for women by the quota, five female candidates were elected to the parliament, increasing the overall share from 12% to 15% (Cuthbert, 2016).

In preparation for the local elections to be held in 2017, the government published the Governorate Councils Districting Bylaw in the Official Gazette on 15 December 2016. The bylaw divides the Kingdom into 145 constituencies, with a total of 270 seats. The size of the governorate council varies between 41 seats in the governorate of Amman and 14 seats in the governorate of Aqaba (Jordan Times, 2016). The draft bylaw has been criticised by observers, including the Al Hayat Center for Civil Society Development, as it may generate some imbalances in the representation of certain districts:

- In the absence of clear standards and criteria, the bylaw has ignored existing administrative units in the drawing of electoral districts.
- The decision about the number of seats allocated per district suffers from a lack of clear standards, and results in significant differences in the political weight of local communities in different governorates, which may ultimately result in distorted development strategies at the governorate level. For instance, while the districts of Sahab, Al Jeeza, Al Mowaggar and Na'our in Amman account for 28% of total seats, their combined population does not exceed 7% of the total population of the capital city.
- No criteria have been defined for the members who will be appointed by the central government.

Open government in practice: Enhancing current participation practices at central and local levels

The assessment in this section is based on 17 answers to a survey that the OECD received from members of the Network of Civil Society Organisations for Open Government at the Local Level in Jordan ("Network of CSOs") between 26 July and 6 October 2016, as well as replies to a questionnaire from the ministries with a key stake in the decentralisation process (e.g. MoPIC, MoI, MoMA) and the municipalities of Ajloun, Al Salt, and Deir Alla. The questionnaire designed for government largely mirrors the questions raised in the CSO survey, and hence complements the assessment in the previous section with an analysis of actual open government and engagement practices.

Towards clear rules for consulting, engaging and receiving feedback from citizens

The constitution guarantees the right of petition and stipulates that Jordanians shall have the right to address the public authorities on personal matters affecting them, or on what is relative to public affairs in the manner and conditions prescribed by law (Article 17). Since 2013, the Legislative and Opinion Bureau (LOB) has been obliged to publish any draft legislation on its website[9] for no less than 10 days to enable citizens and the private sector to provide comment (Regulation No. 5/2013, Article 9). The regulation was introduced as part of Jordan's first National Action Plan for the OGP (OECD, 2013). While this is an important step towards involving non-governmental stakeholders in the policy cycle, the OECD Regulatory Policy Outlook 2015 underlines that stakeholders should be given sufficient time to respond to the consultation. For instance, at the EU level, the minimum duration amounts to 12 weeks whereas U.S. agencies often provide 30 days or more depending on the complexity of the proposed regulation (OECD, 2015). The Ministry of Public Sector Development (MoPSD) offers a web-based complaint system through which sector-specific requests are forwarded to the line ministries. Line ministries have one week to clarify with the MoPSD whether the request was addressed, which can, if necessary, raise a pending case in a report submitted to the Prime Minister's Office. According to the MoPSD, the annual number of requests received since 2013 is decreasing, and in 2016, 94% of all requests were solved. The third action plan for the OGP commits the MoPSD to developing a smartphone application and telephone hotline to increase the access of citizens for submitting complaints by July 2018.

The survey results suggest that, in parallel to the formal procedures described above, informal meetings between government officials and non-governmental stakeholders take place on an ad hoc basis. These meetings are typically initiated by the government and open to selected non-governmental stakeholders, but rarely to the wider public (OECD, 2013). In line with good practice in the United Kingdom (see Box 4.6), Jordan could consider clearly determining the duration of public consultation exercises and the procedures to participate, and raise awareness in order to ensure that a maximum number of interested parties are able to participate. In this regard, line ministries could make more extensive use of existing manuals to guide policy makers, such as the "Participatory Approach to Strategic Planning in the Public Sector" (2014), which was prepared by the MoPSD and circulated by the Prime Minister to all ministries. A set of common principles applied widely across the public administration can reduce the risk of a fragmented approach to public consultation, which bears the risk of discouraging citizens from becoming involved.

The experience with the Code of Practice on Consultation in the United Kingdom (see Box 4.6) shows that a clear set of principles can contribute to increasing the transparency, inclusiveness and efficiency of consultation activities.

Box 4.6. Guidance on consultation: The case of the United Kingdom

Prior to replacing it with the much shorter "Consultation Principles" in 2012, the United Kingdom had a detailed "Code of Practice on Consultation", which aimed to "help improve the transparency, responsiveness and accessibility of consultations, and help in reducing the burden of engaging in government policy development."

Although not legally binding, and only applying to formal, written consultations, the Code of Practice constitutes a good example of how a government can provide its civil servants with a powerful tool to improve the consultation process. The 16-page Code of Practice is divided into seven criteria, which are to be reproduced as below in every consultation.

Box 4.6. Guidance on consultation: The case of the United Kingdom *(cont.)*

- Criterion 1. When to consult: Formal consultation should take place at a stage when there is scope to influence the policy outcome.
- Criterion 2. Duration of consultation exercises: Consultations should normally last for at least 12 weeks, with consideration given to longer timescales where feasible and sensible.
- Criterion 3. Clarity of scope and impact: Consultation documents should be clear about the consultation process, what is being proposed, the scope to influence and the expected costs and benefits of the proposals.
- Criterion 4. Accessibility of consultation exercises: Consultation exercises should be designed to be accessible to, and clearly targeted at, those people the exercise is intended to reach.
- Criterion 5. The burden of consultation: Keeping the burden of consultation to a minimum is essential if consultations are to be effective and if consultees' buy-in to the process is to be obtained.
- Criterion 6. Responsiveness of consultation exercises: Consultation responses should be analysed carefully and clear feedback should be provided to participants following the consultation.
- Criterion 7. Capacity to consult: Officials running consultations should seek guidance on how to run an effective consultation exercise and share what they have learned from the experience.

Sources: UK Government (2016), *Consultation principles 2016*, www.gov.uk/government/uploads/system/uploads/attachment_data/file/60937/Consultation-Principles.pdf; UK Government (2008), *Code of conduct on consultation,* www.bis.gov.uk/files/file47158.pdf.

Informal channels to inform citizens about engagement opportunities prevail

All surveyed entities inform citizens about new opportunities to participate on their website (e.g. MoPIC, MoI, MoPSD, Deir Alla, Ajloun). However, a visit to the website of the MoI shows that it does not list any engagement opportunity other than a general "complaints and suggestions" section. From the online interface, it is also unclear which department within the MoI has the task of dealing with citizen feedback. The lack of a transparent contact section may hamper citizens' use of the opportunities available online to send formal requests. Except for the MoI, all entities report using social media (e.g. Facebook) to provide information. Most entities make use of (traditional) mass media, such as newspapers, TV or radio, to raise awareness for engagement opportunities.

Informal relationships between government officials and specific stakeholders in society (e.g. phone calls, direct contacts) tend to play a significant role for raising awareness, however, such an approach is limited to a group of (government) selected participants. In line with these findings, more than half of all responding CSOs state that they ask friends at the governorate level.

CSOs and citizens seek interaction with central and local decision-making centres

At the central level, a majority of CSOs interact with ministries and parliament. Around a third has established some form of collaboration with the Royal Court. The regular contact with ministries is reflected by the fact that a majority of CSOs report contacting public officials on a weekly basis, while CSOs interact less frequently with members of Parliament and the Royal Court.

At the subnational level, the methods applied by local authorities to interact with CSOs and citizens can vary between municipalities (e.g. regular meetings of the "Municipality Friendship Group" in Deir Alla; ad hoc meetings with citizens in Ajloun and in Al Salt to discuss immediate service needs). CSO activity at the subnational level focuses on the executive decision-making centre, both at the governorate (governor) and the municipality level (mayor). Another preferred target for CSOs seeking influence are local development units (LDUs) and other service providers, whereas members of the Executive Council (governorate level) and the elected municipal council seem to play a less important role in this regard.

Vulnerable groups require specific attention: The example of youth engagement

Engaging vulnerable groups in society, including young men and women, is of particular concern in a country where around 70% of the population is below 30 years of age. Despite their access to the world via new digital technologies, and a variety of civil society activities to foster their involvement in local civic life (e.g. volunteering), the lack of structures and institutions to make young people's voices heard and foster their integration in decision-making processes is a major reason for the disengagement of many from politics today (OECD, 2016b).

The transformation of the former Higher Council for Youth and Sports into the Ministry of Youth in 2016 was a positive step to direct new attention to the specific challenges young people are facing. It is the stated objective of the ministry to integrate youth participation in political, social and cultural life, and to develop new channels to close the communication gap between both sides (Ministry of Youth Jordan, 2016). According to the Ministry of Youth, a new National Youth Strategy 2017-25 is currently being elaborated to improve the co-ordination of youth-related policies and services across different departments. Since its transformation, the ministry has invested significant efforts into improving outreach to young people through social media (as of February 2017, the Twitter account has 1 200 followers). These efforts cannot obscure the fact that young people continue to be side-lined in political decision making that affects their future. The Jordanian political analyst, Amer Sabaileh, notes that youth are not represented in the political system unless they have benefited from privileged access (Konrad-Adenauer-Stiftung, 2016).

While the disenchantment of youth from politics constitutes a major challenge (e.g. low turnout in elections, lack of awareness of government and parliamentary work), promising (grassroots) initiatives have been built in the run up to the 2016 parliamentary elections and beyond. For instance, Shaghaf, which formed in June 2016, held candidate debates at the local level to raise the transparency of election promises and hold future members of parliament accountable. The initiative is composed of young Jordanians from across the Kingdom, including poorer cities such as Zarqa and Jarash, and has rapidly grown to almost 5 000 activists, 40% of whom are young women (Yom and Al-Khatib, 2016).

Youth-led associations in Jordan have proven their innovative potential and maturity to become a partner in the open government agenda of the government. Box 4.7 presents the "Diwanieh" debate approach, organised by Leaders of Tomorrow, which is committed to the idea that more spaces for open and free dialogue are to be built, in particular at the local level, to foster critical thinking and encourage citizens from all backgrounds to take part in political, economic and social discussions.

Box 4.7. Creating a forum for open dialogue at the local level: The example of "Diwanieh"

Diwanieh is an initiative created by the Jordanian youth-led organisation Leaders of Tomorrow which aims to create open, free, and critical debates to encourage open dialogue. The debates in public spaces bring together opinion leaders, local experts, government representatives, representatives from political parties and community members to discuss relevant socio-political issues.

The open and free debate platform aims to encourage young Jordanians to take part in political, economic and social discussions and build their skills, including critical thinking, research, public speaking and persuasive communication.

Since its inception, Leaders of Tomorrow reports that over 9 000 citizens have participated in 22 large-scale public debates across the country.

Source: Leaders of tomorrow (2017), *Diwanieh webpage*, www.leadersot.org/initiatives/diwanieh/ (accessed 17 February 2017).

So far, youth (led) associations and youth demands are absent in the open government discourse in Jordan. The examples of Finland[10] and Tunisia[11] illustrate that the National Action Plan for the OGP can be used to anchor youth-related commitments and, given the cross-sectorial scope and ambition of the plan, expose them to government-wide attention and international scrutiny (see Box 4.8).

Box 4.8. Youth in the open government agenda in Tunisia

Tunisia's second National Action Plan for the Open Government Partnership aims to adapt innovative, participatory and transparent approaches in the design and implementation of public policies. With commitment 11 ("Developing new mechanisms to promote interaction with the youth and enable them to pursue dialogue about public policies"), the plan acknowledges the readiness of young men and women to become agents for open government principles and practices, and the need to create effective mechanisms in this respect.

By July 2018, the plan foresees:

1. The development of an e-platform for youth to provide feedback on the delivery of public services.
2. The creation of local councils with representatives from CSOs and government and a "significant presence" of young people to establish a mechanism through which young people can express their demands and priorities, to which (local) government ought respond.

Source: Republic of Tunisia (n.d.), *Open Government Partnership: 2nd National Action Plan 2016-2018*, Ministry of Public Service and Governance, https://www.opengovpartnership.org/countries/tunisia.

Closing the feedback loop: Public information and evaluation activities are scarce

While almost all entities report informing citizens always, or at least in more than 50% of cases, about the outcomes of their participation, it is questionable if the actual information provided is of high value. For instance, both the MoPSD and MoF stress that other than the number of participants and aggregated information on the nature of comments, no information is collected. Furthermore, these results are exclusively communicated within the ministry and among the participants. In the Ministry of Health, only the number of participants is made public.

Through the Monitoring and Evaluation Unit, and with the support of the Communication and Media Unit, the MoPSD reports using a variety of evaluation methods, including internal assessments, surveys and independent assessments conducted by NGOs. In the MoH, monitoring and evaluation is conducted on a six months basis, such as through internal assessments and surveys among citizens. The last international evaluation was organised by the World Health Organisation in 2013. However, little comparative information is available to assess the level of responsiveness of government officials.

Leverage decentralisation reform to foster open government and genuine citizen participation at the local level

As discussed in Chapter 2, decentralisation reform has been on the political agenda in Jordan for more than a decade. King Abdullah II has played an important role in reminding each new government that implementing decentralisation is a national priority for fostering popular participation and local democratic governance. In his letter to the former Prime Minister, Abdullah Ensour, of 29 March 2014, which precedes Jordan 2025, he reiterates the need to enhance local governance and implement decentralisation with a view to ensuring a just distribution of development gains by giving priority to governorate development programmes (Inform, 2015).

The rationale behind the reform, which is to allow for a more participatory and citizen-driven approach in the development process, has remained the leitmotiv, while different concepts to reorganise the subnational layers of government have been discussed. The Executive Development Programme 2016-18 places the current reform in the context of the broader democratic transformation process in Jordan, stating that engaging a variety of groups in society in the development process will improve government performance and foster a wider set of open government principles (e.g. transparency and accountability). These will improve citizens' livelihoods, reduce local development disparities and promote democratic development across different regions.

The sense of urgency conveyed by the Royal Court resonates with the perception among the members of the Network of CSOs that reform is a priority both for the government and the citizens of Jordan.[12] The country's legacy as a highly centralised state with strong tribal affiliations calls for a context-sensitive approach. Considerable differences between the governorates and municipalities exist in terms of the economic weight and composition of the population, as well as regarding the participation of non-governmental stakeholders in local decision making and available capacities. Therefore, the tools and mechanisms applied to realise the King's vision of a development process that is driven by the grassroots should be sensitive to specific circumstances in each region. Local community engagement may take a different form in highly populated urban areas than in rural, impoverished and culturally more conservative regions.

The evolution of the institutional framework at the subnational level and its impact on the relationship between government and citizens

The creation of elected local councils at the governorate and district level is the most prominent institutional change introduced by the 2015 Decentralisation Law (DL) and Municipality Law (ML). In the words of the Executive Development Programme 2016-18, it presents the most tangible commitment by the Government of Jordan to realise the vision of "[i]nitiating local development across the Kingdom's governorates through an effective and accountable decentralised system that responds to the needs of citizens in local areas and provides services to them at the highest levels of efficiency and effectiveness in partnership with them and within available resources".

With the decentralisation reform, the new reality at the local level in Jordan will be characterised by a largely deconcentrated system of day-to-day service delivery, and a more active stance of the local level in the national planning and development process. For both processes, the procedures for local non-governmental stakeholders to participate in the assessment of local needs, and partner in the implementation and evaluation, are yet to be defined. The bylaw for the elected governorate councils, which was approved in December 2016, provides limited clarification in this regard.

The bylaw stresses that the governorate council shall meet at least once every month upon the invitation of its chairman. The council meetings shall be open to the public, unless the council decides otherwise (Article 9). At its first meeting, the council elects the members of five permanent (thematic) committees. Each permanent committee is composed of four to seven council members who alone have the right to vote on the issues that fall under the competence of the committee (Article 17). For each governorate, a local society committee is tasked with studying the basis for improving public service delivery, communicating with local societies on all levels to discuss service needs, and fulfilling any other task delegated by the council (Article 16).

The bylaw for the elected local councils is expected to be finalised in 2017. Their proximity to citizens has created expectations that policy making and service delivery will become more inclusive and responsive to local requirements. However, some scepticism prevails among CSOs as to whether the elected councils will indeed act as a local parliament with adequate resources and capacities to represent the interests of local community members and encourage new forms of popular participation. OECD experience shows that concerns related to the additional financial and human resource needs of local elected councils (and potential voting fatigue) can be addressed by clearly defining and communicating their mandate regarding the elected body at the higher (i.e. governorate council) layers of government.

The creation of elected councils is a first and crucial step for Jordan in the process of replacing centralised planning by a bottom-up approach to the identification of local needs. According to MoPIC, LDUs, once transformed into directorates (see Chapter 2), will feature a directorate in charge of liaising with citizens and CSOs. This mechanism could, if effectively interlocked with the elected local officials, overcome the current ad hoc approach to popular participation. The dominance of the central level in addressing the day-to-day (service) demands of citizens in their local community, however, may risk slowing down the rise of a new administrative culture in which CSOs and citizens refer to their elected local representatives as a first choice.

As discussed in Chapter 2, the delivery of public services remains largely in the hands of the line ministries and their deconcentrated entities (directorates) in the governorates. Through the governor, the central level is expected to continuously exercise significant influence over local affairs. Furthermore, the financial dependence of many municipalities on central grants and donor support suggests that the scope of action for elected local representatives will still be limited. If the decision-making power remains vested outside the subnational elected bodies, CSOs and citizens are likely to direct their attention towards the ministries and their deconcentrated entities and, in many cases, Parliament, to benefit from the strong tribal affiliations that link many parliamentarians to their constituency. The experience with the so far directly elected municipal councils suggests that in the absence of sufficient resources, and the dominance of the central level in determining local needs, there is a weak incentive for local CSOs to form partnerships with elected subnational bodies.

Given the absence of strong transparency and accountability mechanisms at the subnational level to date, a certain degree of central oversight in local affairs is reasonable. However, vast centralised power over the subnational layers of government risks slowing down the rise of a new administrative culture in which citizens address their demands to elected local representatives. In this system, the lines of accountability tend to be blurred, especially between the entities at the different subnational layers and the Ministry of the Interior and the Ministry of Municipal Affairs. If citizens feel that their participation has little impact on the decision-making process, they may be discouraged, as would be the emergence of a genuine culture of open and participatory governance.

Towards a culture of open and democratic local governance in Jordan: Living diverse forms of democracy

By virtue of its smaller size and the proximity of policy makers and citizens, local governance can offer greater prospects for the use of direct and representative democracy, as well as a more direct participative democracy (Cretu and Cretu, 2014). Local democracy cannot and should not be narrowed down to casting a ballot on election day. As such, the subnational level offers the potential for new and innovative forms of engaging citizens and strengthening transparency and accountability mechanisms (OECD, 2016a).

The creation of elected governorate and local councils in Jordan, the institutional centrepiece of the reform process, provides a new momentum to strengthen local democracy in its various forms (e.g. representative, deliberative and direct forms of engagement), and increase the performance of local government. It also holds the potential of creating a shared sense of responsibility among citizens for the development of their community, and increases the legitimacy of otherwise contested political decisions in a context of scarce resources (e.g. urban planning).

The 2017 local elections: A test for representative democracy

The first elections of the governorate and local councils are expected to take place in August 2017, and have raised high hopes that the needs of local communities, in particular those of vulnerable groups, will be better represented in public life. The first significant change that must be noted is an increasing number of elected local representatives. Whereas the number of elected representatives in the governorate council is to be determined by specific regulations (Article 3, DL), the 2015 ML stresses that the number of representatives in the municipal councils should be no fewer than seven members, including the mayor, and that there shall be no fewer than five members per local council (Article 3). However, it remains to be seen whether or not a higher number of elected local authorities will indeed increase legitimacy and citizens' trust in the government.

Previous election rounds at the municipal level in Jordan were held in 1995, 2007 and 2013, and point to a downward trend in voter turnout (from 50% to 30% between 2007 and 2013). The very low turnout in Amman (10.5% in 2013) accounts for much of the weak participation in the past (Al Monitor, 2013). Since 2007, elections have been supervised by the Independent Elections Commission. Understanding the factors that shape voter turnout in local elections is critical for tailoring awareness campaigns and similar activities to specific groups in society, in particular the disengaged. Box 4.9 presents evidence from New Zealand and other OECD countries in this regard.

Box 4.9. Factors shaping turnout in local elections: The example of New Zealand

Low turnout in local government elections is a challenge that Jordan shares with many OECD member countries. In New Zealand, for instance, average voter turnout in local elections is approximately 30% less than turnout for parliamentary elections.

A study conducted by Local Government New Zealand identifies some of the factors shaping turnout in local elections in New Zealand. The study sheds light on structural issues, as well as the characteristics of the population that can influence voter behaviour.

The study finds that:

- Turnout tends to be higher in local governments with smaller populations. Between 2010 and 2013, voter turnout in metropolitan councils (more than 90 000 inhabitants) and provincial councils (20 000-90 000) decreased, while it increased in rural councils (fewer than 20 000), where turnout already tended to be higher in 2010.
- Participation in local elections increases with age. The pattern that younger voters are less likely to cast their vote than the electorate in general has been discussed before (OECD, 2016c). For instance, in OECD countries, voter turnout among 18-to-24 year-olds in national parliamentary elections is, on average, 17% lower than for adults aged 25 to 50 inclusive. Relative turnout among young people is particularly low in France, the Slovak Republic, Estonia, and the United Kingdom.

The findings add to international research suggesting that voting tends to be associated with higher levels of education, property ownership or at least having lived at the same address for a reasonable length of time and civic education/awareness.

The analysis also finds that, from an international perspective, turnout tends to be higher in systems in which local government has a large range of responsibilities and functions, compared to systems which have a small number of responsibilities. This pattern suggests that the incentive for citizens to invest time into comparing candidates, casting the ballot and monitoring the performance of local authorities is positively related to the "salience", which describes the role and the relevance of the local government.

Sources: Local Government New Zealand (n.d.), *Local democracy: Quick facts*, www.lgnz.co.nz/assets/Uploads/Elections-Fact-sheet-16.pdf;
OECD (2016c), *CO4.2: Participation rates of first-time voters*, OECD, Paris, www.oecd.org/social/family/CO_4_2_Participation_first_time_voters.pdf.

The 2015 DL introduces a 10% quota for women in the elected governorate councils. The Cabinet may appoint 15% of the number of elected members, provided that one-third of appointed candidates are women. In the municipal councils, which will be composed of the members of the local councils who obtained the highest votes, at least 25% of its members must be women.

Candidates of the elected councils must be at least 25-years-old, and, in the case of the governorate councils, have been Jordanian for at least ten years. The minimum age is considerably higher than for most OECD countries, such as Australia, Canada, Germany, Italy and the United Kingdom, in which citizens can run for office in regional and local elections once they reach 18. According to the CIA World Factbook, around 55% (2015) of the population are below 25, therefore, this criteria risks undermining the fair representation of the specific demands and needs of young men and women. Initiatives to enhance youth participation in electoral processes (e.g. organisation of school parliaments), such as by Afaq Jordan for Development and Training, a youth organisation based in the governorate of Al Mafraq, are critical for supporting a young generation to become active citizens with the skills to hold local representatives to account. The existing infrastructure at local level (e.g. youth centres) and programmes (e.g. youth parliaments are operational in some governorates) could be used more effectively to raise awareness and encourage young people to run.

The quota for women in the governorate and municipal councils guarantees a welcome minimum level of inclusive representation, which can contribute to changing traditional norms and perceptions. The current practice in the elected municipal councils shows that despite a significant under-representation of women, the gender gap tends to be considerably smaller than in centralised government bodies. In 2014, for instance, the average gender gap in the municipal councils was 44% (72.2% men; 27.8% women) compared to 78% in the Cabinet, 76% in the House of Representatives, and 56% in Labour Unions (Department of Statistics, 2014).

Figure 4.1. Gender gap in local councils in Jordan (2014)

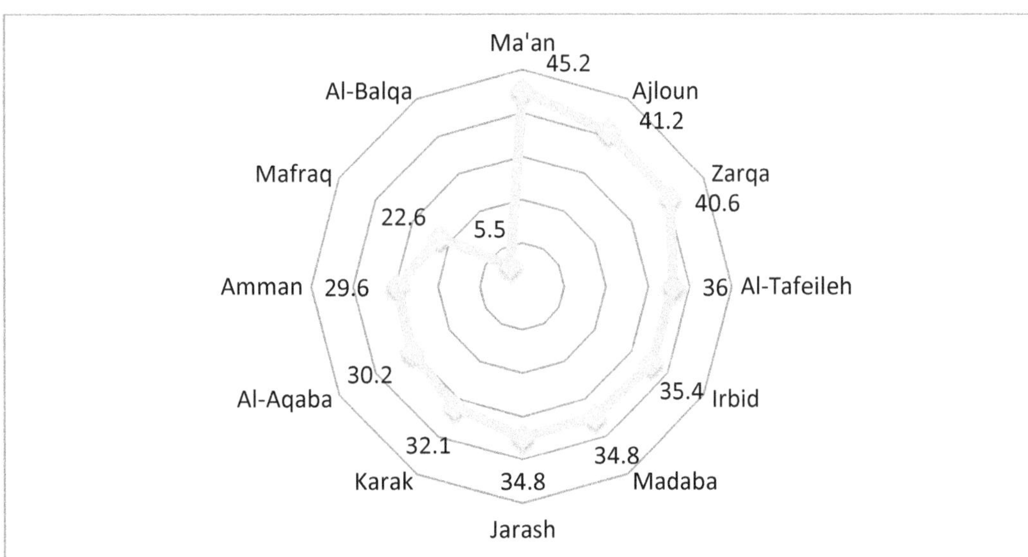

Note: Gender gap = (%) Male - (%) Female.

Source: OECD's own work based on: Department of Statistics (2014), *Gender gap*, www.dos.gov.jo/dos_home_e/main/population/gender/policy/2014/10.pdf.

Elected councils may offer new avenues for the representation of marginalised groups in society. For voters to make an informed choice, in particular those with little experience or interest in democratic procedures and less educated groups, they must have a thorough understanding of why their participation in elections matters. As trust in and the satisfaction with the performance of elected representatives in the national parliament tends to be low in Jordan, awareness campaigns should be organised well ahead of the elections to foster broad participation.

Despite efforts to foster the creation of political parties through the 2015 Election Law, tribal affiliations tend to determine the voting preference, particularly in more rural areas. Experiences in the past have led to some scepticism as to whether the opportunity to elect representatives at the governorate and district levels will fundamentally change this pattern. It must be noted that the elected councils will not automatically lead to a fairer and more equal representation of citizens' needs.

Consultation, active participation and evaluation beyond election day

Periodic elections are a mandatory but not a sufficient condition for a culture of open and democratic local governance to materialise. This requires the daily commitment and effort of local representatives, civil servants and civil society actors to bargain and seek compromises. A healthy democratic culture rests on a vibrant civil society and active citizens to ensure a "living democracy" in which opportunities for citizens to access information and participate in consultations (e.g. open consultations, citizen fora, advisory sessions, use of e-participation tools) go hand in hand with mechanisms to monitor government performance. As local governments come closer to citizens, the potential of open consultations, new forms of engagement and partnership approaches is highest at the local level.

The Executive Development Plan 2016-18 acknowledges the need to organise awareness raising activities among and build communication channels between local authorities, CSOs and citizens. However, general optimism towards the objectives of the reform cannot disguise the scepticism among civil society representatives as to whether or not the government is indeed serious about allowing a bottom-up approach. So far, many CSOs have been present in a merely symbolic way in the absence of a structured dialogue.

There are good practices for successful deliberative approaches in the day-to-day activities of the municipalities in Jordan. In Deir Alla, the decision of where a school should be built was prepared in collaboration with a voluntary committee, which featured representatives from the local community. The voluntary committee was given the right to set the priorities, which resulted in building up mutual trust and the acceptance of local authorities and community members. The challenge for governorates and municipalities in Jordan is to institutionalise this kind of citizen participation and engagement in the development process to ensure sustainability and build trust, in particular in the interaction with the newly elected bodies at the governorate and district level.

In most Latin American countries, for instance, local citizens councils were established for this purpose. Councils usually have a mandate to advise the elected council on specific issues, such as planning, housing or selected policy areas (education, social affair). The implementation of the plans and policies falls under the responsibility of the municipality (see Box 4.10). Evidence from Latin America illustrates that the performance of the councils depends on the availability of sufficient capacities and the openness of local officials to take their advice into due account.

Box 4.10. Latin America's local citizen councils

Since the 1980s, governments in Latin America have developed a new relationship with their citizens in which they can participate more actively in the decision-making process. They have achieved this, in part, by creating local citizen councils.

Although local councils take on different names and forms across the region, they share common features. Generally, they gather different sectors of civil society, such as academics, civil or community-based organisations and the private sector, and join them with local political authorities in a single body, where they collaboratively make public policies or design development programmes. They also typically share a common goal of strengthening democracy and the quality and responsiveness of public policies at the local level.

In some cases, the creation of local councils is mandated by the constitution (e.g. Peru's Constitution - Title IV, Chapter XIV on Decentralisation) or a national law (e.g. Mexico's National Water Law mandating the creation of Basin Councils), while in others they have emerged at the initiative of local governments and citizens (e.g. Colombia's Medellin's Youth Municipal Councils).

In general, local councils in Latin America are formed by elected representatives of various social, political, and sometimes economic sectors, which shows the importance of the capacity and will of the actors involved in the councils, especially the local governments' open attitude towards citizen participation.

Local councils in Latin America follow two basic models in terms of the variety of thematic areas they tackle. They can debate and decide on comprehensive development plans that cut across many sector-specific concerns, such as the Peruvian Participatory Development Plan (*Plan de Desarrollo Concertado*). In other countries, local councils are created to deal with specific thematic areas, such as social policy, environmental preservation, urban governance or public service provision, such as Local Health Management Councils in Paraguay.

Source: OECD (2016a), *Open Government: The Global Context and the Way Forward*, OECD Publishing, Paris, http://dx.doi.org/10.1787/9789264268104-en.

The example of the provincial Council of Biscay in Spain (Box 4.11) illustrates how the use of innovative tools has resulted in more accountable, transparent and efficient service delivery. This could be of great interest for Jordan given its young and tech-savvy population, as well as the e-Government Strategy 2014-2016 which calls upon the government to be proactive in soliciting citizens' opinions and feedback through social media, discussion forums, web logs, surveys and polls and live chats. According to Internetworldstats, 5.7 million people in Jordan used the Internet in June 2016 (72.4% of the population) and there were 4.8 million Facebook subscribers in June 2016 (62%) (Internetworldstats). The World Bank estimates that around 54% of the population in Jordan uses the Internet, compared to an average of 44% in MENA countries.[13]

Box 4.11. Opening municipalities in the province of Biscay in Spain

The provincial Council of Biscay in Spain has developed an innovative approach that regroups all of the province's municipalities, and grants citizens a decisive role in improving local policies and contributing to the quality of services in the region. Based on the concept that "a modern institution has to be close and accessible to its citizens", the council commits itself to "continue working on spaces of co-operation and social participation in order to be able to be systematically accountable, transparent and efficient."

The provincial Council of Biscay developed an easy-to-use website (http://zabaltzen.balmaseda.net/es/portada/) as well as a smartphone application, called "Udala zabaltzen" (Opening Municipalities), which allows citizens to report flaws in infrastructure, for example potholes or sanitation facilities in improvable conditions. The website and application offer citizens the possibility to provide a detailed localisation of the reported problem, which facilitates a swift transfer of this information to the office responsible. Each of the reported required improvements is updated as soon as the problem is solved, which exposes the provincial council, the municipality and the office in charge to public scrutiny.

As one of the first local administrations, the province of Biscay moved from e-government to open government, which, according to the provincial Council of Biscay's definition, is based on the three pillars of transparency, participation and collaboration. Among the features available on its website, citizens can exchange opinions directly with the mayor of each municipality and make their needs and suggestions heard in a direct exchange. On some occasions, the provincial council has opened online surveys to all citizens to identify the need for new infrastructure facilities or other potential improvements. In order to enhance transparency and accountability at the local level, the province publishes information on public procurement.

Source: BiscayTik (n.d.), "Diputación Foral de Bizkaia", www.bizkaia.eus/home2/archivos/DPTO1/goazen2030/Bizkaia2030_CAST.pdf.

With the upgrade of the local level and the role of non-governmental stakeholders in the national planning and development process, existing e-participation and m-government tools could be mainstreamed and used across all municipalities with a view to benefit citizens with low or no income, seniors, disabled and persons who live in rural and non-serviced areas (e.g. the existing Mobile Gateway, which offers 40 informational and interactive services to citizens and businesses including inquiries regarding utilities, airline schedule, traffic violations, property tax, vocational license, and weather condition).

The first steps towards facilitating participatory planning at the subnational level in Jordan have already been undertaken. According to the Ministry of the Interior, a regional electronic information system was developed with USAID three years ago, which will be accessible online to all communities and encourage participatory planning. The system is currently being tested in Irbid governorate. In addition to effective (information and communication) tools, examples from Indonesia and Costa Rica point to the importance of strong legal and institutional frameworks to encourage popular participation with the involvement of local communities in national planning and development (see Box 4.12).

Box 4.12. Engaging citizens at the local level in the national planning and development process

In **Indonesia**, the primary legal vehicle that supports citizen participation is Law No. 25 of 2004 on National Development Planning, which seeks to "optimise public participation." The law establishes the national development planning system and delineates the public's ability to participate formally in the process via the Multi-Stakeholder Consultation Forum for Development Planning process (*Musyawarah Rencana Pembangunan, or musrenbang*). While the *musrenbang* process is an important opportunity to involve the public in determining development priorities across all levels of government, both government and CSO representatives have noted its limitations, primarily around ensuring public inputs are taken into account and in identifying the correct CSO partners.

The *Tejiendo Desarrollo* programme in **Costa Rica**, promoted by the office of the First Lady, provides a good example of how citizens can be involved in all stages of the policy cycle at the subnational level. The main components of the programme are the creation of development processes in specific territories, and the elaboration of a National Policy for Regional and Territorial Development with the participation of citizens. The programme is anchored in a solid legal framework for citizen participation in local affairs. The Municipal Code establishes the municipal council's obligation to promote the active, conscious and democratic participation of the people in the decisions of the local government, and gives a prominent role to popular consultations, such as popular initiatives, referenda and town hall meetings (Cabildos). These activities are protected in the bylaws to the Constitution (Laws 8491 and 8492 from 2006), which include the right to referenda, popular initiatives and petitions.

Sources: OECD (2016d), *Indonesia, OECD Open Government Review*, Highlights, OECD, Paris, https://www.oecd.org/gov/open-gov-review-indonesia.pdf;
OECD (2016e), *Open Government in Costa Rica*, OECD Publishing, Paris, http://dx.doi.org/10.1787/9789264265424-en.

The 2015 DL and ML foresee a more prominent role of the subnational layers of government and non-governmental stakeholders in shaping the development process. A new set of skills and competencies is required to ensure that both local populations and local public officials can exercise their new mandate effectively and in a partnership approach (active citizenship, use of planning tools, etc.). In the northern region of Morocco, support programmes for participatory planning were carried out in more than 230 rural communes and municipalities to streamline the new administrative approach and improve the operations of municipal staff and local civil society actors involved in drawing up communal development plans (see Box 4.13).

Box 4.13. Participatory planning as a performance catalyst in the north of Morocco

In the northern region of Morocco, participatory planning is part of an approach that emphasises the involvement of local populations and local public officials in local development and decision-making processes.

This policy has been driven forward by several initiatives, in particular:

- The launching of the National Initiative for Human Development (NHRI) in 2005, based on local development which is strongly associated with a participatory approach.

Box 4.13. Participatory planning as a performance catalyst in the north of Morocco *(cont.)*

- The policy of decentralisation by the state that aims to reinforce the role of regional governments (*collectivités territoriales*) and elected local officials.
- The 2009 Municipal Charter, which strengthened the role of communal councils (*conseils communaux*) in decision making regarding local socio-economic development and in the management and development of their territory.
- The 2011 Constitution, which highlights fundamental principles of decentralisation, such as subsidiarity, free administration, co-operation and solidarity.

Support programmes for participatory planning were carried out in more than 230 rural communes and municipalities with fewer than 35 000 inhabitants between 2009 and 2015 by the General Directorate for Local and Regional Authorities of the Ministry of Education, in conjunction with the Northern Development and Promotion Agency and the Targa-Aide Association. The departments of local governments (collectivités locales) in the prefectures and provinces concerned have also benefited from this support.

The programme focused on streamlining the administrative approach and improving the level of operationality of municipal staff and local civil society actors involved in drawing up communal development plans. This was done through the strengthening of municipal capacity in strategic and participatory planning, and the affirmation of the transparency of the municipality's action regarding its citizens.

The different stages of the programme are presented below:

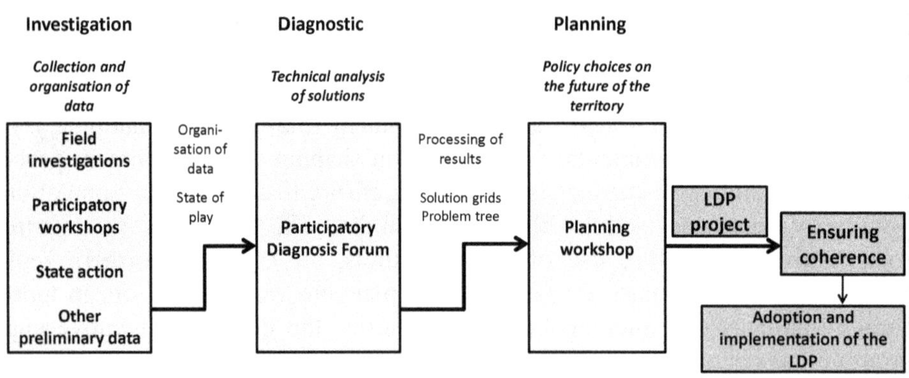

Through this approach, knowledge and capacity in strategic planning have been strengthened. All municipalities prepared a six-year Municipal Development Plan (MDP) with two triennial programmes and a mid-term evaluation. In addition, municipalities have gained a better knowledge of their territory thanks to the preparation of communal maps (road networks, the douars - the villages forming the commune, the location of social facilities, etc.).

The collaboration between the three layers of subnational government (municipality, province/prefecture and region) promoted by the new organic laws covering regions and municipalities (July 2015) is expected to further improve territorial planning and co-ordination between the development policies to increase the efficiency of deployed resources.

Source: OECD (2017), Guide de pratiques sur la gouvernance locale au Maroc, Paris, forthcoming.

As the concrete mechanisms for popular participation in the service delivery and national planning cycle still need to be identified, it remains to be seen at what point CSOs and citizens will be able to shape the process. Low levels of satisfaction with the quality of public services in the municipalities suggest that under the new legal framework, citizens could play a more active role in exercising scrutiny over the performance of service providers, and hence increase transparency and accountability. Independent local media outlets and independent state institutions can act as partners in raising awareness, avoid the misuse of resources, and ultimately contribute to improving the access to and the quality of education, health and other services.

The creation of a system to assess the progress made in implementing the governorate plans is expected in the near future. As Jordan advances in translating the new legal framework into practice, it should consider how to move from ad hoc consultation with the public to more comprehensive forms of interaction, including how to enhance the role of CSOs and citizens in monitoring public service delivery at the subnational level. The need of a substantial investment in building capacity amongst participants and methodological support in participatory evaluation can be offset by higher legitimacy and the acceptance of decisions (OECD, 2009).

New partnerships between local authorities and community members

In addition to an enhanced representation and deliberative participatory approaches, the current reform process holds the potential to foster direct democratic procedures in Jordan. Direct democratic elements of decision making can refer to citizen engagement through methods such as referenda, citizen initiatives, petitions or participatory budgeting schemes. While this approach is not meant to replace local authorities as the final decision maker, it can usefully complement representative and deliberative approaches, and create trust between local authorities and community members.

In a pilot programme with three municipalities, the Ministry of Municipal Affairs has implemented participatory budgeting in practice with what it says are satisfying results. As the examples from the municipality of Sfax in Tunisia and the city of Paris in France show (see Box 4.14), involving citizens in the allocation of a share of the city or district budget to concrete projects can increase the legitimacy of government action and even result in decreasing levels of tax evasion. It ensures that public money is spent in line with the priorities of the (active) electorate and provides a training ground for turning transparency, efficiency, accountability and civic engagement into practice.

Box 4.14. Participatory budgeting at the local level: Experiences from Sfax (Tunisia) and Paris (France)

The 2015 OECD Recommendation on Budgetary Governance explicitly calls on governments to "ensure that budget documents and data are open, transparent and accessible" and to "provide for an inclusive, participative and realistic debate on budgetary choices".

Over recent years, the trend towards participative budgeting has extended internationally and has been taken up with success in a number of OECD member countries and non-member economies. In practice, progress at the national level has been limited to date, with more activities and innovations emerging at the level of cities and municipalities.

Box 4.14. Participatory budgeting at the local level: Experiences from Sfax (Tunisia) and Paris (France) *(cont.)*

Sfax, Tunisia

The allocation of public budgets at the level of municipalities has traditionally been decided by local authorities behind closed doors. This has caused the increasing disengagement of community members from local politics, and fuelled the feeling that elected officials were disconnected from their reality. In light of the lack of trust in local authorities, many citizens refrained from paying local taxes, stressing that they were unsatisfied with the quality of public services and the lack of transparency in financial matters.

In 2015, the municipal council decided to release three million dinar (around USD 1.3 million) to be allocated to investments in roads, street lighting and pavement construction through a participatory budgeting approach. This exercise built on three phases:

1. Communication and awareness campaign (e.g. press release) in collaboration with Gesellschaft für Internationale Zusammenarbeit (GIZ) and a local NGO.
2. The municipal territory was divided into residential areas. In each, citizen fora, animated by a neutral facilitator and featuring a diverse representation of societal groups, were organised discuss concrete projects. In each residential area, one man, one women and one young person were elected to represent the area in the forum of delegates. Almost 2 000 citizens participated in the fora.
3. Forum of delegates: The forum agreed on a total of 25 projects and set up priority criteria for their implementation. The projects selected by the citizens were included in the draft budget for 2016, which was voted on by the municipal council in July 2015.

On a global level, various cities and municipalities have experimented with different forms of participatory budgeting schemes, including in Porto Alegre (Brazil), Paris (France), New York (USA), Toronto (Canada) and elsewhere (OECD, 2016a). In Newcastle (United Kingdom) and Boston (USA), efforts to involve citizens in the allocation of a share of the city's budget were specifically designed for teenagers and young adults. In many cases, the voting process brought young people for the first time to the ballot box (OECD, 2016b).

Paris, France

Since 2014, the municipality of Paris has given its citizens the opportunity to decide on the use of 5% of its investment budget, which amounts to EUR 0.5 billion in 2014-20. The aim is to involve citizens in municipal politics to foster social cohesion and to learn their preferences. It builds on the principles of open government and promotes a stronger relationship between citizens, their representatives and the public institutions. In the 2015 edition of the participatory budget, participation was deepened by providing citizens with the opportunity to propose projects that would then be voted on (Mairie de Paris, 2015). The project tries to harness the creative ideas of Parisians through the following process: 1) Parisians propose their ideas for investment projects on a website; 2) the municipality evaluates the feasibility of the proposal; and 3) project proposals are submitted to a vote.

Sources: Guidara A. (2015), *Le Budget Participatif: Un pas vers la démocratie locale en Tunisie (l'expérience de la commune de Sfax)*, www.leaders.com.tn/article/18292-le-budget-participatif-un-pas-vers-la-democratie-locale-en-tunisie-l-experience-de-la-commune-de-sfax; OECD (2016a), Open Government: The Global Context and the Way Forward, OECD Publishing, Paris, http://dx.doi.org/10.1787/9789264268104-en.

The successful pilot project conducted by MoMA provides an example that other municipalities in Jordan could follow. It combines the practical learning experience of participating in a democratic procedure with assuming actual decision-making power and responsibility, and hence represents the kind of popular participation that decentralisation reform seeks to promote. Good practice examples and success stories can help in overcoming potential resistance or scepticism among local authorities and community members.

Assessment and recommendations

The validation of the 2015 Decentralisation Law and Municipality Law is a significant step towards reinforcing local governance, and holds the potential of moving forward the open government agenda at the level of governorates, municipalities and districts. With the approval of bylaws regulating the election and function of the governorate councils, work on training programmes for local public officials, and awareness raising activities at the governorate level, the Government of Jordan has initiated a series of urgent measures to translate the new legal framework into practice ahead of the local elections in August 2017.

This chapter discusses the links between the current decentralisation reform process, the open government agenda and the broader democratisation agenda in Jordan. It illustrates the mutual reinforcement mechanisms that exist between the three agendas, which culminate in the King's vision that "political development should start at the grassroots level, then move up to decision-making centres". The current reform holds great potential to encourage the emergence of a "culture of governance based on innovative and sustainable policies and practices inspired by the principles of transparency, accountability, and participation that fosters democracy and inclusive growth" at the local level. With the creation of elected councils at the governorate and local level, there is a momentum for a coalition of local public officials and civil society actors to foster representative, deliberative and direct forms of citizen participation. The involvement of local CSOs, citizens and other non-governmental stakeholders in identifying service needs and policy priorities, and the monitoring of government performance, can increase transparency and accountability mechanisms, which have, so far, suffered from severe shortcomings.

However, it must also be noted that many of the detailed procedures and chains of responsibility are still to be defined. Despite a generally positive attitude towards the objectives of the reform process among CSOs and most government officials, some scepticism prevails as to whether the government is indeed serious in allowing for a bottom-up process to planning and development and new forms of citizen participation. For instance, criticism focuses on the limited attention that has been devoted to increasing popular awareness and grassroots support during the reform process. For some CSOs, the government's orchestrated approach is perceived as a tool to stimulate "defensive democratisation" (i.e. concessionary democratic reforms to pre-empt more fundamental challenges to the status quo), which is unlikely to vitalise greater citizen participation, transparency and accountability (Identity Center, n.d.).

This chapter points to two critical determinants for the success of the reform. First, it stresses the need to improve the overall context for open and participatory government across the different layers of government (e.g. access to information framework, a review of decisions affecting the freedom of the media and expression, and the operational freedom of civil society). It reflects that a vibrant civil society is critical for increasing popular awareness and grassroots support for the reform, and, as soon as the local councils begin their work, holding representatives to account. Second, the Chapter highlights the need to establish effective tools and mechanisms strengthen representative, deliberative and direct forms of citizen engagement at subnational level.

In his recent visit to the Ministry of Interior, the Prime Minister stressed the urgency of raising awareness for the law and the future function of the governorate council. The Prime Minister suggested the prospect of organising debates in the governorates regarding the preparation of the state budget to experiment with the interaction between the councils and central government (Watnjo, 2016). Led by the Ministry of Political and Parliamentary Affairs, a national dialogue to raise awareness for the decentralisation reform was initiated in December 2016, featuring meetings with local authorities and community members in each governorate. The sustainability of these initiatives will be critical for ensuring that the current reform process will be understood as a unique opportunity for citizens to shape development in their region. According to the Ministry of the Interior, the Inter-Ministerial Committee in charge of the reform is currently preparing capacity building programmes for different target groups (e.g. youth, CSOs, private sector).

In pursuing the objective of improving the state-of-play for open government in Jordan, and to lever the decentralisation reform to increase popular participation, transparency and accountability at the subnational level, the Government of Jordan could consider the following recommendations:

Turning commitments into results: The process towards a culture of open and inclusive governance

Jordan's membership of the Open Government Partnership

- **Consider formulating a single national open government strategy** to overcome fragmented approaches and foster a whole-of-government approach across the different levels of government. The strategy should build on a national vision for how open government can contribute to broader policy objectives, such as those identified in Jordan 2025. The evidence for such a strategy should be gathered through a collective process starting at the community level (e.g. local elected councils), before being consolidated in the municipalities and governorates and ultimately at central level. Parliament, civil society, the private sector, independent state institutions, media and academics should be involved in a clear and transparent procedure.
- **Upgrade the role of the parliament and the subnational level in the national open government agenda** by organising large-scale training programmes for parliamentarians and local authorities, in particular for the elected representatives in local, municipality and governorate councils and relevant directorates in the LDUs. Local authorities could become involved in the National Commission, which is tasked with elaborating the country's National Action Plan for the OGP.
- **Foster a culture of monitoring and evaluating programmes to increase transparency and accountability**. The creation of an independent reporting mechanism to assess the progress in delivering on open government commitments should be encouraged to increase public scrutiny.

Access to information

- **Consider revising laws and regulations that may impede the effective use in practice** (Protection of the State's Secrets and Documents Law No. 50, 1971) in line with the objective of the 3rd National Action Plan for the OGP to "strengthen the legislative framework governing access to information."
- **Consider amending the Law of Access to Information to extend its scope to the subnational level**. Access to reliable government data and information is a precondition for local media, CSOs and independent state institutions to exercise effective scrutiny over the performance of state institutions at the subnational level in delivering public services and spending decisions.
- **Define clear criteria as to what information is considered "classified", "secret" or "protected by other legislation"** to provide guidance for public officials and increase legal certainty for citizens and businesses. Periodic reviews by an independent agency, which could be discussed by Parliament, could provide information on the use of the right in practice, indicate potential violations and support the creation of a community of practice.
- **Organise an awareness campaign targeting public officials, Parliament, the media, civil society and citizens** with a view to explaining the critical importance that access to reliable information plays in achieving broader policy objectives (e.g. increase the access to and quality of public services).

Freedom of the media and freedom of expression

- **Conduct a review of recent regulations and decisions affecting the freedom of media and freedom of expression** in line with the commitment stressed in the 3rd National Action Plan for the OGP to "strengthen the framework governing the freedom of the media". Independent investigations and reporting by journalists present important pillars for long-term stability and democratic development in Jordan. The criteria for imposing media bans or restrictions on news content should be clarified and disseminated widely to increase transparency and legal certainty for journalists, CSOs and citizens.
- **Foster the emergence of independent local media outlets** (e.g. radio programmes, newspapers, online) to stimulate a culture of debate and dialogue at the community level and to increase the diversity of available information channels. A new diversity of traditional and new media can play a significant role in promoting active citizenship and increasing the level of transparency among existing and future power holders in the governorates and municipalities.
- The need for a broad alliance of watchdogs over central and local political affairs **Foster a genuine culture of monitoring and evaluation among all levels of government, as well as governmental and non-governmental bodies**, to ensure that scarce resources are allocated for their intended purpose. In this respect, the role of the legislative and main oversight agencies should be redefined and upgraded with a view to addressing overlapping responsibilities (e.g. co-ordinate work plans, avoid parallel investigations and duplications, and encourage a culture of sharing information among the Anti-Corruption Commission, the National Audit Bureau and the Ombudsman Office) and the lack of capacity.

- **Increase transparency in the allocation of grants by members of parliament at the subnational level**. For instance, a dedicated database could be created following the example of France (http://data.senat.fr/dotation-daction-parlementaire/) to be able to trace back the grants suggested by members of parliament for parliamentary action, beneficiaries and the resources allocated.
- **Strengthen decentralised control mechanisms by seeking partnerships with independent local media and CSOs and** educating citizens against the hazards of corruption.

Budget transparency

- **Establish a formal mechanism through which CSOs and citizens can participate in the budget process**, in particular at local level, to tailor the allocation of public expenditure to their needs and priorities. Experiments with participatory budgeting schemes at the subnational level (e.g. Ministry of Municipal Affairs and three pilot municipalities) could be replicated on a bigger scale to foster a sense of participatory policy making in practice, in particular among the disengaged and vulnerable groups in society.

Legal status and operational freedom of civil society

- **Request the Registration Management Council to justify the rejection of an application** by a written statement. This requirement would increase the transparency of the application procedure and increase legal certainty among CSOs to operate legally.
- **Organise a national consultation process about the potential amendments of the 2008 Law No. 51 on Society** to increase awareness among civil society organisations and ensure that all relevant stakeholders can raise their voice and potential concerns. Moreover, these amendments should be reconsidered in light of the critical role that CSOs, particularly at municipal and district level, play in providing services to neglected groups in society

2016 Election Law

- **Raise awareness among citizens about the work of Parliament to increase public interest and scrutiny over its activities**.
- **Organise a nationwide awareness campaign to inform citizens about the impact of the bylaws related to the election of the governorate** (e.g. Governorate Councils Districting Bylaw) **and local councils,** in collaboration with local stakeholders from media and civil society to encourage all segments of society, including vulnerable groups, to participate in the 2017 local elections Specific activities should be organised to raise awareness among youth and other groups in society with a lower interest in voting. Initiatives such as *Naseej* (fabric), which brought together 130 young people from different governorates to enhance youth participation in the 2016 parliamentary elections, illustrate that promising citizen-driven initiative have been underway in this regard.

Open government in practice: Enhancing current practices across the different levels of government

- **Formalise citizen consultation to overcome ad hoc approaches and open up participation across the different levels of government to new groups and close the feedback loop.**
- **Review the channels and tools used by government entities to inform the public about consultation and engagement opportunities.** Provide clear indications on who will deal with citizen feedback, and create social media accounts while continuing to use traditional mass media. Awareness for existing manuals (e.g. "Participatory Approach to Strategic Planning in the Public Sector") should be increased so that they become a reference document public officials.
- **Create mechanisms and institutions to make vulnerable segments of society a partner in the open government agenda and the national development process.** The fact that almost 70% of the population in Jordan are below 30 years of age suggests that engaging youth in public life and policy making should be a priority for the government. The examples of Finland and Tunisia illustrate that the OGP National Action Plan can feature youth-related commitments and may, due to the cross-sectorial scope and ambition of the plan and the international scrutiny provided by the OGP, act as an effective lever to turn commitments into actual practice.
- **Reinforce existing mechanisms to collect citizen feedback on the performance of public service delivery and quality**, such as the Central Government Complaints System and the citizen satisfaction survey conducted by the King Abdullah II Centre of Excellence. Support new initiatives, such as the development of an individual Customer Service Charter for each government institution (Ministry of Public Sector Development). A more regular use of surveys could help close the feedback loop, which would increase transparency and ultimately the quality of public services. For this purpose, all relevant information from surveys or consultation activities should be made public.

Leverage the decentralisation reform to foster open government and genuine citizen participation at the local level

- **Increase popular awareness and grassroots support for the ongoing decentralisation reform** in line with the current efforts undertaken through the national dialogue (Ministry of Political and Parliamentary Affairs). The role of the Network of Civil Society Organisations for Open Government at the Local Level in Jordan could be upgraded so that its members act as the link between government and other local CSOs in raising awareness for the reform and its practical implications for local governance and CSO activity.
- **Apply a context-sensitive approach to fostering a culture of open and participatory government at the local level.** Based on a strategic assessment of the available open government capacities and the maturity of open government practices in the governorates, municipalities and districts, a guide could be elaborated to support local authorities and non-governmental stakeholders to implement open government principles and practices, with a view to fostering inclusion and diversity.

- **Build up effective capacities and tools for use by the directorates responsible for liaising with CSOs and citizens** inside the LDUs and among the elected members of the governorate and local councils. Local public officials, both elected and appointed, should have access to training in order to implement a participatory approach to assessing local needs in collaboration with CSOs and citizens. Existing institutions, such as the National Institute for Training, could elaborate training modules that link engagement practices to the broader objective of reinforcing mechanisms for greater openness, transparency and accountability.

Towards a culture of open and democratic local governance in Jordan: Living diverse forms of democracy

The 2017 local elections: A test for representative democracy

- **Foster the equal participation of women in local decision making** through mentoring programmes that link female candidates and women holding office could encourage female candidates to run for local or governorate councils, and would ultimately result in a more balanced participation of women in local councils.
- **Support initiatives to enhance youth participation in local elections and create institutional mechanisms** through which they can play a constructive role in the identification of needs and priorities in their community. The organisation of school parliaments and similar initiatives can raise awareness of the importance of local elections in Jordan's democratisation process. Existing infrastructure, such as local youth councils, could be modernised and used more effectively to empower them to apply open government principles and democracy in practice.

Consultation, active participation and evaluation beyond election day

- **Foster a culture of civic engagement, volunteering and political participation at the local level** by including a civics component in the school curriculum to teach children about the rights and responsibilities of each citizen, as suggested by Jordan 2025.
- **Formalise the participation of non-governmental stakeholders** (e.g. CSOs, citizens, private sector, academia) **in determining development priorities**. Depending on the available capacities and characteristics in each municipality (size, geography, demography, etc.), the most adequate approach may vary between more and less institutionalised forms (e.g. advisory committees for CSOs or specific groups in society vs. survey) and the reliance on traditional (e.g. gatherings with local authorities) and more innovative forms (e.g. online surveys, use of social media). Neither a one-fits-all solution for each municipality, nor a narrow focus on one particular approach, is likely to encourage non-governmental stakeholders to participate in the national planning and development process.
- **Create a website and social media presence for each municipality and use digital technologies more systematically to inform the local community about its work and opportunities for engagement.** The online presence could feature the organisation chart, a complaint mechanism to allow for a direct response from local authorities, the minutes of meetings from the gatherings of the municipal and district councils, access to relevant administrative documents, and other

useful information. The creation of a joint online presence of all municipalities could be considered to encourage the flow of information and good practice across administrative boundaries.

- **Encourage innovative engagement practices at the municipal and governorate level** by establishing a category in the National Honours Program, the creation of which is foreseen by Jordan 2025, to reward Jordanians for their contribution to Jordanian society, for outstanding partnership approaches between CSOs or citizens and local government.

New partnerships between local authorities and community members

- **Replicate experiments with participatory budgeting schemes** to involve a larger number of citizens in the allocation of a share of the municipality or district budget. Citizens should be involved from the very beginning of the process (e.g. identification of projects) to create the necessary buy-in and interest.

Notes

1. The results reflect the answers received from 17 members of the Network of Civil Society Organisations for Open Government at the Local Level in Jordan ("Network of CSOs") received between 26 July and 6 October 2016.
2. The OECD, in partnership with Al-Hayat Center for Civil Society Development, supported the organisation of the two workshops to raise awareness of the open government agenda and the draft plan among Jordanian CSOs.
3. Article 21 (a) of the Anti-corruption Law of 2006; Article 9 of the Financial Disclosure Law of 2006; Article 68 of the Civil Service bylaw of 2007; Decree by the Prime Minister (13/11/1/2776 on 13 February 2008) instructing government officials not to hand out any information to the press except through the Minister or the Deputy Minister.
4. http://data.senat.fr/dotation-daction-parlementaire/.
5. www.gbd.gov.jo/en/Page/Index/citizen-guid.
6. As of April 2017, the amendments have not been approved by the Council of Ministers.
7. Under the Single Non-Transferable Vote (SNTV) system, each voter casts one vote for a candidate while there is more than one seat to be filled in each electoral district. The candidates with the highest votes fill the position which can create negative incentive for political parties to form.
8. This electorate tends to vote for the political arm of the Muslim Brotherhood, the Islamic Action Front (Economist Intelligence Unit, generated on 13 May 2016).
9. www.lob.jo/List_LawsLegislations_Public.aspx.

10. www.opengovpartnership.org/sites/default/files/OGP_Action_Plan_Finland-2015_2017.pdf.

11. www.opengovpartnership.org/countries/tunisia.

12. The results reflect the answers received from 17 members of the Network of Civil Society Organisations for Open Government at the Local Level in Jordan and the questionnaire sent to ministries with a key stake in the decentralisation reform (e.g. MoPIC, MoMA, MoI, MoF, MoPPA, MoPSD) and selected governorates and municipalities.

13. http://data.worldbank.org/indicator/IT.NET.USER.P2?locations=JO-ZQ.

References

Ababsa, M. (2013), *Atlas of Jordan - History, Territories and Society*, http://books.openedition.org/ifpo/4560.

Al-Dabbas, Dr. A. (2008), *Right to Access to Information In the Hashemite Kingdom of Jordan*, National Center for Human Rights, www.nchr.org.jo/english/ModulesFiles/PublicationsFiles/Files/Information-Eng1%20%282%29.pdf.

Al-Samadi, Tamer (2013), Jordan's Local Elections See Low Turnout, Al Monitor, 29 August, www.al-monitor.com/pulse/politics/2013/08/jordan-elections-low-turnout.html.

Bertelsmann Stiftung (2016), *Facts on the European Dimension of Displacement and Asylum: Jordan*, July, http://www.bertelsmann-stiftung.de/fileadmin/files/BSt/Publikationen/GrauePublikationen/EZ_Factsheet_Jordan_07_16_ENG.pdf.

Bertelsmann Foundation (2016), Transformation Index, www.bti-project.org/en/index/.

BiscayTik (n.d.), "Diputación Foral de Bizkaia", www.bizkaia.eus/home2/archivos/DPTO1/goazen2030/Bizkaia2030_CAST.pdf.

CIA World Factbook (2017), Jordan, last update: 12 January, www.cia.gov/library/publications/the-world-factbook/geos/jo.html.

Crețu, V. and Crețu, N. (2014), "How to build local open government?", European Public Sector Information Platform, Topic Report No. 2014/7, July 2014, www.europeandataportal.eu/sites/default/files/2014_how_to_build_local_open_government.pdf.

Cuthbert (2016), *Women gain ground in Jordan election despite yawning gender gap*, www.theguardian.com/global-development/2016/sep/23/jordan-election-women-gain-ground-gender-gap.

data.senat.fr (n.d.), Dotation d'action parlementaire, http://data.senat.fr/dotation-daction-parlementaire/.

Department of Statistics (2014), *Gender gap*, Department of Statistics Jordan, Amman, www.dos.gov.jo/dos_home_e/main/population/gender/policy/2014/10.pdf.

European Union (2016), *Election Observation Mission, The Hashemite Kingdom of Jordan, Parliamentary Election, Final Report*, European Union, Brussels, https://eeas.europa.eu/sites/eeas/files/eu_eom_jordan_2016_final_report_eng.pdf.

Freedom House (2017), Freedom in the World report. Populists and Autocrats: The Dual Threat to Global Democracy, https://freedomhouse.org/sites/default/files/FH_FIW_2017_Report_Final.pdf.

Freedom House (2016), *Jordan, Freedom of the Press Index*, https://freedomhouse.org/report/freedom-press/2016/jordan.

General Budget Department (n.d.), Citizen Guide to the Budget, www.gbd.gov.jo/en/Page/Index/citizen-guid.

Ghazal, M. (2014), *Over 60% of news in major Arabic dailies taken from Petra, press releases — report*, Jordan Times, Amman, www.jordantimes.com/news/local/over-60-news-major-arabic-dailies-taken-petra-press-releases-%E2%80%94-report.

Government of Finland (n.d.), *Finland - Open Government Action Plan 2015-2017*, www.opengovpartnership.org/sites/default/files/OGP_Action_Plan_Finland-2015_2017.pdf.

Government of Jordan (2016), Executive Development Program 2016-18 . n.a. online, www.mop.gov.jo/Pages/viewpage.aspx?pageID=103.

Guidara A. (2015), *Le Budget Participatif: Un pas vers la démocratie locale en Tunisie (l'expérience de la commune de Sfax)*, www.leaders.com.tn/article/18292-le-budget-participatif-un-pas-vers-la-democratie-locale-en-tunisie-l-experience-de-la-commune-de-sfax.

Human Rights Watch (n.d.), *World Report 2016 - Events of 2015*, www.hrw.org/sites/default/files/world_report_download/wr2016_web.pdf.

Huntington and Nelson (1976), *No Easy Choice: Political Participation in Developing Countries*, Harvard University Press, Cambridge, Mass.

Identity Centre (2016), *Integrity Coalition for Elections Observation, 18th House of Representatives, Elections 2016, Final Observation Report*, http://identity-center.org/sites/default/files/elections%20final%20report.pdf.

Identity Center (n.d.), *Policy Paper: Building Grassroots Participation for Decentralisation*, www.identity-center.org/sites/default/files/Identity%20Center%20Policy%20Paper%20-%20Decentralization_0.pdf.

Inform (2015), *Jordan 2025*, Ministry of Planning and International Cooperation, Amman, http://inform.gov.jo/en-us/By-Date/Report-Details/ArticleId/247/Jordan-2025.

Inform (2013), e-Government Strategy 2014-2016, Ministry of Planning and International Cooperation, 15 April, https://jordan.gov.jo/wps/wcm/connect/56d75661-abb5-4ecb-8826-67a1c3ee30df/e-government_strategyjo_draft.pdf?mod=ajperes.

Inform (2012), 2012 National Integrity Charter and Action Plan, Ministry of Planning and International Cooperation, Amman, http://inform.gov.jo/Portals/0/Report%20PDFs/7.%20Role%20&%20Performance%20of%20Government/iii.%20National%20Integrity%20Systems/2012%20National%20Integrity%20Charter%20and%20Action%20Plan.pdf.

International Budget Partnership (2015), *Open Budget Survey 2015, Country Summary Jordan*, www.internationalbudget.org/wp-content/uploads/OBS2015-CS-Jordan-English.pdf.

International Center for Not-for-Profit Law (ICNL) (2017), Civic Freedom Monitor: Jordan, Last update: 4 January, www.icnl.org/research/monitor/jordan.html.

ICNL (n.d.), Law of Societies (No. 51 of 2008) as amended by Law No. 22 of 2009, unofficial translation, www.icnl.org/research/library/files/Jordan/51-2008-En.pdf.

Internet World Stats (n.d.), *Middle East Internet Users, Population and Facebook Statistics 2017*, last update: March 6, 2017, www.internetworldstats.com/stats5.htm.

Khouri, R. G. (2016), *Shutting Arab minds and mouths may lead to disaster*, 29 September, www.jordantimes.com/opinion/rami-g-khouri/shutting-arab-minds-and-mouths-may-lead-disaster.

King Abdullah II (2005), *Address by His Majesty King Abdullah II To the Nation Announcing the Decentralisation Plan*, 26 January, https://kingabdullah.jo/en/speeches/nation-announcing-decentralisation-plan.

Konrad-Adenauer-Stiftung (2016), Jugend und Politik in Jordanien, Länderbericht, http://www.kas.de/wf/doc/kas_45143-544-1-30.pdf?160511095809.

Law on the Election of the House of Representatives (n.d.), No (6) of 2016, www.iec.jo/sites/default/files/2ParliamentaryElectionLawMay2016EN.docx%20%281%29_0.pdf.

Law on Municipalities 2015 (n.d.), Law No 41 of 2015, www.iec.jo/sites/default/files/2015%20Municipalities%20Law%20EN.pdf.

Law on Decentralisation 2015 (n.d.), Law No 49 of 2015, www.iec.jo/sites/default/files/2015%20Decentralisation%20Law%20EN.pdf.

Leaders of tomorrow (2017), *Diwanieh webpage*, www.leadersot.org/initiatives/diwanieh/ (accessed 17 February 2017).

Legislative and Opinion Bureau (n.d.), List of draft laws and regulations, www.lob.jo/List_LawsLegislations_Public.aspx (Arabic).

Local Government New Zealand (n.d.), *Local democracy: Quick facts*, http://www.lgnz.co.nz/assets/Uploads/Elections-Fact-sheet-16.pdf.

Middle East Eye (2016), *Amman bans independent coverage of Jordan's royal family*, http://www.middleeasteye.net/news/jordan-bans-media-publishing-about-royal-family-531467385.

Ministry of Public Sector Development (2014), Participatory Approach to Strategic Planning in the Public Sector, Ministry of Public Sector Development, Jordan.

Ministry of Youth Jordan (2016), Presentation made by representatives from the Ministry during consultation meeting on 15 September 2016 at the OECD in Paris.

MoPIC (2016), *Jordan's Third National Action Plan 2016-2018 under the Open Government Partnership Initiative*, Ministry of Planning and International Co-operation www.opengovpartnership.org/countries/jordan.

OECD (2017), Guide de pratiques sur la gouvernance locale au Maroc, forthcoming.

OECD (2016a), *Open Government: The Global Context and the Way Forward*, OECD Publishing, Paris, http://dx.doi.org/10.1787/9789264268104-en.

OECD (2016b), *Youth in the MENA Region: How to Bring Them In*, OECD Publishing, Paris, http://dx.doi.org/10.1787/9789264265721-en.

OECD (2016c), *CO4.2: Participation rates of first-time voters*, OECD, Paris, www.oecd.org/social/family/CO_4_2_Participation_first_time_voters.pdf.

OECD (2016d), *Indonesia, OECD Open Government Review*, Highlights, OECD, Paris, www.oecd.org/gov/open-gov-review-indonesia.pdf.

OECD (2016e), *Open Government in Costa Rica*, OECD Publishing, Paris, http://dx.doi.org/10.1787/9789264265424-en.

OECD (2015), OECD Regulatory Policy Outlook 2015, OECD Publishing, Paris, http://dx.doi.org/10.1787/9789264238770-en.

OECD (2013), *Regulatory Reform in the Middle East and North Africa: Implementing Regulatory Policy Principles to Foster Inclusive Growth*, OECD Publishing, Paris, http://dx.doi.org/10.1787/9789264204553-en.

OECD (2011), *Government at a Glance 2011*, OECD Publishing, Paris, http://dx.doi.org/10.1787/gov_glance-2011-en.

OECD (2010), "Background document for session 1 OECD Guiding Principles for Open and Inclusive Policy Making", expert meeting on Building an open and innovative government for better policies and service delivery, OECD, Paris, 8-9 June 2010, www.oecd.org/gov/46560128.pdf.

OECD (2009), Focus on Citizens: Public Engagement for Better Policy and Services, OECD Publishing, Paris, http://dx.doi.org/10.1787/9789264048874-en.

The Hashemite Kingdom of Jordan (2014), The Open Government Partnership – Second National Action Plan for Jordan, www.opengovpartnership.org/sites/default/files/Jordan%20-%20Second%20National%20Action%20Plan%2C%202014%20-%202016_1.pdf.

The Hashemite Kingdom of Jordan (2012), *The Open Government Partnership - Jordan: National Action Plan*, www.opengovpartnership.org/sites/default/files/legacy_files/country_action_plans/OGP%20Action%20Plan-Jordan-Final-April%202012_0.docx.

Transparency International (2016), *People and Corruption: Middle East and North Africa Survey 2016*, Transparency International, Berlin, https://issuu.com/transparencyinternational/docs/2016_gcb_mena_en?e=2496456/35314511.

Transparency International (2015), *Table of results: Corruption Perceptions Index 2015*, www.transparency.org/cpi2015/#results-table.

UNESCO (n.d.), Access to Information: The Right of Everyone in Jordan, http://en.unesco.org/events/access-information-right-everyone-jordan-0.

Reporters Without Borders (n.d.), *2016 World Press Freedom Index*, https://rsf.org/en/ranking.

Republic of Tunisia (n.d.), *Open Government Partnership: 2nd National Action Plan 2016-2018*, Ministry of Public Service and Governance, www.opengovpartnership.org/country/tunisia/action-plan.

UK Government (2016), *Consultation principles 2016*, www.gov.uk/government/uploads/system/uploads/attachment_data/file/492132/20160111_Consultation_principles_final.pdf.

UK Government (2008), *Code of conduct on consultation,* www.bis.gov.uk/files/file47158.pdf.

Watnjo (2016), Prime Minister: "Implementation of Decentralization measures will be undertaken before September", in Arabic, www.watnjo.com/news-3095.html.

World Intellectual Property Organization (WIPO) (n.d.), Law No. 8 of 1998 on Press and Publications, in Arabic, www.wipo.int/edocs/lexdocs/laws/ar/jo/jo055ar.pdf.

World Bank (n.d.), Internet users (per 100 people), Jordan and Middle East & North Africa, http://data.worldbank.org/indicator/IT.NET.USER.P2?locations=JO-ZQ.

Yom, S. and Al-Khatib, W. (2016), How a new youth movement is emerging in Jordan ahead of elections, Washington Post, 14 September, www.washingtonpost.com/news/monkey-cage/wp/2016/09/14/how-a-new-youth-movement-in-jordan-is-emerging-ahead-of-elections/?utm_term=.058c8c336ca4.

Annex A.

The French experience of decentralisation[1]

Decentralisation is a French word for both a political concept in French politics from 1968–1990, and a term employed to describe the results of the evolution of the spatial, economic and institutional organisation of France.

In the French experience, territorial decentralisation concerns devolution by giving territorial authorities in France separate and defined responsibilities and resources, and providing for the election of representatives by the citizens of those territories. This is different from deconcentration, which is when the central government aims to improve efficiency by delegating certain policies and powers to a centrally nominated representative: the Prefect (*Préfet*).

Currently, the French decentralised administration is divided vertically in four different layers of administrative and political structures:

- The communal level (*Commune*): with a total of around 36 000 municipalities.
- The inter-communal structures (*Intercommunalité*): where several communes can unite to implement special fields of public policies.
- The department (*Département*): with 101 in mainland France and overseas.
- The region (*Région*): numbering 27 until 31 December 2015, and 18 afterwards.

A short history of French decentralisation

In French history, and in contrast to other European countries such as Italy or Germany, the State preceded and created the Nation. The French State quickly became very centralised, and, with the beginning of the French Republic after the French Revolution of 1789, the first territorial organisation with the communes and the department was designed to be a copy of the national republican model. The mayors were the first representatives of the State, and had little autonomous power before becoming representatives of a local community. The office of Prefect, one for each department, was created in 1800 by Napoleon Bonaparte with extensive powers of control at the local level.

The decentralisation laws passed on 10 August 1871 and 5 April 1884 gave the attribution of powers to elected department councils and municipal councils. This first decentralisation was built upon pre-existing structures and on the image of the organisation of the State. Until the 1982 decentralisation laws, the department-elected councils had very limited powers and were effectively under the stewardship of the department's Prefect as the local representative of the state.

Until the 1980s, centralisation remained the dominant force in French politics, despite failed attempts of reformers in the past, and the spirit of decentralisation took a long time to penetrate the political and administrative culture of France's ruling elites. In 1981, the socialist President François Mitterrand was elected; followed by the election of a socialist majority in the national legislature. The left was to lead a socialist experiment that would change the distribution of power and resources within French society for the first time under the Fifth republic. On 2 March 1982, the first law to set off the first wave of decentralisation reforms was implemented, and by 1986, there were 40 laws and 300 decrees. The 1982 law passed by the government of Pierre Mauroy introduced three new elements:

- The administrative stewardship of the Prefect was replaced by a legal check and balance system exercised by the administrative courts and the regional courts of audit with the help of the Prefects.
- Departmental executive power was transferred from the Prefect to the President of the departmental-elected Council.
- The creation of regions with full powers and recognition as territorial collectivities.

The 1983 laws, the so-called Gaston Deferre Laws, voted on 7 January and 22 July defined the responsibilities of the new administrative bodies and how they would be financed.

The goal of decentralisation in France was first and foremost to break the cycle of the central welfare State mentality and ensure that industrial and urban development would entail dynamism rather than "*dirigisme*" (State managed economy). It further sought to revitalise the peripheral regions politically, administratively, and economically, and make local government more efficient. The concomitant political result was to force local politicians to become more responsible for their decisions and to have enough productive jobs in the peripheral regions so that fewer people would depend on State-financed welfare.

The French administrative system is vertically subdivided between four main levels: communes, inter-communal structures, departments and regions. Particularly relevant are the communes, departments, and regions, which are governed by democratically elected councils and executives. The first stage of decentralisation immediately transferred the traditional powers of the Prefect to newly created regions and to the departments, both of which became local forms of government with decision-making powers. Regions and departments gained the freedom to organise technical and public services. The communes, whose mayors traditionally had executive powers, gained even more subtle autonomous powers, most of which strengthened the traditional duties of mayors, such as the right to deliver building permits. The Prefect still remains the sole representative of the central state's interest in the French territory, but the loss of power was considerable.

In 2002 and 2004, the second wave of Territorial Decentralisation was set in motion by Prime Minister Jean-Pierre Raffarin. The 28 March 2003 change to the French Constitution introduced the principle of financial autonomy for territorial collectivities, and of the words "region" and "decentralisation" in the French Constitution in Article 72. The changes also introduced the possibility of holding local referendum and the right to petition. The constitutional changes strengthened the two core principles of decentralisation: free administration, and autonomy of decision for local governments. However, in reality these two concepts have several technical limitations.

The 2003-2004 decentralisation saw the transfer of administrative functions to subnational (local) government, specifically those related to economic development. The regions are now in charge of regional economic planning and policy, industrial development, and professional education. The departments are responsible for some health and social services, secondary education infrastructures (although teaching remains a state prerogative) and transportation (until 2017, where the responsibility will be transferred to the regions). The communes retain traditional duties regarding municipal services and primary education infrastructures, with the addition of land-use plans and the issuing of building permits.

In 2013, a third wave of reforms began in order to allow regions and the departments to specialise in different aspects of governance, and to reinforce the regions. Reforms also aim to merge different regions and intercommunal structures to reduce their number.

Between 1982 and the present day, a withdrawal of the state from the territories has been observed, with the creation of new levels of responsibilities on a bigger scale, such as the region, in order to address the new challenges of globalisation. In France, as in some other European countries, there is a slow decrease in participation in elections, especially local elections. This may be due to the ever-increasing mobility of the population, which means that the bonds between the citizen and their local institutions have become looser.

The financial aspects of decentralisation

The total budget of the French decentralised administration represented EUR 229.8 billion in 2015.

In 2015, EUR 131 billion of local spending was covered by taxes and excise, set and raised locally. The main taxes are:

- property tax and land tax (24%)
- business tax (20%)
- local amenities tax (16%)
- insurance and gasoline tax (14%)
- property transaction tax (8%).

This level of tax autonomy is not common in OECD countries, where tax autonomy is around 30% on average.

There are also various other smaller taxes (which account for 18%):

- public transport contribution
- tourist tax
- advertising tax
- gambling tax
- other taxes.

The decentralised administration also relies on government transfers and grants. In 2015, these transfers represented EUR 45 billion, of local spending, 7 billion less than their 2012 peak. The grants cover the increased spending of local authorities due to the transfer of responsibilities from the central to local government during the successive decentralisation phases, and to insure the equalisation of the financial resources under various criteria.

Grants and transfers from the state fall into three categories:

- grants and subsidies for current spending
- grants and subsidies for investments
- compensation for the transfer of responsibilities, for both current spending and investments.

Local authorities are free to spend these resources as they want. However, due to the ever-increasing cost for the state of these grants, a Stability Pact was put in place in 1996, and later replaced by the European Growth and Solidarity pact in 1999. In 2013, for the first time since the beginning of decentralisation in 1982, state grants have begun to decrease.

Loans are the third biggest source of resource for local government in France. This debt represents EUR 178.5 billion, with 20 billion of new loans in 2015. Local authorities do not need to seek central government authorisation to borrow money, but all resources from loans can only be spent on investments and never on current spending. This is called the golden rule, and is only relevant for local decentralised authorities in France and not for the central state where wages, especially in the educational area, are the main budget.

The remainder of local government resources (11%) comes from rents, duties and European structural funds.

The financial resources of the decentralised authorities rely on a fiscal system based mostly on a property system, with property and land taxes calculated on the estimated rent value of the property.

The different levels of decentralised administrations

The region

The regional councils

In 2014, the French Parliament (the National Assembly and the Senate) passed a law that reduces the number of regions in Metropolitan France (mainland and Corsica) from 22 to 13. The new regional map took effect on 1 January 2016. France was, until 31 December 2015, divided into 27 administrative regions, 22 of which are in Metropolitan France, and five of which are overseas. The island of Corsica enjoys a special status, but is considered a region in mainstream usage.

The mainland regions and Corsica are each further subdivided into departments, ranging in number from 2 to 13 per region for the metropolitan regions. The overseas regions consist of only one department each. The term region was officially created by the Law of Decentralisation of 2 March 1982, which also gave regions their legal status and an elected assembly: the regional councils (*Conseil Régional*).

The Law of Decentralisation introduced regional administrative areas reminiscent of the historic French provinces, although Normandy was until the last reform divided into two entities, and some historic provinces were merged together, such as Provence, the Alps, and the Côte d'Azur.

Unlike European federal States, such as Germany, the French regions lack separate legislative authority and legislative autonomy, meaning that they cannot write their own statutory laws. They levy their own taxes and in return receive a decreasing part of their budget from the central government, which also gives them a portion of the taxes it levies. The regions also have considerable budgets managed by a regional council made up of representatives voted into office in regional elections every six years.

The regional councils were first created by law on 5 July 1972. Originally, these councils were simply consultative bodies consisting of the region's national parliamentary representatives, plus an equal number of members nominated by the departments and communes. The decentralisation programme of 1982-1983 allowed the direct election of the regional councils, which first took place in 1986, and increased their powers.

The third wave of reforms induced by the law of 7 August 2015 enabled the regions and the departments to specialise, meaning that they lost their general competence clause. The region is now principally in charge of:

- Regional economic planning and policy, industrial development.
- Professional education and high schools, but without the management of the teachers and the school programmes.
- Professional education for the unemployed.
- Transportation outside of cities with interurban busses, regional trains, school buses for high schools. They can be also responsible for some local ports and airports.
- Environmental protection with several special plan organisations, including for example the blue-green infrastructure.

The region and the department have still shared responsibilities regarding the following public policies:

- culture
- sport
- tourism
- regional languages.

The Regional Economic, Social and Environmental Councils (RESEC)

A Regional Economic, Social and Environmental Council *(Conseil Économique, Social et Environnemental Régional - CESER)* works with each regional council for a given region, and assists in governance through the reports it issues.

Each RESEC comprises four colleges representing companies, self-employed professionals, trade unions, associations and other bodies involved in community life in the region, and experts. Members are appointed by a decree of the Prefect every six years.

It is mandatory to consult RESEC on any budget related documents and strategic plans for the region.

The President of the regional council may refer matters to RESEC for an opinion or report on any given topic. RESEC may also issue opinions of its own accord on any matters of regional interest, or may be called on by the Prefect to analyse government initiatives in the region.

Although RESEC performs the same functions in every region, their number of members, depending on regional population, and composition of groups are not always the same. Each RESEC reflects key economic and social interest groups in its region. They promote partnerships, contribute to balanced growth throughout the region, and encourage unity and solidarity as a source of social innovation, prevention and regulation.

The departments

In the administrative divisions of France, the department is one of the levels of government below the national level ("territorial collectivities"), between the administrative regions and the communes. There are 96 departments in metropolitan France and 5 overseas departments, which are also classified as regions.

The departments are further subdivided into 335 *arrondissements*, which again are divided into cantons; the latter two have no autonomy and are used for the organisation of police, fire departments and elections. The departmental councils are the elected assemblies of the departments and are elected by universal suffrage.

A law passed on 22 December 1789 established an assembly in each department, known as the Council of the Department. This law was repealed on 4 December 1793. It was restored as the "law on the division of the territory of the Republic and its administration" on 17 February 1800, in which the "General Council of the Departments" was formed. The members of the General Council were not elected by suffrage until 1833. They were elected by universal suffrage from 3 July 1848. Until the 2 March 1982 law of decentralisation, the department Prefect also served as the department state representative and the department executive. Since 1982, the President of the Council has been the department executive body. The law of 26 February 2008 means that there must be at least a single candidate of each gender in a department council election elected by a two-person team in each Canton. In March 2015, the name of the General Council was changed to Departmental Council.

The third wave of reforms induced by the law of 7 August 2015 enabled the regions and the departments to specialise and they lost their general competence clause. The department competences were reduced to the benefit of the region.

According to the law of 7 August 2015, the departments are now in charge of:

- Intercity roads (*routes départementales*).
- Some social policies and welfare allowances.
- Secondary school (for children between 11 to 15 years-old) infrastructure and maintenance, but not for the teaching and school programmes and degrees.

As mentioned earlier, the region and the department have shared responsibilities regarding the following public policies:

- culture
- sport
- tourism
- regional languages.

The communes

The 36 000 communes

A French commune may be a city of 2.2 million inhabitants, such as Paris, a town of 10 000 people, or just a 10-person hamlet. Communes are typically based on pre-existing villages and facilitate local governance. With the exception of the municipal *arrondissements* of the largest cities, such as Paris, Lyon and Marseille, the communes are the lowest level of administrative division in France. They are governed by elected officials, the mayor and the municipal council (*Conseil Municipal*), with extensive autonomous powers to implement national and local policies. Since 1871, the mayor has been elected by the members of the elected municipal council.

As of January 2015, according to the National Institute of Statistics (INSEE), there were 36 681 Communes in France, 36 552 in metropolitan France and 129 overseas. This is considerably higher than any other European country, and accounts for around 40% of all the Commune-level administration in the European Union. In January 2016, due to voluntary merges with strong financial incentives from the central State, this number decreased to 35 885, and this tendency is expected to continue in the coming years.

According to the law of the 7 August 2015, the communes now are responsible for most matters regarding the life of the commune, especially:

- primary schools and pre-school
- local roads
- local police and public order
- urbanism
- local ports and canal
- housing
- cemeteries
- culture and sport equipment and incentives policies
- local social services
- local public transportations
- gas and electricity networks.

Several increasing responsibilities can be delegated to the intercommunality (*intercommunalité*), such as waste collection or transportation. The law also makes it mandatory for the intercommunality to manage other areas, such as economic planning, development, housing projects, and environmental protection.

The intercommunal structures, or intercommunality

"Intercommunality" denotes several forms of co-operation between several communes. Such co-operation made its appearance at the end of the 19th century in a law on 22 March 1890, which provided for the establishment of single-purpose intercommunal associations. This means that several municipal councils can pool resources to implement public policies and services more effectively, especially when there are easy economies of scale to make, when the cost of a policy or equipment is too high to be borne by a single commune, or when such a policy or equipment would benefit several communes (a swimming pool or a library, for example). French lawmakers have long been aware of the inadequacy of the communal structure inherited from the French Revolution for dealing with a number of practical matters. Therefore the law of 12 July 1999 "relating to the improvement and simplification of intercommunal co-operation (*Établissement Public de Coopération Intercommunal* or "EPCI") in the so called Chevènement law, aimed to strengthen and simplify this principle by helping more collective actions of the communes.

In recent years, it has become increasingly common for communes to unite in intercommunal consortia for the provision of public services, such as waste collection and water supply. Suburban communes often team up with the city at the core of their urban area to form a community responsible for managing public transportation, or even administering the collection of local taxes. Almost all the French communes are now involved in intercommunal structures.

The Chevènement law has been extremely successful in the sense that a majority of French communes have now joined the new intercommunal structures. There is a national aim to integrate every commune in an intercommunal structure. On 1 January 2016, there were more than 2 000 intercommunal structures.

There are two types of intercommunality:

- Structures without fiscal power, which are the loosest form. This category mainly includes the traditional syndicates of communes. Communes gather and contribute financially to the syndicate, but the syndicate cannot levy its own taxes. Communes can leave the syndicate at any time. Syndicates are set up for a single purpose (most commonly waste management and water/energy distribution), or to deal with several matters. These structures are on the decline.
- Structures with fiscal power, which number around 2000. There are several structures with fiscal power:
  - The Community of communes (*Communauté de Communes*), aimed primarily at rural communes.
  - The Community of Agglomeration (*Communauté d'Agglomération*), aimed at towns and middle-sized cities and their suburbs.
  - The Urban Community (*Communauté Urbaine*), aimed at larger cities and their suburbs.
  - A more integrated form, The Metropole has been created for the French major cities. The Metropole can have increased responsibilities and tasks taken from the department and the regions.

These four structures are given varying levels of fiscal autonomy. The Community of Agglomeration, the Urban Community and the Metropole have the greatest fiscal autonomy, with the same level of taxation across the communes of the community. Communities of Communes have the fewest compulsory areas of competence, leaving the Communes more autonomous. Urban Communities and Metropoles are required to manage most matters (for instance, all public spaces, most equipment, and energy networks), leaving the communes within with less autonomy.

Due to strong pressure from the State, the number of intercommunalities fell on 1 January 2017 from more than 2000 to 1265. At the same time, their responsibilities will be multiplied by five in the following few years, going from 2 mandatory competencies in public policies before 2014 to more than 10 in 2020, including water supply, water sanitation, tourism, management of travellers and nomadic communities.

One major and often cited problem with intercommunity is that the representatives of intercommunal structures are not directly elected by local citizens, but by representatives of each individual commune in the intercommunal structure. As a consequence, civil servants and bureaucrats set and implement the agenda, with the elected representatives of the communes only endorsing key decisions. However, in 2014 there was a first attempt to make intercommunality members elected more directly, and when "Lyon metropole" was transformed into a real territorial collectivity by merging with a part of the "Rhone department", a new direct electoral system was created, which will be implemented for the 2020s elections.

The administration of the decentralised administrations

The elected councils and their presidents

The local council assemblies of the four layers of decentralised authorities are either elected (communes, department, or region) or designated members from an elected assembly (intercommunality). They do not have appointed members. Because of this four layer system, there are around 500 000 elected representatives in a population of 66 million in France. These elected officials can have financial compensation if the council they are members of approve. The compensation levels are fixed by law and limited by the demographic size of the structure and the role of the member in the assembly (president, vice-president, etc.). The purpose of this financial compensation is to limit the temptation of corruption and to make these responsibilities available for individuals with mixed social backgrounds.

The representatives of the local assembly have, by law, a right to be informed in order to vote on the matters within their sphere of competence. In some cases, such as for the budget, the documents that have to be transmitted and the deadlines are clearly defined by law. The representatives also have the right by law to be trained in order to complete their tasks.

The elected representative members sometimes have, depending on the population of the administrated territory, special powers and responsibilities:

- The mayor of the commune is also an agent of the state and the head of the communal assembly. As part of the responsibility as an agent of the state, the mayor is responsible for the registry office, public order and the organisation of elections. As part of the responsibility as chief of the communal assembly, the mayor has to prepare and implement the decisions of the elected communal council. The mayor is the head of the local administration and responsible for the budget. The mayor can delegate under their monitoring and responsibility some missions to other members of the assembly, such as one or several deputy mayors. The mayor can also delegate their right of signature to any member of the administration, such as the general manager, head of the administration. The mayor is also the chief of the local police.
- The president of an intercommunality, departmental or regional structure has almost the same kind of powers, and is elected by members of the elected council. The president has to prepare and implement the decisions of the elected council,

and is head of the administration. The president is responsible for the budget and can delegate, under monitoring and with their responsibility, some tasks to other members of the assembly who bear the title of vice-presidents. The president can authorise any member of the administration, such as the general manager or any director, to sign on their behalf.

The laws of 5 April 2000 and 22 January 2014, which address the plurality of local and national offices, forbid anyone to be member of more than one local executive and parliament office. If so, they can be suspended or revoked in a special case by a disciplinary procedure, and by a decision of the Prime Minister or the council of ministers in cases of a revocation.

The means of action of local decentralised authorities

Decentralised authorities can manage their public policies with several legal tools. They can organise public services the way they see the fit for local interests, except when mandated by the law.

According to French and Europeans legislations, decentralised authorities can provide public services in four different ways:

- By their own civil servant, in an internalised way but with different possible levels of autonomy.
- By public procurement.
- By delegation of public services with a private, a semi-private or a fully public company or by a public private partnership.
- By making an agreement with local or national voluntary associations or non-governmental organisations (NGO).

The decentralised authorities can vote for special financial or material benefits and allowances for private persons or companies in a clearly defined frame of national law for private persons, or European decisions for companies and economic operators.

The documents and decisions produced by the local assemblies are public and often available on the website of each decentralised authority. The debates of the council are public and sometimes available online.

The budgeting process and budgeting cycle

The budget is built by respecting accounting norms designed for every level of decentralised administration and based upon international norms. The budgetary process is identical for every decentralised administration.

Budget preparation has to take into account the information given by the state, particularly regarding the expected level of income of the different taxes, the level of the different grants, and transfers regarding the national budget. The state also defines spending objectives, particularly concerning social expenditures. The law make it mandatory to have a budget in real equilibrium, as creating loans is only allowed to finance infrastructures that enrich the collectivity assets. Considering these previous elements, the local administration and the local assembly work together to evaluate the needs, the upcoming projects and the evolution of the salaries of civil servants in the decentralised administration. A short and medium-term risk assessment is also conducted in order to evaluate the financial, social and organisational risks of public policies and projects. There is usually a multi-year programme for the different projects in order to plan and organise investments during the elective mandate.

Decentralised authorities cannot create new taxes, however, they can adjust some rates in a restricted frame for the taxes under their responsibility. Some expenditures are mandatory. The collection of most taxes is a mission of the local branches of the Ministry of Budget.

After the first phase there is a debate concerning the general budgetary orientations two months before the budget is put to a vote. This debate is mandatory and allows discussions on the upcoming projects of the year between the majority and the opposition in local councils.

When the general budgetary orientation debate is complete, the budget has to be voted on and accepted before the 15th of April of the year of its implementation. The budget is usually voted on in December, shortly before the year of its implementation.

After the vote, the draft budget is sent to the local representative of the state, the Prefect, in order to check if the draft respects the legal budgetary framework. If a budget is not voted on and accepted in time by the local assembly, or if it does not respect the legal framework, the Prefect has powers to make amendments, sometimes with the technical help of the regional court of account.

The budget can be modified during the calendar year of its validity in order to adapt it to the actual expenditures of the structure, to any unexpected event, or to new sources of spending or income. Those modifications are also checked by the Prefect services, with the technical help of the regional court of account.

During the calendar year, expenses are made inside a strict and clear workflow involving the local representative of the Ministry of Finance, who is responsible for the account of the decentralised administration.

During the following year, the decentralised administration has to vote on the "administrative accounting" before 30 June. Administrative accounting is compared with the accounting held by the local representative of the Ministry of Finance, called the "public accountant". These accounts are also checked by the Prefect with, in complicated cases, the technical help of the regional court of account.

All of these documents, as with most public official documents since the law of 17 July 1978, are public and mostly available on each decentralised authority website. The debates of the council regarding the budget are held in public and are often available online.

Organisation and management

The organisation and the decision-making process

Most decentralised administrations have an organisational chart and some internal procedural guidelines to define the responsibilities of the different parts of the administration. According to Article 72.3 of the French Constitution, decentralised authorities are free to organise themselves. The administration is often organised as follows:

- At the top, the elected executive head of the assembly is the mayor of the commune or the president. This person can be assisted by a variable number of deputy mayors or vice presidents. Vice-presidents sometimes specialise in several technical themes, such as education, economics or culture.

- The elected executive head of the assembly is the head of the administration and chooses a secretary general or a general manager to manage the administration.
- To organise the political agenda of the elected executive head, a cabinet some of whom may specialise in technical aspects, assists the chief or director of the cabinet.
- The secretary general or general manager is sometimes assisted by a varying number of deputy secretary generals or deputy general managers. At least 40% of deputies must be women. These deputies can be specialised in one or several public policies, and are managing the operating service of the administration. The general manager and their deputies have a special status and can be revoked at will by the elected executive head of the assembly.
- Under deputy general managers, services are organised with specialised directors or heads of departments and civil servants. Most have civil servant status, which guarantees them a working stability, along with a set of special rights and obligations.

The civil servant status

The French Civil Service (*fonction publique française*) is the corps of civil servants (*fonctionnaires*) working for the French government or decentralised administrations. Not all employees of the state and public institutions or corporations are civil servants. However, the media often incorrectly equates "government employee" or "employee of a public corporation" with *fonctionnaire* (civil servant).

The French public service consists of three main sections:

- State civil service (central administrations, regional and departmental services of the state, public establishments of the state).
- Territorial civil service (civil servants of the communes, departments and regions).
- Hospital civil service (administrative, medical and nursing staffs of public hospitals).

The local government civil service (*fonction publique territoriale*) was created in 1984 as part of the decentralisation process. It includes almost all employment in local government structures such as communes, departments and regions.

Regarding the organisation of the civil service, the categories described below are used for hierarchical purposes, to clarify employment conditions, and to calculate salaries:

Category => Corps/employment framework =>Grade => Class =>*Echelon*

A category is divided in several corps or employment framework, corps or employment framework are divided again in several grades, those grades are divided in classes and those classes are divided further in "echelon".

Civil servants are split on the basis of level of responsibility and education. There are three main categories from A to C in decreasing order of educational level required. Civil servants in Category A occupy highly skilled or managerial positions and have a higher education degree. Category B comprises agents in mid-level management tasks and requires a *baccalauréat* (end of secondary school degree). Category C includes personnel dedicated to day-to-day administrative and technical tasks. Within each category, every civil servant belongs to a corps or an employment framework for the local government civil service. The high ranking civil servants are commonly labelled as A+.

Corps or employment frameworks consist of civil servants ruled, managed and promoted according to their particular status, supplementing the general statutory rules. Corps or employment frameworks refer to a job family and qualification.

Civil servants have duties. Failure to carry these duties out may result in disciplinary action, possibly revocation. According to the law of the 13 July 1983, and numerous jurisprudence, the main duties are:

- Full commitment to professional activity: a civil servant should devote their full professional activity to their appointed task. A civil servant may, in addition to their regular activities, accomplish certain tasks, such as teaching, arts, or competitive sports, with the permission of the administration if remuneration is involved.
- Morality: it is not possible for a person to be a civil servant if they have been convicted of a crime that is incompatible with their functions. In exceptional cases, certain aspects of the private life of a civil servant may be deemed incompatible with their functions. For instance, it is inappropriate for a member of the police or the judiciary to live with a delinquent partner. Appreciation of what is appropriate or not is largely a matter of case law.
- Duty of reserve: a civil servant should not by their actions or declarations cause harm to the institutions. Generally speaking, a civil servant should always refrain from enunciating personal opinions in a manner that could be construed as expressing the official opinion of the French government, a public or local institution. This is more relevant for higher managerial positions.
- Hierarchical obedience: a civil servant must accomplish the orders given by their hierarchical supervisor, unless those orders are evidently illegal and contrary to public interest. While the hierarchical authority is normally responsible for assigning civil servants to positions and evaluating their work, certain corps of civil servants follow specific rules regarding the management, evaluation and discipline of their members.
- Professional discretion: civil servants must not reveal private or secret information that they have gained in the course of their duties.
- Honesty: civil servants must not use the means of their professional disposal for private gain. They must report any illegal activities that they witness and they must disobey illegal instructions.
- Neutrality: civil servants must be neutral regarding religious or political opinions, origin, or gender, and should refrain from expressing their own personal opinions.

This frame of duties for the civil servant has been improved in the law of 20 April 2016, which introduces various innovations, such as:

- Whistleblower protection.

- A stronger control of conflict of interests.

Most local civil servant positions are open to citizens of the European Union. Certain positions that involve the main powers of the State, such as the Police, are open only to French citizens. Some positions, such as university professors and researchers, are open to anyone, regardless of citizenship.

In contrast to the general rules concerning workers, civil servants do not sign contracts; their situation is defined by statutory and regulatory law, most notably the General Statute of Civil Servants (*Statut Général des Fonctionnaires*).

The general rule is that civil servants are recruited through competitive exams, which are either:

- External: reserved to candidates fulfilling certain conditions of diplomas and age.
- Internal: reserved to civil servants in certain positions.
- External "third way": reserved to candidates with certain professional experience and age.

The most common method of recruiting is to organise written and/or oral competitive exams in subjects pertaining to the tasks to be accomplished. In all cases, a committee ranks candidates by order of preference. For some top managerial positions, such as the secretary general and deputies in a local administration, nominations are at the discretion of the local executive.

The pay of a civil servant is composed of:

- A base pay known as "*traitement*".
- Possible overtime pay.
- Possible bonuses, which depend on the particular job assignment and possibly the individual worker.

The base pay or "*traitement*" is, for most civil servants, fixed by multiplying an index by the value of the index point in Euros. The value of the index point is set nationally. The index depends on the corps, rank and seniority in rank (*échelon*). New laws introduce special financial incentives for merit and productivity.

There are special rules for the pay of elected officials at the national and local level, and government ministers.

The local government civil service are trained and educated by the National Centre for the Territorial Civil Servant (CNFPT: *Centre National de la Fonction Publique Territoriale*). For high-ranking civil servants, the A+ (territorial administrators) are educated after a competitive exam at the National Institute for Territorial Studies (INET: *Institut National des Études Territoriales*) in Strasbourg for 18 months.

High ranking civil servants of the state, such as Prefects, are educated after a competitive exam at the National School for Administration (ENA: *École Nationale d'Administration*) in Strasbourg for 24 months.

The process of a career can be flexible, and someone may change from state service to local service and vice versa.

The management of the decentralised administration

Originally, the management of public local administration was inspired by the traditional hierarchical way of managing the State administration inspired by military organisation.

With the laws of 1982, the decentralised administration gained the power of self-organisation, meaning that the methods of management became more diverse. A number of French decentralised administrations integrated the principles of new public management. This system emphasises the concept that ideas and practices used in the private sector can be applied to the public sector.

New public management is viewed as a more efficient means of attaining the same product or service; where citizens are viewed as customers, and public servants/administrators hold the title of Public Managers. New public management tries to realign the relationship between expert managers and their political superiors by creating a parallel relationship. Under new public management, public managers have incentive-based motivation and greater autonomy (as opposed to a regulated outcome per scenario, regardless of situation). New public management tries to integrate the best methods for international management, such as American and Japanese schools, and to adapt them to the characteristics of the public administration.

Although French public management is still largely driven by traditional pyramidal organisations, it tries to be open to new ideas and concepts in management and government, with new public management the dominant force since the early 2000s.

The Prefect and deconcentration in France

Known until recently for a centralising tradition, France is a country where decisions were largely taken in Paris and implemented throughout the country by state-appointed representatives. This is still partly true, but much has changed, especially since 1982.

The historical background of deconcentration, before the decentralisation laws

The Prefect succeeded the intendants of the Kings of France, responsible for enforcing the King's orders in the provinces.

On 22 December 1789, the French Constituent Assembly created the first 83 Departments. The office of Prefect was then created in 1800 by Napoleon Bonaparte. In 1871, the General Council gradually received its own areas of competence; however, the Prefect still had to approve the decisions taken. Then, as further changes came in, the General Council was given new powers, including the power to adopt its own budget and raise taxes. It also obtained the end of the Prefect's authority over certain decisions.

No regime in France has challenged the existence of the office of Prefect. This has made changing and modernising the administration easier. The existence of representatives who were appointed and could be dismissed by the Council of Ministers has made it easier for ministers to successfully pursue their initiatives.

Provided that departments complied with statutes and regulations, they had their own remit, notably in the health and social spheres, infrastructure, help for small communes, transportation (especially school transportation), the environment and sport. Their freedoms, however, were limited by the need for state financial help to enable them to act in their areas of competence, especially on health and social matters, even though their assemblies had the power to raise certain taxes.

The Prefect was still the departmental executive. However, while this position had still allowed the Prefect to impose their view at the beginning of the twentieth century, it was no longer the case at the time of the 1982 reform. The budget prepared by the Prefect needed to be passed by the departmental assembly, however, the assembly was increasingly using its power to contribute to its preparation and influence choices. Consequently, the Prefect had to reach a compromise in order to get the budget approved. The Prefect used to discuss the proposed budget with the General Council chairman, finance committee and a number of other local leaders, so that there was a degree of co-management and co-operation, in short, the beginnings of decentralisation. The amount this took place varied from department to department.

The 1982 reform of decentralisation and deconcentration

The 1982 reform involved both decentralisation and deconcentration. Acts passed in 1982 and 1983 brought about a new division of powers between the state, regions, departments and communes. Subsequent legislation further increased the department's reserved powers. The Prefect thus lost part of their power over certain decisions previously taken by the state, particularly concerning the establishment and upkeep of *collèges* (schools catering for pupils aged approximately 11-15 years), health and social programmes, and capital spending on sport, the environment, fire services, transport, etc.

Although under the 1982 laws (and later the 1992 law) the departmental assemblies were assigned new powers previously exercised by the state, in political terms, the essence of the reform came with the transfer of the executive to the department council president, who now prepares and carries out the decisions of the departmental assembly, especially regarding the budget. The representative of the state can no longer intervene in the management of the department's areas of competence.

The department no longer receives subsidies from the state for projects within its remit. This also used to be a way for the Prefect to exert influence. The state now allocates one appropriation for capital investment and another for operating costs to the departments. The departmental assembly is free to use this allocated funding as it sees fit.

At the same time as decentralisation, the government decided to implement a policy of administrative deconcentration by strengthening the authority of its agent, the Prefect. This was undertaken to prevent decentralisation undermining the influence of the government's representative in the department and enable decisions to be brought closer to citizens.

The state's representatives in the departments now head the local services of the various ministries. Only the military authorities, judicial services, national education, the work inspectorate and taxation administrations escape this rule. All other services have been placed under the authority of the Prefect, who chairs all the local administrative committees, and is the only authority with the power to commit state expenditure in the department. The Prefect may delegate their signature to the heads of the directorates (*Directeurs Départementaux*), but such delegation must clearly mention the powers delegated.

Despite these increased powers, the Prefect still has to do the bidding of the government, which, today, as before, appoints and, if so desired, replaces the Prefect. Although the Prefect must respect the remit of the department's elected representatives, they must also prevent them from encroaching on the state's powers, which highlights the fact that decentralisation and deconcentration require a balance that is sometimes hard to find.

The legal oversight by the Prefect and public order

Although the Prefect no longer has any control over the opportunity of the decisions taken by the departmental council, or any other decentralised authority in the exercise of its powers, they can refer to the courts any decision deemed against the law, and the court will rule on this question. This gives the Prefect some influence over the decentralised powers, as they can raise any concerns about the legality of locally-voted acts with, for example, the departmental council president. The Prefect can submit any act adopted by a local council to the administrative courts, if the Prefect deems this act illegal. It is not a control of the appropriateness or the political dimension of the decision, but only of its respect of the law.

The Prefect cannot refer a decision to the court in one case but not in another identical one: the law must be the same for all.

The Prefect knows and acts as the "government public relations officer" in their department. The Prefect must provide information and explain the government's policy. This borders on the political, however, as the law applies to everyone, it is logical for its implementation to be explained to local leaders and the public. While the Prefect must defend a statute passed by Parliament, in order to protect authority, the Prefect must be prudent and not promote bills, which is not always understood by some politicians.

The Prefect is responsible not just for implementing and enforcing legislation, but also for respecting and ensuring others respect the law. The Prefect may have to interpret a central administration's *circulaire* (*circulaires* have the status of regulations if they contain instructions to civil servants) that seeks to apply the legislative text in a questionable way. It is also important for Prefects to report back to the government on local reactions to government policy.

The office of Prefect is a system of command and leadership that operates through the Prefect's personal authority, and their authority over the representatives of the various ministries in the department. The Prefect must be able to respond to events and cope with the demands of any situation calling for authoritative action. In addition, the Prefect must resolve problems and conflicts, getting administrative, economic and social leaders to agree.

The Prefect is responsible for the respect of law and order in the department, and in this sphere carries the full authority and sovereignty of the state. This requires a leader capable of personally taking responsibility and directing operations under grave circumstances. The police and the gendarmerie (military force charged with police duties in rural areas) are under the Prefect's authority. The Prefect authorises or bans demonstrations. Maintaining public order does not only involve ensuring public peace, but also civil defense by the protection of people and property from natural, industrial, technological and accidental hazards, as well as crime prevention and the war on terrorism. Consequently, the Prefect has to prepare state services in the department for all eventualities, especially the management of serious accidents and consequences of natural disasters. It is the Prefect whom the public will hold accountable.

The regional Prefects

The region is the largest administrative division in France, each made up of 2 to 13 departments. Above the departmental Prefects, there is a regional Prefect. However, this civil servant is not superior in rank, even though the administrative powers exercised allow a certain authority over departmental Prefects. The government has only one official representative in each department: the Prefect.

The regional Prefect combines this office with that of departmental Prefect in the region's capital city. The regional Prefect has the same function to the regional assembly as the departmental Prefect regarding the departmental council in being responsible for judicial oversight. The regional Prefect has the same authority over the heads of the regional directorates of the ministries as a departmental Prefect over the heads of the departmental directorates. The role is to co-ordinate and to allocate state funding between the departmental Prefects in the region.

The regional Prefect must take any initiative suitable to promote the economic and social development of the region within the general context of the government's town and country planning policy. The regional Prefect ensures the co-ordination required to implement national policies.

The role of the regional Prefect has been strengthened with the latest reform of deconcentration after the decree of 16 February 2010. Since the regional level is the usual level for nationwide state policies, the power of regional Prefects has grown compared to local Prefects. The regional directions of the ministries' services have also been reinforced. The regional Prefect now has a pivotal role in the enforcement of most national policies, except matters of safety and security, which are still managed at the department level.

Changes in the relationship between the state and local government

Logically, each level of government (state, region, department, intercommunality and commune) should finance operations in its own areas of competence with its own resources from its own taxes. However, this is not always the case since the state does not finance activities outside its own remit, which requires local authorities to help fund some central government projects, especially in the context of the contract between the state and the decentralised authorities[2] (*contrats de plan État-Régions*). For example, local authorities that wish to develop their local road networks have paid a significant percentage of the costs of main, nationwide roads. Local authorities have also contributed to the building of university and research premises under some national plans, even though the state is responsible for higher education.

Financial constraints have led the state to seek increased funding in order to carry out its own projects. This has contributed to raising local taxation. These forms of cross financing can lead to confusion about responsibilities. At the regional and departmental level, the task of the Prefect is consequently rendered more complicated because it is necessary to ask for funding for state-run projects from many partners. Limiting such cross financing should be a major aspect of future reforms of the state organisation. There were attempts recently to limit cross financing between decentralised authorities (2010, 2014 and 2015 laws), however, there is still a lot to be done regarding cross financing between the state and local authorities.

The relationship between a Prefect who represents central government and locally elected representatives with different political orientation could, in theory, be a challenge.

However, this does not generally prevent them working together. The locally elected representative is aware that the Prefect represents a government chosen by universal suffrage and, similarly, the state representative is aware that the local representatives have also been elected through universal suffrage and must be able to take decisions freely under the powers entrusted to them by the law and the constitution. It is on this basis of mutual recognition that the 1982 reforms on decentralisation and deconcentration have become a reality and operate satisfactorily.

The indispensable control of the use of public money in French decentralisation

The fight against the corruption of decentralised officials and civil servants

The first tools for the fight against corruption are transparency and open data policies. Every decision made by local authorities has to be public since the law of 17 July 1978, and therefore these decisions are now usually published on the local authorities' websites.

A developing trend on transparency for high-ranking civil servants and members of the local executive has been carried out with:

- Mandatory Statement on high-ranking civil servants and members of the local executive of other commitments (professional or personal).
- Mandatory declaration of assets at the beginning and the end of their office period.
- For the local level, declarations are public on request, however, it is illegal to publish asset declarations.

These declarations were introduced with the law of 11 October 2013 after several corruption scandals, and have helped to improve the accountability of politicians and high-level civil servants.

If those enforcing the decision of a local politician are civil servants with a good education background, sufficient salary and job protection, they will be more prone to say no to corruption or illegal instructions. The civil servant status is therefore a guarantee.

More democracy in the use of public money

Transparency and open data policies regarding documents on budgets and accounts of the decentralised authorities help citizens to know the true situation. An increasing number of decentralised authorities take a pedagogical approach to informing citizens of the use of public money through online or paper publications.

Two other instruments of participation have been increasingly used in local governance: local councils and participatory budgeting. Decentralised authorities are using those tools, for example, the region Poitou-Charentes has used both methods:

- Councils of local citizens have given advice and observations on the policies implemented by the region.
- Participatory budgets in high schools financed by the region have taken place to educate young people on democratic life.
- Participatory democracy is also used for management inside the regional administration in case of major changes with the selection of a pool of civil servants giving advice to the president and top management of the region.

These tools are also used on a voluntary base in communes.

The legal fight against misuse of public money and the regional court of account

According to Article L211 of the code of the financial jurisdiction, there are various systems for controlling and managing local decentralised administration on three keys points:

- accounting control
- budgetary control
- management control.

For accounting control there is a principle of separation of authorising officers and accountants. The decentralised administration cannot use any money directly, instead it is in an account managed by the Ministry of Finance. When the decentralised administration wants to spend money it has to prove that it can legally pay (bills, official's acts), and the Ministry of Finance officer makes the credit transfer after proper controls.

Most of the decisions, especially those regarding the budget, are controlled by the Prefect in order to check legal correctness, such as the quality of documents, respect of the legal deadlines, respect of some basic budgetary rules, and respect of the different signatures right.

Some in France have protested against this limitation of the autonomy of the decentralised authorities, however, this control is also considered useful by having the central state as a "watchdog" to avoid a degradation of quality in local administrations.

Budgetary controls are also carried out by the Regional and Territorial Chambers of Accounts (RTCAs) system. RTCAs are independent courts that rule on the accounts of public accountants, examine management, and audit the budget operations of decentralised authorities and their public institutions. Since 1982, the rules of RTCAs have been amended and adjusted by a significant amount of legislation aimed at extending their competence and strengthening their proceedings. RTCAs have the following tasks:

- Court review: The fundamental duty of financial courts is to judge the accounts of public accountants to ensure compliance with the rules of performance for income and expenditure and the principle of separation of authorising officers and accountants. The RTCAs hand down legal rulings, such as verdicts or orders on the accounts presented to them. Public accountants may be held personally and financially liable by the regional court in a number of instances:
  - If a deficit or missing funds have been noted.
  - If income has not been recovered.
  - If an expense has been improperly paid.
  - If the public body has had to compensate a third party because of the public accountant.
- Management review: RTCAs review the management of regional authorities and bodies within their remits and attributions (Article L. 211-8 of the code of the financial jurisdiction). Audits are undertaken either on the initiative of the RTCA

as part of its annual audit programme, or at the request of the local authority of the Prefect. RTCAs examine each of the following aspects, in order:

- Correctness, i.e. compliance with the law on expenditure and public contributions.
- Economical use of public funds.
- Effective use of public funds.

- Auditing of budget transactions: The Prefect may refer the budgetary situation of a local authority or public institution to the Court. The Court provides its expertise as an independent authority and expresses opinions.
- National court of audit *(Cour des comptes)* and RTCA joint investigations: RTCAs often work with the French national court of audit in thematic investigations on a wide variety of subjects. Usually, this work leads to the publication of public thematic reports.

Every document regarding this system has to be online in order to let the local communities know the result of the audits on the principles of transparency, open data and open government.

Territorial reform in France: 2013-2015[3]

Within the last few years, the French territorial administration, which is thought to be – and is – very difficult to reform, has seen a lot of territorial reform changes. After an unsuccessful attempt from a right-wing government in 2010, in 2012 a left-wing government decided to restart the process of reforms. These reforms are being implemented in 2016 and 2017, and this implementation will continue until 2020, unless new laws come and change the framework once again. However, the whole structure will stay roughly as it used to be: the French decentralised administration is still divided into four different layers of administrative and political structures.

During the 5th Republic, and after a victory of "No" in a 1969 referendum on the question of decentralisation and the creation of the region, a failure that continued for every referendum on this subject until now, there were three major periods of reforms in French local administrations: 1982-1985, 2003-2005, and 2013-2015.

The first two waves were periods of a large "decentralisation of powers" from the state to pre-existing local structures. They created a more decentralised France, symbolised by some amendments to the Constitution in 2004 to acknowledge the relative autonomy of local powers.

The third wave, however, although it involved some aspects of decentralisation (European funding and parts of employment policy were given to the regions), it was more oriented towards a rationalisation of structures, a redistribution of competencies between the local administrations, and a new financial constraint that sometimes has been interpreted as a "re-centralisation", although this is somewhat exaggerated.

Since 2013, the third wave of reforms aims to allow the regions and the departments to specialise, strengthen the regions, and merge different regions and inter-municipalities together to reduce their number and make them fit for the new practices of increased mobility of people, goods and capital.

Although others laws were passed at the same time, for instance to reinforce the status of elected representatives and increase their diversity, three main laws made this change possible:

- "Modernisation of Territorial Public Action and Affirmation of the Metropoles" (27 January 2014): created 13 "Metropoles", Nice was already in place, and Nancy was created later. Others are now willing to join, including the "Metropole de Lyon", which replaced both the intercommunality and the Department within its boundaries.
- "Delimitation of the regions, regional and departmental elections and modifying the electoral agenda" (16 January 2015), which merged 16 regions into 7; decreasing the total number from 27 to 18.
- "New Territorial Organisation of the Republic" (7 August 2015) which transferred some competencies from departments to regions, gave more prescriptive powers to the regions, transferred some competencies from communes to intercommunalities, and rationalised their map (from 2 100 to around 1 300).

A change of the structure: Fewer entities, but still four layers

The different layers of decentralised administrations were all challenged in the last three years:

The regions: A historical change

As with the whole territorial reform, the change of the region map was not part of the presidential programme of François Hollande in 2012, but a reform that has been discussed for many years. Think tanks and parliamentary reports had often called for reform in order to make French regions more powerful on a European scale. Nonetheless, there was no prepared map to replace the old regional organisation.

In January 2015, following a debate on the subject in the Senate where many senators declared a wish for bigger regions in order to avoid competition between regions and fewer small departments, the President of the Republic, François Hollande, declared his intention to decrease the number of regions through mergers.

In April 2015, for his first declaration in front of Parliament, the newly appointed Prime Minister, Manuel Valls, made the target even more specific: he wanted to divide the number by two in mainland France (oversees were not directly concerned), leading to an objective of 11 to 12 regions (13 eventually). The principles to make the exercise more simple were to avoid changes of departments from one region to another (although it could theoretically happen later) and to make a proposition on a statistical basis (by the national administration), even if political pressure was very high as most regional presidents belonged to the same political party as the President of the Republic.

In June 2015, after a very short debate within the country, with considerable declarations from the regions themselves (only some, including Upper and Lower parts of Normandy, which used to be divided between Haute-Normandie and Basse-Normandie, Bourgogne and Franche-Comté, and Auvergne and Rhone-Alpes, were willing to merge together), and a lot of high-level lobbying, a new map was proposed by the president and released to the regional media before its official presentation to the Cabinet (council of ministers) on 18 June 2015.

The debate in Parliament, with the Ministry of Interior and, significantly, not the Ministry of Decentralisation, speaking at the bench to defend the law, led to some changes from the Presidential proposal:

- The proposed merge between Picardie and Champagne-Ardennes was replaced by a merge between Picardie and Nord-Pas-de-Calais, and Champagne-Ardennes joined Alsace and Lorraine. It later became Hauts-de-France and Grand Est (regions chose their own names after the regional elections).
- The proposed merge between Centre, Limousin and Poitou-Charentes was replaced by a bigger merge between Aquitaine, Limousin and Poitou-Charentes, which later became Nouvelle-Aquitaine. This new region is close to the historical Aquitaine of the middle ages, and is as vast as a country such as Austria or Portugal. The region Centre remained as it was, as did Bretagne, Pays de la Loire, Ile-de-France, and Provence-Alpes-Côte-d'Azur. Corsica and overseas regions were left apart.

In order to be implemented during the next regional elections, the date has to be postponed from March to December 2015, as it is a Republican tradition to leave around a year between a change in the constituencies and the date of the elections.

The elections system has not been changed, nor has the number of elected regional council members. However a new guarantee of a least two elected members per department has been added to ensure that new big regions will not lose ties with their vast territory.

Eventually, the law relative to the "delimitation of the regions, regional and departmental elections and modifying the electoral agenda" (16 January 2015) merged 16 regions into 7, decreasing the total number from 27 to 18.

Some departments have experienced some changes, but most remain unchanged in their boundaries.

The departments that existed from the end of the 18th century remained basically unchanged during the 19th century – with the exception of the Ile-de-France Region, their boundaries were thought to make it possible to go from any part of the department to its centre (the "Prefecture") and back by horse within a day – however, they do not correspond to the actual mobility of people today.

For this reason, even though departments were given new powers during the first two waves of reform, many think tanks and even official reports, for instance the "Freeing French Growth" report released by the Jacques Attali commission in 2008, call for their suppression or merger with the regions, or even with the intercommunality.

In April 2015, the Prime Minister and the President, said they were in favour of such a reform in the long term. However, it would take a change in the Constitution as departments are mentioned in the Article 72, and then a majority of 3/5 in the national Congress, or a politically risky referendum. After a consultation of each political party, the executive gave up on this reform and decided only to transfer some competencies from the departments to the regions, to merge intercommunalities that will be able later to replace the departments in their role of helping the communes, especially the rural ones, and to experiment with only some changes in department boundaries.

These experiments are mainly:

- The creation of the Metropole of Lyon: since 2015, the department has been merged with the intercommunal structure, meaning that for the first time, representatives of a "supra-communal structure" are directly elected. The social competencies of the former departments are now closely linked with competencies on economic development or housing from local powers. Some observers call for similar changes, whether in every Metropole (15 now, may be 19 later), or at least in some (Grand Paris and Aix-Marseille-Provence being the most logical, even if not the easiest).
- The "Corsica model": the island of Corsica is a territorial government (collectivité territoriale), but is considered a region in mainstream usage. By 2018, there would be a merge between the "region" and the two departments. This would be a unique collectivity with many powers that may increase the already growing feeling of regionalism, but also reduce territorial fragmentation in an island composed of 300 000 inhabitants.

However, attempts to develop this model by suppressing one layer – the department – will fail unless the municipal sector organises itself with the development of intercommunalities.

The intercommunalities

In the 2000s, financial incentives were implemented to accelerate the move towards the creation of intercommunalities (*Établissement Public de Coopération Intercommunal* or "EPCI"). Nonetheless, very rich and very poor regions remained sometimes without a full cover, as rich communes usually do not want to get closer to poor areas. A law passed on 16 December 2010 made it mandatory for every commune to join an EPCI by 2014. This was almost complete, but with very different sizes of EPCI from one department to another, and with some small EPCIs barely able to sustain themselves.

Due to a new map of intercommunality, their number fell dramatically on 1 January of 2016, decreasing from more than 2 000 down to below 1 300. The new EPCI will mostly correspond better than before to the new inhabitants' way of life, such as transportation. However, it will be a difficult task to lead these new EPCI to merging different identities and local legitimacies.

At the same time, a more integrated form of intercommunality has been created for France's major cities with Metropole status. The Metropole can have increased responsibilities and tasks taken from the department and the regions. After Nice, created in 2012, the law of 27 January 2014 created Metropoles in Paris, Aix-Marseille-Provence, Lyon (the three with different special status, Lyon being the most integrated), Lille, Strasbourg, Grenoble, Toulouse, Montpellier, Bordeaux, Nantes, Rennes, Brest, and Rouen in 2015. Nancy urban community was also transformed by decree into a Metropole in 2016, and a new law is prepared to allow Orleans and Dijon (the only capitals of mainland regions without the status of Metropole), but also Saint-Etienne and Toulon (which are bigger cities than the previous ones) to be transformed into Metropoles.

The communes

As of 1 January 2015 there were 36 681 communes in France, 36 552 in metropolitan France and 129 overseas. This is a considerably higher total than that of any other European country, and around 40% of all commune-level administration in the European

Union. In January 2016, due to voluntary merges with financial incentives from the state, this number fell to 35 885, and this tendency should continue over the next few years. In some parts of some regions, especially in Normandy, Pays de la Loire and Bretagne, all communes of one intercommunality decided to merge into one new commune. This may be a good way to completely mutualise services, but mayors have to overcome people's fear of ancient communes disappearing.

The new communes were created on 1 January 2016, and mergers were numerous in western-northern and eastern parts of France, but very rare in the centre and the south.

A change of the competencies and the balance of powers between local administrations

The law of 7 August 2015, "New Territorial Organisation of the Republic", gave specificities to the regions and the departments as they lost their general competence clause.

The regions are now principally in charge of:

- Regional economic planning and policy, industrial development.
- Professional education and high schools (but not the management of the teachers and the school programmes), professional education for the unemployed.
- Transportation outside of cities (intercity busses, regional trains, school buses for high schools), sometimes they are responsible for some local ports and airports.
- Environmental protection with special plans organisation.

The departments are now in charge of:

- Intercity roads (routes départementales).
- Some social policies and welfare allowances.
- Secondary (or middle/junior high) school (except teaching and school programmes),

In the governmental version of the law, when it was adopted by the Cabinet and before the hundreds of amendments in Parliament, intercity roads and secondary schools were supposed to be transferred from departments to regions. However, only transportation has been transferred, and the departments have ceased to share competency on economic development.

The regions and departments still have shared responsibilities regarding public policies considered to be very sensitive: culture, sport, and tourism.

In France, the problem of co-operation between the four administration layers has been addressed for a long time through a complicated scheme of contracts, the main being the *Contrat de Plan État-Régions*, which included other local authorities, despite the name. However, it has recently appeared that these contracts were not sufficient for limiting the rising competition between territories, which has been emphasised by globalisation.

Thus, new tools have been invented, such as prescriptive regulatory plans in economic and territorial development invented by the New Organisation of Territorial Republic law in August 2015. In this case, the region is given authority to make local plans – after a large consultation – that are compatible with its own plans and vision. Although some integrative planning has been implemented since the 1990s in Île de France, the region where Paris is located with 10 million inhabitants, in Corsica and overseas, this kind of integrative planning at a regional level is relatively new in other French regions. Regions have been given the power to organise local economic and urban development with recent laws, especially the New Organisation of Territorial Republic law, which merged seven different types of schemes dealing with environmental, transportation and development problems.

This kind of planning may be very useful for regulating the housing market and making sure that buildings are concentrated where networks (roads, public transportation, high quality electricity, services, high speed internet) already exist or can be extended at a reasonable cost (financial, environmental and social costs). Such regional view reveals is crucial at a time where the consumption of good land – the best for agriculture is located close to the cities – is accelerating because of urban sprawl.

These new rules will not be easy to accept for local powers. But there is a need to clearly define responsive a clear leadership of the region in order to avoid excessive localism or egoism.

Another tool for local co-operation are the regional conferences of public action (CTAP in France), with representatives of each layer to co-ordinate the implementation of competencies, with or without the help of the Prefect. These were created by the law of 27 January 2014, and inspired by the successful experiment of such assemblies (although with fewer entities involved) in Bretagne (the ancient "B16" was the reunion of the biggest 16 local administrations of this region).

Intercommunality gets new competencies

Several responsibilities can be delegated by the communes to the intercommunality, such as waste collection or transportation, but the law also makes it mandatory for the intercommunality to manage other areas, such as economic planning and development, housing projects, or environment protection. Their competencies will be multiplied by 5 in a 5 year period (2015-2020), going from 2 mandatory competencies before 2014 to more than 10 in 2020, including water supply, wasted water, tourism, and travelling communities.

Communities of Communes have the fewest compulsory areas of competence, leaving the communes more autonomous, while urban communities and metropoles are required to manage most matters (for instance: all public spaces, most of the equipment, energy networks), leaving the communes with less autonomy.

International perspective and conclusion

The French experience of decentralisation is distinct in various aspects from other models of decentralisation. French decentralisation appeared quite recently, in a country with a very long history of State centralisation. The French state appeared before the French nation, which is in contrast to, for instance, the decentralisation history of Germany or Italy. Unlike Spain and the United Kingdom, French decentralisation is almost free of pressure from populations with a strong cultural identity fighting for more autonomy, although there is an increasing movement in Corsica. Other areas with a strong cultural identity, such as Britany, the Basque country or Alsace, are not expressing a wish for more autonomy or even independence. Unlike the case of most Eastern European countries, such as decentralisation in Poland, French decentralisation came independently following pressure from the European Union. French decentralisation came from the will of the central power to delegate more responsibility in logic of democratic improvement and of better wealth sharing between each part of the country. The French experience of decentralisation is not free from criticism. The multi-layer structure is often considered too expensive and not efficient enough to answer economic, environmental and social challenges. However, this has led to a trend towards the fusion of structures, which should improve the situation. The slow decrease of state-funded grants and allowances is putting a lot of pressure on decentralised authorities to improve internal processes.

As with many European countries, there has been a decrease of public participation in local elections in recent decades, and a tendency to vote for political parties labelled as far right and populist. This can be explained by the fact that the increasingly mobile populations of European countries feel less concerned by local (except at the Commune level) than national and global issues. The evolution of a society in motion is shaping Europeans countries, and France in particular, and the challenges of the coming times for the French experience of decentralisation will be to reinforce public participation in elections and the decision-making process.

The French experience of decentralisation may be interesting for developing or emerging countries due to the following aspects:

- The slow evolution of French decentralisation makes it easier to imitate.
- The role of the Prefect kept a possibility for central oversight of local political evolutions.
- The regional court of accounts and the various budgetary limits and regulations provide limitations to financial risks for the entire country.
- By preserving the power and the control of the central state, on the opposite of the more developed systems of federations, the French model of decentralisation can ensure stability and a more sustainable and safer path for democratisation at the local level.

Notes

1. The report has been written by: **Jean-Louis Rocheron**, territorial administrator and Deputy Finance director in the Region Nouvelle-Aquitaine in Poitiers, France. He is lecturer in public finances at the University of Poitiers. With the precious help of **Jonathan Morice**, territorial administrator and Deputy Director of development and planning in the Region Bretagne, in Rennes, France. He was technical advisor in the cabinet for the Minister of Decentralisation in Paris from 2013 to 2016.
2. *Contrats de plan*, drawn up at Regional level, lay down the major economic and social priorities for the Region and set out the relevant action programmes, which the plan's signatories (State, Regional authorities) are committed to finance.
3. This section was drafted By J. Morice.

Annex B.

The Spanish decentralisation model[1]

Background: The territorial organisation of the State in Spain

In just thirty years, Spain has evolved from a state with a highly centralised territorial model to a multi-layered state that consists of the national government, the autonomous communities and local government. This state structure founded upon autonomous communities was established in 1978. Certain elements may be in need of adaptation to reflect the historical, political and economic evolution that Spain has undergone since then (including alterations in matters such as the definition of autonomous communities' powers and changes in how they are financed, and the institutional design of local government). However, some instruments within this state system have proven themselves effective in the process of decentralisation.

Article 137 of Spain's Constitution defines the territorial distribution of public power in the country, and provides for the establishment of a state with three levels of government:

- National government.
- Autonomous communities: 17 autonomous communities and 2 cities, Ceuta and Melilla, with autonomy statues.
- Local government: including municipalities, provinces and islands.

The analysis below focuses on the local government level, although there will be numerous references to the system of autonomous communities. First, it reviews the historical evolution of the decentralisation process in Spain. Second, it takes a close look at the defining tenets and phenomena that shape the institutional profiles of local government: the principles of local and democratic autonomy, the fragmentation of the types of local government that exist in Spain and the practices of infra-municipalism and inter-municipality. Third, it discusses the regulation of local governments from a three-fold perspective, examining the national level, autonomous community level and local legislation. Fourth, it offers an account of the local electoral system, including the electoral rules governing city councils and provincial councils. Fifth, it analyses the institutional system of municipalities and provinces; and sixth, it looks at the model for the exercise of local power and government financing, which has undergone significant legal reforms as a result of the economic crisis that began in 2007-2008. For example, the national government enacted laws such as 27/2013, passed on 27 December 2013, which called for the rationalisation and enhanced sustainability of local governments, and the Organic Law 2/2012 on Budgetary Stability and Financial Sustainability. Both of these measures were met with widespread rejection by Spanish municipal governments, autonomous communities and a range of organised social groups, who have filed as many as 10 lawsuits branding the laws unconstitutional. To date, this has led the courts to declare a significant portion of the local government reform measures carried out in 2013[2] as unconstitutional.

A review of the historical evolution of decentralisation in Spain

Although Spain is one of the oldest states in Europe, tension between the centre and the periphery has been constant throughout its history. The rule of the Catholic Monarchs saw the conquest of Granada in 1492 and of Navarra in 1512, which represented the beginning of the Spanish state. The marriage of two rulers, Isabella of Castile and Ferdinand of Aragon, resulted in the union of kingdoms that brought together the territories that now make up Spain.

This personal union meant that the institutional and legal peculiarities of each of the kingdoms immediately vanished. They remained formally intact throughout the rule of the Hapsburg dynasty and disappeared only with the ascendency of the House of Bourbon to the Spanish throne under Phillip V. He issued the *Nueva Planta* Decrees of 1707 and 1714, which abolished the self-government rights of the territories of Catalonia, Aragon, Majorca and Valencia, all of which had been loyal to the other pretender to the throne, the Archduke Charles of Austria.

However, the Basque Country and Navarra were allowed to maintain their rights to self-government in gratitude for their loyalty to the French monarch. Spain took shape as a legally and institutionally integrated state with the issuing of the *Nueva Planta* Decrees and the import of the French organisational model by the House of Bourbon, which marked the centralisation of power.

The 19th and 20th centuries saw new outbreaks of tension between the centre and the periphery, as the balance of power swung back and forth. The constitutional texts from this period traced a general trend towards a greater concentration of power in central government, with the fleeting exception of the draft constitution for the First Republic, written in 1873. Later, the 1931 Constitution of the Second Republic enshrined an integrated state model that allowed regions and municipalities some autonomy. Under the auspices of this Constitution, Autonomy Statutes were passed in 1931 for Catalonia, and in 1936, after the start of the Spanish Civil War, for the Basque Country. The Autonomy Statute for Galicia was approved in a referendum in 1936, but it was never passed by Parliament. The end of the Civil War prompted the annulment of the Catalan and Basque Autonomy Statutes, as well as the special self-government arrangements of Guipúzcoa and Vizcaya. Only Alava and Navarra were able to retain these privileges, thanks to their loyalty to the victorious side in the Civil War.

The Political Reform Law, passed on 4 January 1977, brought about the unusual transition away from the Franco regime. Spanish voters gave this law their approval in a referendum, paving the way for the general election that was held on 15 June 1977 and the subsequent passage of the Constitution on 27 December 1978.

It was taken for granted that the new Constitution of 1978 would set up a system of autonomous regions, and this idea was among the few principles, along with the notions of a democratic state and the monarchy, that were resolved at the time with little debate.

Catalans and Basques pushed for a larger degree of regional autonomy, and from the very beginning incorporated calls for more regional power into their political platforms. The reasons for this can be found in the distinctive characteristics of these regions, where there were deeply rooted political traditions of autonomy.

Unlike in the past, however, at the time of drafting the new Constitution, all of the country's political parties endorsed the principle. Other regions at the time also experienced pro-autonomy movements. However, the predominance of these proposals was driven namely by a wish to do away with the centralist nature of the old regime, whose political identity had been marked by the political and administrative dominance of the central government. Added to this was a desire to connect political decentralisation with democracy. A concern that would remain at the forefront of the process of planning for political autonomy, was opposition to offering greater autonomy to Catalonia and the Basque Country than to other regions, which was seen as potentially discriminatory.

It is clear that there was an overall consensus on the introduction of a system of regional autonomy, however the basic framework of such a system was not explicitly provided for. Instead, this consensus was built upon more general principles, which made it easy to maintain the agreement while leaving questions of content to be resolved later on by the individual autonomy statutes and the practice of constitutional law.

Local governments in Spain

General characteristics

Local autonomy

Article 137 of the Spanish Constitution grants municipalities, provinces and islands the right to manage their respective interests. This proclamation is viewed as an "institutional guarantee" of local autonomy. Along these lines, the Spanish Constitutional Court, in one of its first decisions, established that this clause means that for certain institutions, such as municipalities and provinces, "the setup of the institutions is the responsibility of the ordinary legislator, constrained only by the indispensable core principle of the essence of the institution guaranteed by the Constitution". However, "the institutional guarantee does not provide for any specific content or any permanently determined sphere of power, but rather for the preservation of an institution in a form that is recognisable in terms of the image of such an institution, as defined by society at any given time and in any given place".

Local autonomy can thus be shaped and designed by the ordinary legislator, with the proviso that the "essential content" or the "core" idea of local government is always respected. Applying this perspective, "essential content" represents a baseline that all laws much respect in order to ensure the "recognisability" of local institutions.

This view of local autonomy as an institutional guarantee is reflected in Law 7/1985, passed on 2 April 1955, which establishes the framework for local government. However, the principle has been the subject of widespread criticism due to its negative perspective on the definition of local autonomy, a state of affairs that has caused "local autonomy" to be defined at various times as either a constitutional guarantee, an optimisation command, or a constitutional principle.

The democratic principle

The democratic principle is explicitly recognised and enshrined in Article 1.1 of the Spanish Constitution, which states that "Spain is hereby established as a democratic state". The contents of the principle are dual in nature, connecting with both the notion of procedural democracy and that of material democracy, although the two concepts are difficult to separate. With procedural democracy, the Constitution itself acts to guarantee democracy via mechanisms including the rules that regulate the election of officials to representative democratic institutions, such as Parliament, autonomous community legislative assemblies, city councils and provincial councils. Meanwhile, in material democracy, the Constitution also guarantees democracy through its explicit recognition of material rules, such as those that provide for fundamental rights.

According to the concept of municipalities and provinces, which the 1978 Constitution defines as basic and necessary organs of local government, the democratic principle, understood in both material and procedural terms, is imbued with the function of transforming local organisation into something different from what it had been before. A joint, systematic reading of Articles 1.1, 23, 137, 140 and 141 of the Constitution would seem to lend itself to this interpretation, given that democracy is herein defined as a form of organisation in which the will of the people is the source of legitimacy for political power and those who reach and exercise this power. From such a premise, it can be argued that from the beginning the democratic principle transformed the nature of local autonomy. The preamble of the Local Government Framework Law is more explicit, saying that local government should be understood in light of this principle, and from the perspective of the core Constitutional principles that shape the state as a whole.

From these premises, it is possible to arrive at the following systematic list of the characteristics of local governments:

- Local governments, and especially municipal governments, are set up to be a model of representative democracy, under which council members have direct democratic legitimacy, according to Article 23 of the Spanish Constitution.
- The democratic constituencies of local representatives have a direct influence on the legislation passed by these officials, especially when it comes to municipal ordinances and regulations.
- As citizen participation is the direct source of local officials' democratic legitimacy, it is thought to provide additional legitimacy to decisions taken by plenary sessions of local councils, although participation is not an autonomous mechanism for the legitimacy of these decisions.

Types of local governments

Municipalities

Municipalities are the basic entities of the territorial organisation of the state and the most direct channels for citizen participation in public affairs. They serve as an institutional outlet for the autonomous management of the interests of their communities. Their existence is explicitly enshrined in Articles 137 and 140 of the Spanish Constitution, which define the essential characteristics of municipal governments.

There are currently 8 124 municipalities in Spain, of which about 85% have fewer than 5 000 inhabitants and 11% have between 5 000 and 20 000 inhabitants, the remaining 4% have a population of over 20 000.

Municipalities are not evenly distributed throughout the various autonomous communities, owing to the distinctive style of settlement that has been present throughout Spanish history. The country's central plateau has the greatest number, but the least populous municipalities. For example, the autonomous community of Castile and León boasts 2 248 municipalities, 2 000 of which are less than 1 000 people.

Provinces

Article 141 of the Constitution defines provinces as local entities made up of groups of municipalities and serving as territorial divisions for the purposes of carrying out the activities of the state. Provinces are autonomously governed and administered by the provincial councils, which must be democratically representative.

Spain currently has 50 provinces, groups of which make up the country's autonomous communities. Castile and León has nine provinces, more than any other autonomous community; Andalusia is next with eight. In the autonomous communities made up of a single province, namely Asturias, Cantabria, Navarra, La Rioja, Madrid and the Region of Murcia, there is no governing body in the form of a provincial council, and these functions are taken on by the corresponding autonomous community governments, as will be discussed further below.

There is a specific regime for the islands: for the Balearic Islands, the Consells insulars of Majorca, Menorca, Ibiza and Formentera take responsibility for the administration of the island whereas in the Canary Island the Cabildo Insulares of El Hierro, La Palma, La Gomera, Tenerife, Gran Canaria, Fuerteventura and Lanzarote are responsible of each territory.

Other local governments

a) *Comarcas* (counties)

Along with provinces (Article 141.1) and islands (Article 141.4), the Constitution also allows for other possible types of government entity spanning multiple municipalities. Article 141.3 establishes the possibility of creating groupings of municipalities other than provinces. Article 152.3 states that "by grouping bordering municipalities together, the [Autonomy] Statues may establish their own territorial divisions, which will enjoy full legal status". Founded upon this explicit Constitutional provision allowing for the creation of *comarcas*, the Autonomy Statues of all the autonomous communities, except the Canary Islands, the Balearic Islands, the Basque Country and Navarra, make mention of these entities.

The Local Government Framework Law (referred to by its Spanish initials, LBRL) was drafted in light of these Constitutional provisions and the Autonomy Statues, and devotes two of its sections to the discussion of *comarcas*: Article 42 and Additional Provision 4.

Under Article 42, *comarcas* can be created under two conditions. First, there must be a minimum degree of consent from the municipalities involved. A *comarca* cannot be created over the objections of at least two fifths of the municipalities that are to make it up, provided that these municipalities account for at least half of the area's population. Second, the assumption of responsibilities by the *comarca* must not bring with it any loss in the abilities of the municipalities involved to provide the minimum services required of them by Article 26 of the law, nor must it strip said municipalities of their roles in the areas set out in Article 25.2. The makeup and operation of the governing bodies of the *comarcas* are also required to be representative of the city councils involved.

Elsewhere in the law, Additional Provision 4 grants the Catalan parliament permission to divide the whole of the territory of Catalonia into *comarcas*, without regard to the consent of individual municipalities. The reasons underlying this exception to the specific provisions outlined in Article 42.2 are specified in the text of the Additional

Provision itself: first, the fact that Catalonia "had in the past organised its territory as a whole into *comarcas*," and second, because the autonomous community's statute "called for the division of the territory as a whole into *comarcas*".

Despite the legal provisions discussed above, only three autonomous communities have made use of *comarcas* in the organisation of their territories. In order of increasing importance they are: in the autonomous community of Castile and León, Law 1/1991, passed on 14 March, created the *Comarca* of El Bierzo.[3] In Aragon, Law 10/1993 on the creation of *comarcas* in the region, passed on 4 November, a process of dividing the autonomous community's territory into *comarcas* was begun, culminating in the passage of 32 laws providing for the creation of the 33 *comarcas* that were originally envisioned in the passage by the Aragon government of Legislative Decree 1/2006 on 27 December, replacing the previous law from 1993.[4] Finally, in Catalonia, Law 6/1987 on the *comarcas* of Catalonia passed on 4 April, and was followed on 16 December 1987 by Law 22/1987. These set up and organised the division of Catalonia into *comarcas* and provided for the election of *comarca* councils. These laws were implicitly replaced by Legislative Decree 4/2003, passed on 4 November, which represented the approval of a new text of the Catalan *Comarca* Organisation Law.[5]

b) Metropolitan Areas

The LBRL defines metropolitan areas as "local entities made up of the municipalities located in large urban areas with various population centres that are economically and socially linked in such a way as to render necessary joint planning and co-ordination of certain services and activities".

The existence of an inter-connected metropolitan area does not necessarily lead to the founding of a metropolitan governing body to provide services or manage general interests. However, it is becoming increasingly common for such areas to make use of other legal formulas that do not bind cities together in the same way as an official metropolitan area. They may take forms such as *mancomunidades* (inter-municipalities), consortia and inter-city agreements, all solutions that apply associations or voluntary agreements in order to meet metropolitan-level service provision needs in urban areas.

This type of local entity is governed by regular autonomous community legislation, under the provisions of Article 43 of the LBRL, which says that these corresponding laws are to determine the form of the individual government and administrative bodies, provided that within these institutions "all the municipalities in the area are represented". The economic setup and the sphere of action of these institutions must also guarantee "the participation of all the municipalities in the decision-making process", as well as a "fair distribution of the financial burden". This legislation must list the services the institution will offer and the other work it will carry out, as well as the procedures through which this will be done.

Due to the political disagreements that tend to predominate, the history of metropolitan area institutions in Spanish cities has not been particularly positive, which has given rise to mutual suspicion between member municipalities and between the cities and their autonomous communities. There are some historical precedents in local Spanish law for this kind of entity, namely the prior existence of bodies such as Greater Valencia, the Metropolitan Corporation Greater Bilbao, COPLACO in Madrid and the Barcelona Metropolitan Corporation. Currently, the country has only four entities of this sort. In Catalonia, Law 31/2010, passed on 3 August, created the Barcelona Metropolitan Area[6], while Law 2/2001, passed on 11 May, provided for the founding of the Metropolitan Waste Treatment Agency and the Metropolitan Hydraulic Service Agency in Valencia.[7]

c) *Mancomunidades* (commonwealths)

Although the Spanish Constitution does not explicitly recognise the existence of commonwealths, it does contain several provisions that provide an implicit basis for their existence. Among these Constitutional passages are the following: the recognition of the right of association in Article 22, which also applies to legal public entities, and the language in Article 141.3 that allows for the creation of groupings of municipalities distinct from provinces. This freedom of association was significantly strengthened when Spain ratified the European Charter of Local Self-Government in February 1989. Article 10.1 of this agreement states that "Local authorities shall be entitled, in exercising their powers, to co-operate and, within the framework of the law, to form consortia with other local authorities in order to carry out tasks of common interest".

The 1985 Local Government Framework Law builds upon these precepts and recognises commonwealths of municipalities as local entities. Article 3.2 (d) states that municipalities may exercise their right to "associate with other municipalities in commonwealths in order to join together for the purposes of carrying out tasks and services for which they are responsible". Elsewhere, Article 44 grants them status as legal entities and endows them with the capacity to carry out their specified tasks, all under the legal auspices of individual statutes that are subject to the approval of the city councils involved.

These commonwealths of municipalities are contingent local entities, and as such they feature a series of institutional and structural characteristics that have caused Spanish municipalities to frequently make use of them to offer services. There are now 983[8] such entities in the country. Some of the defining characteristics are listed here:

- Commonwealths are the result of voluntary associations that arise from the willingness of municipalities to take part.
- Unlike comarcas and metropolitan areas, these organisations are flexible in terms of their creation and elimination, which can be accomplished without autonomous community legislation.
- As these entities are created through association, they are by definition endowed with the power to organise themselves, in line with the very concept of local self-government guaranteed by the Constitution.
- These local entities are legally recognised bodies, independent of and distinct from the municipalities from which they are formed. This implies the existence of separate governmental structures, as well as of a budget distinct from those of the member municipalities.
- They are entrusted with a series of tasks, such as the provision of services and the carrying out of public works. However, they remain flexible to the extent that their founding objectives can be expanded or reduced through the modification of their statutes.

d) Sub-municipal territorial entities

Law 27/2013 on the rationalisation and sustainability of local administration contained a modification of the older provisions of Article 3 of the LBRL with the effect of eliminating sub-municipal territorial entities from the list of local authorities. The legal status of these bodies was therefore modified as they were no longer considered to have their own independent legal personalities, but instead were defined as separately managed branches of the larger municipal government. This legislative measure was ratified by the Constitutional Court in a decision criticised by municipal governments.

The practical consequences of this change are outlined in an explanatory note written by the Ministry of the Presidency and Territorial Administration for the purposes of explaining the content of the local government reform law. Under Law 27/2013 on the rationalisation and sustainability of local government, sub-municipal territorial entities can now be created only as decentralised agencies of the central municipal government, and do not have the status of independent legal entity.[9] The entities that already existed prior to 31 December 2013 retain their status as local entities with independent legal status, but must present their accounts to the state and the autonomous community or face the possibility of being dissolved. The country currently has 3 170 sub-municipal local entities with independent legal status distributed among the autonomous communities.[10]

Infra-municipalism

The map of Spanish municipalities shows a large degree of fragmentation, which indicates that Spain is a country of small towns, at least in terms of population. As already mentioned, the data show that:

- Of Spain's current 8 124 municipalities, 6 899, or 85%, have fewer than 5 000 inhabitants.
- Some 877 municipalities, or 10.81% of the country's towns, have populations of between 5 000 and 20 000.
- The remaining 339 municipalities are home to over 20 000 people, which are further broken down into the following population ranges:
  - 207 with between 20 000 and 50 000 inhabitants
  - 74 with between 50 001 and 100 000 inhabitants
  - 56 with over 100 001 inhabitants
  - 2 with over 1 million inhabitants.
- In short, 95.81% of Spanish municipalities have fewer than 20 000 inhabitants, and only 4.19% have more. In addition, 5 892 municipalities, or 72.62% of the total, have fewer than 2 000 inhabitants.

This leads to the conclusion that most Spanish municipalities are local entities with limited capacity to manage their own affairs as they fail to meet one of the criteria for the granting of power to local authorities established in Article 2 of Law 7/1985 on the Framework of Local Government, passed on 2 April.

Several contradictory suggestions have been made as to how to deal with this fragmented municipal map. Some are in favour of maintaining the current number of municipalities and argue for a broad interpretation of the democratic principle. Whereas others have proposed a drastic reduction of the number of local governments and appeal to the constitutional principle of effective administrative organisation.

The provisions of Articles 137, 140 and 149.18 of the Constitution grant the state the power to regulate its own structure. These passages formed the constitutional basis for

Article 13.3 of the LBRL, which outlined measures designed to promote the merging of municipalities. However, these measures have yet to be applied throughout the more than two decades that this legislation on local government has been in force. The same applies to the power granted to the autonomous communities under Article 148.1-2(a) of the Constitution. With the exception of the thorough analysis of the status of municipalities in Catalonia conducted in 2001 and published in the Roca Report (whose proposals were met with vehement rejection), the autonomous communities have failed to carry out a single effective measure to reform their territorial structure.

Inter-municipality

In light of the data on infra-municipalism (the existence of local governments in very small towns) and the tendency to maintain the number of municipalities, some have argued for a need to promote ways for municipalities to join together in associations in order to better carry out their responsibilities and serve their local communities. The aim here would be to make use of certain institutional instruments, including those that are flexible (such as consortia) and others that arise from municipalities' authority to form organisations (such as commonwealths) to help meet citizens' basic needs, regardless of the specific territory in which they reside.

Beyond these relationships between local governments, an inter-municipality can take on still other forms, such as a province, which is explicitly referenced in the Spanish Constitution. The constitutional structure of provinces guarantees the presence of an intermediate entity in all autonomous communities that have more than a single province. The relationship between municipalities and provinces does not follow a single, uniform pattern. The realities of public administration in Spain have given rise to the following range of models for these relationships:

- The standard model for autonomous communities with more than province.
- Autonomous communities with a single province in which the usual functions of provincial councils are carried out by the autonomous community governments.
- The Basque Country model, where the county councils have special charters and their own distinct legal status, founded on the first additional provision in the Spanish Constitution.
- The model in the autonomous community of Navarra, which operates in a similar fashion to that of the Basque Country.
- The models of the islands, with island councils that are distinct from provincial councils. This was first underlined in the case of the Balearic Island councils, with the passage in 2000 of the Island Council Act and later with the new Autonomy Statue for the Balearic Islands.

There are differences in terms of public administration between the various autonomous communities. They vary in the strength of their provinces and their governing bodies, provincial councils. For example, the Catalan *vegueries*, the region's traditional administrative jurisdictions, which date from the Middle Ages and whose borders were ratified by a Constitutional Court decision on 28 June 2010. Another example is the expansion of the system of *comarcas* to cover the whole of the territory of the autonomous community of Aragon.

This constitutional model of territorial division of power has brought about a dynamic in which the relationship between autonomous communities and provincial councils can sometimes be a challenge. For example:

- Some autonomous communities have legislation in place to transfer power and financing from their deputation to the autonomous community government.
- A broad interpretation has been made of the co-ordination of activities of the autonomous communities regarding provincial responsibilities.
- With few exceptions, the autonomous communities have made use of the legal instruments at their disposal to devolve powers to their provincial councils.

In addition to the sources of conflict highlighted above, the recent economic crisis has sparked numerous calls for the elimination of the provincial councils in order to cut government spending. It is clear that this debate is far from resolved, and it is impossible to predict its outcome. There is no doubt, however, that it can only be successfully managed with the right attitude of reserved reflection.

Regulations applied to local government

The Constitution

The Spanish Constitution devotes a small number of articles to local government. In addition to the above-mentioned Article 137, Article 140 establishes the following regulations for municipalities:

> *"The Constitution guarantees the autonomy of the municipalities, which shall enjoy full legal personality. Their government and administration shall be incumbent on their respective Town Councils, consisting of Mayors and Councillors. The Councillors shall be elected by the residents of the municipalities by universal, equal, free and secret suffrage, in the manner laid down by the law. The Mayors shall be elected by ten Councillors or by the residents. The law shall regulate the terms under which an open council system shall be applicable."*

Article 141.1 refers to the province, defined here as "a local entity, with its own legal personality, determined by the grouping of municipalities and by territorial division, in order to carry out the activities of the State." Perhaps in order to ensure the stability of the provincial borders, the Article goes on to say that: "any alteration of the provincial boundaries must be approved by the *Cortes Generales* by means of an organic law." Section 2 of this same Article provides that "the government and autonomous administration of the provinces shall be entrusted to Provincial Councils or other Corporations that are representative in character." Section 4 establishes that "in the archipelagos, the islands shall also have their own government in the form of Councils." Meanwhile, Section 3 of the Article allows for the creation of "groups of municipalities other than provinces", which, as explored below, makes possible the formation of super-municipal entities, such as *comarcas*.

Finally, Article 148.1 lists the following among the powers that can be assumed by autonomous communities: "changes in the municipal boundaries within their territory and, in general, the functions appertaining to the State Administration regarding local Corporations, whose transfer may be authorised by legislation on local government".

National legislation

Constitutional jurisprudence states that the tasks of the legislator in the Spanish parliament regarding local government are twofold. First, the legislature must specify "the essential content of local self-government, as explicitly guaranteed under Article 137 of the Spanish Constitution" (STC 148/1991). Second, the parliament is endowed with the power to expand or deepen this "Constitutionally required content" of local self-government by incorporating additional guarantees. The courts have observed that "beyond this minimum content, local self-government is a concept imbued with legal content and thus one that allows for multiple conceptions, all of them valid as long as they respect this institutional guarantee" (STC 46/1992, F.J.2°).

The dual nature of the legislature's duties regarding the laws affecting local government is further explored in Constitutional Court decisions 159/2001 and 240/2006. Here, the Court held that the law on local government:

> *"...may, a priori, contain on the one hand the defining characteristics of local self-government (giving form to the provisions in Article 137, 140 and 141 of the Spanish Constitution, while on the other hand providing legal regulations on the functioning, organisation and structure (among other issues) with regard to local entities. The only elements of local self-government that are explicitly guaranteed by the Constitution can be found in those provisions of the LBRL that are wholly founded upon the Constitution's Articles 137, 140 and 141, with the Law merely acting to make manifest these founding principles. Meanwhile, most of the provisions of the LBRL falls outside the purview of this institutionally guaranteed core, with these sections of the law finding their legal justification in Article 149.1.18(a) of the Constitution, making them distinct from a Constitutional and structural perspective."*

The LBRL operates under Article 149.1.18 of the Spanish Constitution to regulate the structure, functioning and powers of local governments. This law forms the basis for local authority throughout the country, along with the Merged Text on Local Self-government. The legislation that governs local elections, as well as issues regarding no confidence votes on the local level, is under the Organic Law on Electoral Regime (LOREG, Titles I, III, IV and V).

The predominant legislation in the economic and financial sphere is Royal Decree 2/2004, passed on 5 March, which ratified the merged text of the law that regulates local government treasuries. Also relevant in this area are an extensive series of other regulations that touch upon this issue, including: the law on budgetary stability, Law 18/2001, passed on 12 December of that year; Royal Decree 835/2003, issued on 27 June, which regulates the national government's contributions to the investments made by local authorities; Royal Legislative Decree 1/2004, of 5 March, which granted approval to the Merged Text of the Real Estate Registry Law; Order EHA/4040/2004, of 23 November, which approved the basic guidelines for local government accounting; and Order EHA/4042/2004, also of 23 November, which approved the guidelines for the simplified model of local government accounting.

Issues such as legal reform, contracting, management of public assets, and public employment are provided for within the framework of European Law, the Constitutional distribution of powers and the legal evolution and development of the autonomous communities. Among the specific Spanish laws that are based on this foundation are Law 30/1992, of 26 November, on the legal framework for public administration and common administrative procedure; Law 33/2003, of 3 November, on the management of assets on the part of the public administration; Law 30/2007, of 30 October, on public sector contracting; and Law 7/2007, the basic statute governing public employment, among others.

Autonomous community legislation

In the statutory realm, the most recent series of autonomy statues have been characterised by the large degree of attention they pay to the regulation of "local administrations", "local government", etc. To a greater or lesser extent, the autonomy statutes of the Valencian Community, Catalonia, Andalusia, the Balearic Islands and Castile and León all go into some detail when discussing their powers regarding local governments.

This choice of autonomous communities is the result of a series of factors, including the increasingly complex nature of local regulations, the lack of legal means to defend local self-government, and a deficit regarding the participation of local authorities in the decision-making processes of autonomous communities. In recent years, legal scholars have argued for what has come to be colloquially referred to as the "internalisation" of local authority. At its heart, this doctrinal debate is driven by disagreements as to the proper role to be played by the central government legislature in shaping local government and in defining the legal status of local entities, and especially municipalities, in Spain.

Along these lines, the Constitutional Court issued decision 31/2010, of 28 June, which addressed a challenge to the constitutionality of Catalonia's Autonomy Statute. In this decision, the Court placed an emphasis on the "twofold nature of local authority". In practical terms, the Court found that:

> *"...no objection can be made in principle to the inclusion within the Autonomy Statute of an autonomous community, with its role as a foundational institutional law, of fundamental outlines or essential regulations that bind the autonomous community legislature in terms of activities regarding local authorities within the territory of said autonomous community, provided that any such measures are in compliance with statutory provisions, including of course the basic powers reserved for the central government in this area stemming from Article 149.1.18 of the Spanish Constitution, to the extent to which the expression 'the foundations of the legal framework of the public administration' includes local authorities."*

The Court then adds that this leads to the conclusion that it is difficult to argue for the end of the twofold nature of local authority, given that it arises from "the concurrent activities of the central government and the autonomous communities" (Constitutional Court Decision 84/1982, 23 December, F.J.4), such that "in addition to the direct relationship between the central government and local authorities, there is also a relationship, one that is even more natural and closer, between local authorities and their corresponding autonomous communities" (Constitutional Court Decision 331/1993, 12 November, F.J.3). It is inevitable that this situation of concurrent activity is maintained to the extent that the powers exercised by autonomous communities over local authority must comply with the power reserved for the central government in this area under the Spanish Constitution. Thus, any regulation of local authority provided for by autonomy statutes cannot be understood to come at the expense of the relationships that the central government may legitimately establish with all local governments (F.J.36).

The individual autonomous communities exercise their powers in this area through their own laws on local government, which complement the national framework, the LBRL and help ensure that its provisions are carried out. Nearly all of the autonomous communities have their own laws on local government. The exceptions are Asturias and Cantabria, where legislation on local issues can be found in a number of sectoral laws that regulate a range of areas of administrative activities, such as the environment, urban planning, and housing.

Local regulations

The constitutional basis for the regulations that can be issued by local governments can be found in the guarantee of local self-government in Article 137, which is given full expression in Article 4 of the LBRL, the section touching on regulatory powers and self-organisation. There are three key manifestations of this power. First, organic regulations shape the functioning and structure of local governments. Second, local ordinances aim to regulate areas that fall under local authority, as well as local economic and financial matters. Finally, local regulations govern the management of public services for which local authorities are responsible.

It should also be noted that this issue of local regulatory authority has in the past few years taken on a central role in the debate on inter-governmental and intra-governmental relations. Many of the local government reform processes that have been undertaken are intended to confront this issue, as is apparent in the publication entitled White book on the Local Governments reform in Spain (*Libro Blanco para la reforma del Gobierno Local en España).*

The electoral system

Municipal elections

Local elections in Spain are held every four years, using a system in which each municipality is a single electoral district and the number of council members is determined by population, as follows:

City councillors	
Up to 100 residents	3
From 101 to 250 residents	5
From 251 to 1 000	7
From 1 001 to 2 000	9
From 2 001 to 5 000	11
From 5 001 to 10 000	13
From 10 001 to 20 000	17
From 20 001 to 50 000	21
From 50 001 to 100 000	25

In cities with more than 100 001 inhabitants, another council member is added for each additional 100 000 residents, or fraction thereof. One more council seat is included when this yields an even number. The right to active suffrage in municipal elections can be exercised by:

- Spanish adults provided that they are listed on the current electoral census. This rule is subject to three exceptions:
  - Those who have been convicted in a final judicial decision wherein the main or an additional sanction consists of the loss of voting rights during the period of the sentence.
  - Those who have been declared incompetent by a final judicial decision, provided that said decision explicitly states that the incompetence extends to the right to vote.
  - Patients committed to psychiatric hospitals by judicial decree, during the period of time in which they are committed, provided that the judge's ruling explicitly declares them incompetent to exercise the right to vote.
- Residents in Spain whose countries of origin allow their Spanish residents to vote in similar elections, under the terms of a treaty.
- All residents in Spain who are not Spanish citizens but who:
  - Are citizens of the European Union under the terms of Paragraph 2 of Section 1 of Article 8 of the European Union Treaty.
  - Meet all the requirements to become voters under Organic Law 5/1985, of 19 June, on Spain's general electoral framework, and express their desire to exercise the right of active suffrage in Spain.

The following individuals are endowed with the right to passive suffrage in Spanish municipal elections:

- Spanish adults who are of voting age and are not subject to any of the causes of ineligibility set out in Chapter II of Section I of Organic Law 5/1985, of 19 June, on the general electoral regime.
- All residents in Spain who are not Spanish citizens but who:
  - Are citizens of the European Union under the terms of Paragraph 2 of Section 1 of Article 8 of the European Union Treaty, or are citizens of countries that provide their Spanish residents with the right to passive suffrage in their municipal elections under the terms of a treaty.
  - Meet the eligibility requirements under law for Spanish voters.
  - Have not been stripped of the right to passive suffrage in their countries of origin.

Provincial elections

The number council members that correspond to each provincial council is determined by the population of the province, according to the following criteria:

Members	
Up to 500 000 residents	25
From 500 001 to 1 000 000	27
From 1 000 001 to 3 500 000	31
Over 3 500 001	51

When the city councils of the province have been sworn in, the Regional Electoral Board immediately moves to formulate a list of all the political parties, coalitions, federations and other groups that have obtained at least one seat in any jurisdiction. These groups are ranked in order of total votes received.

When this has been done, the Board then assigns seats to parties, coalitions, federations and other groups that have obtained representation by applying the procedure set out in Organic Law 5/1985, of June 19, on the general electoral regime. These seats are assigned according to the number of votes obtained by each political group or other grouping of electors.

The municipal and provincial electoral systems have remained largely unchanged since 1985. However, there have been some proposals to move towards direct mayoral elections by instituting a system with two rounds, similar to the one used in France. There have also been suggestions that the indirect election of provincial council members could be replaced by direct election by citizens. However, these proposals only have minority support, and are yet to be taken up in serious legal reform efforts.

The institutional structure of municipalities and provinces

The organisation of municipalities

In the wake of the reform of the LBRL brought about by the Local Government Modernisation Law 57/2003, of 16 December, there are three possible types of local government: 1) cities subject to the legal regime for municipalities considered to be of large population; 2) municipalities subject to the standard legal regime; and 3) those that are subject to the open council legal regime.

Municipalities with large populations

The "Legal Regime for Municipalities with Large Populations" (Article 121.1 of the LBRL) includes the following categories or types of municipalities:

- Directly, under the provisions of the LBRL itself: municipalities with over 250 000 inhabitants, as well as those provincial capitals that have over 175 000 inhabitants.
- Via an act of the corresponding legislative assembly, at the request of the city council in question: applicable to municipalities that are provincial capitals, autonomous community capitals or the home of autonomous community institutions, as well as those with a population of more than 75 000 inhabitants and that display special economic, social, historic, or cultural circumstances.

Table B.1 describes the list of Municipalities.

Table B.1. List of municipalities with large populations

Autonomous communities	Municipalities with populations over 250 000
Andalusia	Córdoba, Málaga, Seville
Aragon	Zaragoza
Asturias	Gijón
The Balearic Islands	Palma
The Canary Islands	Las Palmas de Gran Canaria
Castile and León	Valladolid
Catalonia	Hospitalet de Llobregat
Galicia	Vigo
Murcia	Murcia
The Basque Country	Bilbao
The Valencian Community	Alicante, Valencia
	Provincial capitals with populations of over 175 000
Andalusia	Almería, Granada
Asturias	Oviedo
Canary Islands	Santa Cruz de Tenerife
Cantabria	Santander
Castile and León	Burgos
Galicia	A Coruña
Navarra	Pamplona/Iruña
The Basque Country	Vitoria/Gasteiz, Donostia/San Sebastián
	Provincial capitals, autonomous community capitals or the homes of autonomous community institutions
Andalusia	*Cádiz, Huelva, Jaén,*
Aragon	*Huesca, Teruel*
Castilla la Mancha	Albacete, Ciudad Real, Cuenca, Guadalajara, Toledo
Castille and León	*Avila, León, Palencia, Salamanca, Segovia, Soria, Zamora*
Catalonia	*Girona, Lleida, Tarragona*
Extremadura	Mérida, *Badajoz, Cáceres,*
Galicia	Santiago de Compostela, Lugo, Orense, Pontevedra
Murcia	Cartagena
La Rioja	Logroño
Valencian Community	Castellón de la Plana
	Municipalities with populations of more than 75 000 inhabitants, and that display special economic, social, historic, or cultural circumstances

Table B.1. List of municipalities with large populations *(cont.)*

Autonomous communities	Municipalities with populations over 250 000
Andalusia	Jerez de la Frontera, Marbella, Vélez-Málaga, *El Ejido, Roquetas de Mar, Algeciras, Chiclana de la Frontera, El Puerto de Santa María, San Fernando, Mijas, Dos Hermanas*
Asturias	*Avilés*
The Canary Islands	Telde, San Cristóbal de la Laguna, *Arona*
Castilla La Mancha	Talavera de la Reina
Catalonia	*Badalona, Cornellá de Llobregat, Manresa, Mataró, Sabadell, Sant Boi de Llobregat, Sant Cugat del Vallés, Santa Coloma de Gramenet, Terrasa, Reus*
Galicia	Ferrol
Community of Madrid	Alcalá de Henares, Alcobendas, Alcorcón, Fuenlabrada, Getafe, Leganés, Móstoles, Parla, Pozuelo de Alarcón, Torrejón de Ardoz, *Coslada, Las Rozas de Madrid, San Sebastián de los Reyes*
Murcia	Lorca
The Basque Country	*Barakaldo, Getxo*
Valencian Community	Elche, Orihuela, Torrevieja, Gandía, Torrent

Note: The municipalities that appear in *italics* meet the requirements under Law 7/1985, of 2 April, The Local Government Framework Law, to be considered municipalities with large populations, but they have yet to be granted that status, either because they have not begun the corresponding process or because they have yet to complete it.

Source: INE (n.d.), National Institute of Statistics, www.ine.es.

Governmental bodies

Municipalities with large populations have the following governmental bodies: the city council, the mayor, deputy mayors and the local government board. Their powers are as follows:

The city council

The city council is made up of the mayor and the rest of the council members, and plays a role as the supreme political body representing citizens in local government. It is presided over by the mayor, who may delegate this responsibility to another council member when he or she deems it necessary. The city council may form committees, which are made up of council members selected by political groups in numbers that are proportional to each group's percentage of seats on the council. These committees carry out studies, issue reports and offer guidance on issues up for debate before the council. Provided that they are delegated with this authority by the council, they may also carry out tasks regarding the approval and modification of city ordinances and regulations (just as committees in the Spanish parliament are able to pass certain legislation). Committees may also be empowered to take action in the management of public services and in the creation of public companies, among other areas.

The mayor

The mayor is the supreme representative of the municipality and exercises a series of functions and powers of a strictly political nature. These duties include the political leadership of the municipal government and public administration, the establishment of guidelines for government activity, the taking of steps to ensure government continuity, the naming and termination of lieutenant mayors, and the publication and enforcement of municipal measures and agreements.

Deputy mayors

They are nominated and can be freely terminated by the mayor; they are chosen from among the ranks of council members. They may also stand in for the mayor in case of vacancy, absence or illness.

The local government board

This body is headed by the mayor and works with the mayor in tasks of political management. One controversial new element of the regulations applied to these bodies is the ability of the mayor to name individuals to the board who are not council members. Local government boards therefore seem to have taken on a character similar to central government cabinets, where ministers are often not members of parliament.

The Spanish legislature enacted this change to local government in order to remake these boards in the image of institutions that exist at higher levels of government (the autonomous community and central governments). The idea was for the board to report as a whole to the city council. For this purpose, the role of board secretary was created. This position must be occupied by a council member, whose tasks include drafting minutes for board meetings and the certification of agreements.

To even further underline the parliamentary nature of local government, the government board is endowed with a lengthy list of executive and administrative functions. Some examples of these tasks include the approval of proposed ordinances and regulations, the approval of budget proposals, the granting of licenses, the approval of job descriptions, and the payment of public employees.

Districts

Districts are established as decentralised public management bodies whose purpose is to improve the management of public affairs and to encourage and further develop processes of citizen participation in municipal issues. However, municipal governments remain single legal entities and are centrally managed. Council members serve as district presidents and are able to use a small percentage of the council's financial resources.

Administrative structure

Among the most noteworthy elements of the regime governing municipalities with large populations is a requirement that has been in place since the modification made to Title X of the Local Government Framework Law via Law 57/2003, of 16 December. Under this provision, municipalities subject to this regime must create a complex series of interlocking institutional bodies, including the following:

- A public legal counselling service.
- A city council for social affairs.
- A body tasked with defending the rights of local residents.
- A body responsible for economic, financial and budgetary issues.
- A body responsible for tax issues.
- A body responsible for internal auditing.

- A body responsible for addressing complaints of an economic or administrative nature.

Standard regime municipalities

Municipalities under the standard regime are subject to a series of regulations:

- The mayor, deputy mayor and city council must exist in all municipal governments.
- The local government board exists in municipalities with populations of over 5 000. This body may also exist in smaller towns as provided for by their respective organic regulations or agreed upon by their city councils.
- Other government bodies, which complement those mentioned above, are established and regulated by the municipalities themselves via their individual organic regulations. Also included here would be any body established under the corresponding autonomous community laws on local authority that may touch upon the creation of organisations in addition to those identified in the LBRL. Special attention was paid to this autonomous community power in the process of the reform of the autonomy statutes, as illustrated by Article 160.1(e) of the Catalan Autonomy Statute, and Article 60.1(e) of the Statute for Andalusia.

Government bodies and their powers

The city council

The mayor heads the city council, which is made up of all the council members, acts as a budgetary body, and exercises oversight of the mayor and his or her collaborators. The council acts in matters that require a quorum or a supermajority, and is also responsible for debating and voting on motions of no confidence in the mayor, should they be put forward.

The government board

This board is made up of the mayor and a number of council members. It is not to exceed one third of the total number of members. They are named and may be terminated by the mayor, upon notification of the council as a whole.

The board's duties consist of supporting the mayor in carrying out his or her responsibilities. Some of these responsibilities may be delegated to the board.

Deputy mayors

They replace the mayor when the mayor's office is left vacant or when the mayor is absent or ill, with the order in which they were named determining the order of succession. The mayor may freely name and replace deputy mayors, choosing from among the members of the board or from among the members of the council if no such board exists.

The mayor

The mayor is the central figure in Spain's current municipal government scheme. He or she acts as the president of the corresponding local government and is elected by the members of the council under the terms set out in the Organic Law on the General Electoral Regime. Current legislation allows for the termination of a mayor through a motion of no confidence, as long as an absolute majority of council members vote in favour of the motion. Because of the key nature of certain municipal government activities, a no confidence vote can also be proposed in connection with the passage or modification of the municipality's annual budget, organic regulations, fiscal ordinances or measures that bring an end to the local processing of zoning instruments.

The reforms were instituted under Law 11/1999, of 21 April; and Law 57/2003, of 16 December, and served to significantly strengthen the role of the mayor, making this figure the central element of municipal government activity. The office is endowed with a series of important powers, and is also assumed to have all other powers, whether of an administrative or a political nature, which are not explicitly assigned to other municipal bodies. With this in mind, and although it may seem like a paradox, it can be observed that in municipalities under the standard regime, the mayor takes on a greater role than in municipalities with large populations.

The open council regime

This regime is a specific instance of direct democracy in which all the residents of a municipality serve as members of a resident assembly (Article 140 CE).

The general norms that apply to this sort of arrangement can be found in Article 29 of the LBRL, which allows for this unusual governmental and administrative regime in municipalities that traditionally and voluntarily employ it, and where such an arrangement is desirable due to geographic location, the requirements of improved public management, or other circumstances. The tasks of local government and administration are the responsibility of the mayor and the resident assembly, which are allowed to operate in accordance with local practices, customs and traditions. Otherwise, they are subject to the provisions of the LBRL and the applicable autonomous community legislation on local government.

Provincial governmental structure

The provincial council is composed of the president and the provincial council members. The government board is headed by the president and a number of council members (not exceeding one third of the total). These members are freely named by the president, who may also replace them at will.

The provincial president is subject to the same rules as the mayors of municipalities under the standard regime, including executive functions, how the president is chosen and terminated, and the mechanisms for no confidence votes.

Vice presidents replace the president when the president's office is left vacant or when the president is absent or ill, with the order in which they were named determining the order of succession. These vice presidents are chosen at the discretion of the president from among the members of the government board.

There is a specific provision in the case of the islands. Each of the Canary Islands features one of the governmental and administrative bodies known as *Cabildos*. The archipelago also has Inter-island provincial commonwealths, which act as instruments for the representation and expression of the interests of the provinces, as established in Article 41 of the LBRL.

In the Balearic Islands there are Island Councils, which are subject to the same dictates under Article 41 of the LBRL as provincial councils in other autonomous communities.

Local government powers

The legal framework governing local government power was subjected to new regulations through the local regime reforms instituted under a measure for the rationalisation and sustainability of local authorities, Law 27/2013, of 27 December.

Below is a summary of the general framework of local government power:

- Section 1 of Article 25 of the LBRL contains a general clause that is phrased in similar terms to those of the original precept. This clause is somewhat more restrictive, however, in that it limits the possibilities for local authorities to carry out activities and offer public services that contribute to meeting residents' needs regarding the terms set out in Article 25 itself.
- Section 2 of Article 25 of the same law features a list of areas for which the Spanish legislature and the autonomous community legislatures are charged with identifying powers to be set aside for municipalities. This new list no longer features some issues that had previously been included, such as consumer defence. This means that municipalities can only act regarding these issues under the following circumstances:
  - When the central government or the corresponding autonomous community government delegates them such responsibility under the terms of Articles 7.3 and 27 of the LBRL.
  - When these activities do not put the overall financial sustainability of the municipal treasury as a whole at risk; when the activity does not amount to an instance of simultaneous execution of the same public service with another part of the public administration; and when the corresponding binding reports are gathered from the relevant administrative body in the area with financial control over the area of new activity, as set out in Article 7.4 of the LBRL.

Articles 148 and 149 of the Spanish Constitution set out the model of the distribution of powers. With these provisions in mind, it is evident that there is nothing to stop autonomous communities in their own sectoral legislation from identifying certain powers that can be set aside for municipalities among the legislative powers reserved for them in their respective autonomy statutes (Sections 1 and 2 of Article 7 of the LBRL).

- Sections 3, 4 and 5 of Article 25 of the LBRL provide municipalities with the following guarantees:
  - The principle of legal reservation, with the legislature having the sole authority to attribute power to municipalities.
  - A mandate for the sectoral, Spanish and autonomous legislatures that requires them, when it is time, to attribute responsibilities to municipalities and to assess the feasibility of providing services at a local level, while bearing in mind the principles of decentralisation, efficiency, stability and financial sustainability.
  - An additional mandate requiring sectoral legislators to include economic reports in any legislation that determines local responsibilities.
  - The requirement that said laws provide for the granting of sufficient resources to guarantee the financial solvency of the municipalities, as long as this does not imply increased expenditure on the part of the public administration.

  - The requirement placed upon sectoral laws to determine the precise municipal power to which they refer, thus guaranteeing that the same power is not also attributed to another part of the public administration, in order to avoid redundancies in powers.

- There are two new elements in the legal regime governing the delegation of powers, as set out in Article 27:
  - The new law includes a guarantee that powers must be delegated when doing so represents an improvement in the efficiency of public management, contributes to eliminating redundancies and is in compliance with legislation on budgetary stability and financial sustainability.
  - The law also links the delegation of powers with the requirement to provide the financing necessary to carry out the activity or service in question.
- Article 7.4 recognises that local bodies can exercise powers beyond those which normally pertain to them or that have been delegated to them, provided that a series of material and procedural requirements are met. The material requirements are as follows:
  - The financial sustainability of the overall municipal treasury, as defined by the provisions of legislation on budgetary stability and financial sustainability, is not to be put at risk.
  - The activity may not amount to an instance of simultaneous execution of the same public service with another part of the public administration.

The procedural requirements consist of the need to issue a series of binding reports prior to undertaking the activity. This is to be done as follows:

- A mandatory, binding report must be issued by the part of the public administration responsible for the area. This report must certify the absence of redundancies.
- A mandatory, binding financial sustainability report must be issued by the part of the administration with responsibility for the financial oversight of the area addressed by the new powers. This report must also be issued prior to the undertaking of any activity, as indicted above. In the case of the autonomous communities of Andalusia, Aragon, Asturias, Castile and León, Galicia, Navarra, the Basque Country, La Rioja and the Valencian Community, the drafting of this report is the responsibility of the autonomous government ministry responsible for the financial oversight of local bodies. For municipalities in the rest of the autonomous communities, the report is drafted by the Ministry of Finance and Public Administration of the Spanish government.

The relationship between municipalities and provinces

Inter-governmental relationships, or relationships between the various levels of government, are a characteristic part of the workings of composite states. These relationships are seen as the foundation of modern public governance and are based upon the principles of collaboration, co-operation and co-ordination.

By way of definition, the principle of co-operation can be said to be at work when various parts of the public administration jointly exercise their powers in spheres of common interest. In Spain, much more than in other European states, references are often made to the phenomenon of "co-operative federalism". This expression conveys the fact that the defining characteristic of the principle of co-operation is that it involves the "joint exercise of powers" by various parts of the administration to resolve a common problem.

In general terms, the defining characteristics of the principle of co-operation are twofold. First, it implies a will to co-operate, as it involves an accord reached between two or more parts of the administration of their own free will. This does not mean, however, that there are not sometimes instances of forced co-operation. Second, it implies the inalterable nature of the control and exercise of the powers of the parts of the public administration that have entered into the relationship.

Based upon this premise, and upon the phenomenon of infra-municipalism described above, in Spain there is an ever more central role to be played by the mechanisms of co-operation between the country's provincial governments and the smaller municipalities within their territories. Thus, the theoretical concept of "local self-government" as the "power of participation" of local bodies in decisions on issues that are relevant to their interests has had certain practical implications. Since the passage in 1985 of the law regulating the structures of local government, the influence of provincial councils has expanded in two distinct directions. First, there has been a new guarantee of a core area of minimum guaranteed powers reserved for provincial governments. Second, there has been recognition of the provincial government's right to act on issues that directly affect its interests.

By way of further definition, part of this "core area of minimum guaranteed powers" set aside for the provinces consists of the ability to lend support to the municipalities located in their territory. This practice takes the shape of economic co-operation in the carrying out of municipal activities and services. The provincial council contributes in these cases by helping to attain financing or employing its own financial resources.

When the Spanish legislature defined the framework of local government in 1985, the core responsibilities of the province were expressed only in terms of the functions of these governmental bodies. This has meant carrying out tasks where the aim is to support other entities and to co-operate and co-ordinate with them, with special attention paid to smaller municipalities. With this function-oriented design of the powers of provincial governments, legislators have strived to accomplish three different objectives:

1. Provincial councils are the governmental and administrative bodies of their respective councils. As such, they act as the ultimate guarantor that municipalities will provide legally mandated basic services. Provinces achieve this aim by acting to address any deficits in the provision of services to residents. They offer municipalities a range of different kinds of support to ensure that everyone in the province has access to these basic services.
2. Provincial councils also act to guarantee the principles of solidarity and fairness between municipalities. They accomplish this through the implementation of public policies designed to guide the processes of economic and social development in their provinces. These policies tend to be planning oriented and include operational plans, special plans, etc.
3. Provincial governments also engage in the provision of public services on the trans-municipal or trans-county level. They do so by creating and carrying out sectoral policies that address certain municipal issues, with a firm emphasis placed upon improving citizens' quality of life.

Bearing in mind this understanding of the objectives that underlie the granting of certain functional powers to provincial governments, the LBRL endows provincial and island governments with the authority to provide municipalities with legal, economic and technical assistance and co-operation. This applies especially to those with greater economic difficulties or with a lesser capacity for public management. The law also specifies that this co-operative function granted to provincial governments means that they must take steps to guarantee "town clerk and magistrate services to municipalities with less than 1 000 inhabitants".

The powers set aside for provincial governments are more clearly outlined by provisions within the local government law itself. The legislation gives provincial governments the task of guaranteeing that city councils are able to effectively carry out their responsibilities. To this end, provincial councils help municipalities with personnel recruitment and training, although the central and autonomous community governments may also provide support in these areas. Upon the request of municipalities, provinces may also assist municipal governments in handling administrative procedures and in conducting their material and management activities.

Provincial governments' co-operative functions are founded on the legal premises above, and their effects are felt in three different spheres of municipal activity: the legal, technical and economic domains.

- Provincial governments may offer the following kinds of legal co-operation measures:
  - Drafting of legal reports and memos in response to questions posed by municipalities with regard to their areas of responsibility.
  - Representation of municipalities in the province before the court in defence of their assets, rights or interests.
- The technical co-operation instruments that provincial governments have at their disposal are as follows:
  - The ability to carry out projects, studies, processes and inquiries touching on municipal responsibilities, all with the aim of helping to improve the functioning of municipal services.
  - Technical assistance in the drafting of language for legal documents, such as regulations and ordinances.
  - Technical assistance with the process of awarding public contracts.
  - Drafting of advice, legal opinions and technical reports with regard to public works, constructions and services that fall under municipal responsibility or are municipal property.
  - Drafting of technical plans for architectural projects, management and closure of public works and facilities, assessment of the technical, human and economic resources that are available, and conducting of feasibility studies.
  - Technical assistance with regard to classified activities.
  - Appraisals, assessments and the corresponding technical reports.
  - Consulting and technical assistance with regard to the municipal census, and sometimes the regular management of census data by the provincial

government when municipalities lack the necessary technical, economic or management capabilities.

- Participation of provincial officials in tribunals or assessment committees engaged in selection processes, and the direct supply of candidates for job vacancies when municipal governments cannot find qualified personnel to fill positions.
- Fielding of requests to nominate magistrates and clerks in disciplinary procedures involving municipal employees, with the exception of national civil servants.
- Online publication of up-to-date information on zoning and urban planning policies, announcements of the opening of these policies to public comment and any public documents that are relevant to the approval or alteration of these policies in municipalities with fewer than 5 000 inhabitants.
- Support in the submission of documentation relevant to areas of municipal responsibility to other public agencies.

- Provincial governments also carry out the following economic co-operation activities:
  - Assistance in tax collection services, in the voluntary and executive periods.
  - Assistance in financial management services to municipalities with fewer than 20 000 inhabitants.
  - Economic and financial consulting via response to requests for assistance, communication, informative visits, and the drafting of reports, opinions and, if necessary, the relevant proposals for resolution.
  - Supplying of information with regard to any questions on economic and financial management submitted by municipalities.
  - Training and consultation on accounting practices for members and employees of local governments.
  - Consultancy on the implementation or modification of local taxes or public fees.
  - Calculation of the financial burden to be incurred when requesting loans.
  - Issuing of economic and financial diagnoses.
  - Drafting of financial rationalisation plans.
  - Carrying out of audits.

When the co-operation functions explicitly recognised in tenets of positive law are put into practice, they can then be subdivided into a wide range of actions that provincial governments are empowered to take on behalf of municipalities.

Thus, from a structural and organisational perspective, there are no universally applicable, uniform rules that apply equally to all provincial governments in Spain. Instead, the principles of self-organisation and financial self-sufficiency are fully on display. It is possible to observe a range of different organisational models regarding the services provided by provinces to municipalities. Although they all comply with basic legislative norms in areas such as contracting and administrative procedure, they vary in terms of the sorts of activities and tasks that they carry out, as can be seen through the examples of the provincial governments of León,[11] Granada[12] and Valencia.[13] This characteristic of the Spanish system has given it a degree of flexibility that has allowed it to be successfully imported to other countries, such as Jordan, which has a multi-layered governmental system and where the municipal level is marked by the geographical dispersion of towns, the concentration of the population in urban areas and the lack of population density in rural areas, and a scarcity of material and bureaucratic resources, etc.

Local government financing

Under Article 142 of the Spanish Constitution, "local treasuries must have sufficient funds available in order to perform the tasks assigned by law to the respective Corporations, and shall mainly be financed by their own taxation as well as by their share of State taxes and those of Self-governing Communities". With regard to this precept, and in relation to Article 137 of the Spanish Constitution, the Constitutional Court[14] has found that this self-government is constitutionally protected both in terms of revenue and public spending. This was taken to mean that local governments must have the overall capacity to determine for themselves their priorities when it comes to public spending. Thus, the concept of local self-government includes full control over local revenue, which may not be subjected to any undue restrictions.

It is clear that the constitutional precept quoted above can lead to certain conclusions about the mechanisms of local government financing. Local authorities are able to raise revenue through their own fiscal initiatives, but they also receive a share of their funding from the central and autonomous community governments. Royal Decree 2/2004, of 5 March, represented the approval of the Merged Text of the Local Treasury Law. This piece of legislation deals with local taxation and central government financing of local entities, providing comprehensive regulations on the resources of local entities and on the system of sharing in central government revenue.

The sources of financing for local treasuries can be broken down as follows: revenue gained from assets and other private law sources, and locally collected fiscal revenue (consisting of fees, special contributions, surcharges applied to autonomous community taxes and other locally applied taxes [real estate taxes, economic activity taxes, road taxes, taxes on the appreciation of the value of urban real estate, and building, facilities and construction taxes]).

More specifically, local governments partly receive their share of central government revenue through the transfer of funds collected via central government taxes. The Spanish government distributes the money it has gathered from income taxes, value added taxes and special manufacturing taxes (on products such as beer, wine, fermented drinks, intermediate products and alcohol and alcoholic drinks). These funds are distributed according to the percentages and mathematical formulas set out in the Local Treasury Law. The Spanish government also divides among local authorities their shares of the Complementary Financing Fund.

In addition to the financing mechanisms mentioned above, the central government uses a variety of other instruments to contribute to local budgets. An example is the Spanish National Economic Co-operation Programme for investment in local entities. Operating under the legal authority of Royal Decree 835/2003, of 27 June, later modified by Royal Decree 1293/2005, of 21 October, this programme finances the following activities: provincial and island co-operation plans for co-operation on local public works and services (whose aim is to collaborate with the creation and improvement of municipal infrastructures, services and facilities); local administration modernisation projects (which are aimed at co-financing local public administration modernisation projects by encouraging the use of information technology in order to improve public management and citizen services and to simplify administrative procedures); and civil society participation projects (whose aim is to bolster the participation of civil society in the improvement of local services).

Other significant sources of investment in local government include the Royal Legislative Decree 9/2008, of 28 November, which created a Nationwide Local Investment Fund and a Special National Fund for the Revitalisation of Local Government and Employment. These funds were provided with a budget of EUR 8 billion, which was to be used to finance urgent activities at the municipal level, with a focus on investments to generate jobs. The Royal Legislative Decree 13/2009, of 26 October, created a Nationwide Employment and Local Sustainability Fund with a budget of EUR 5 billion to be used to finance local government investments in the generation of employment, as well as actions undertaken on a municipal level to contribute to economic, social and environmental sustainability. All of these measures were part of the Spanish government's efforts to combat the economic crisis.

Regarding municipal governments receiving a share of autonomous community tax revenues, despite references (some of which are unambiguous) to this issue in the autonomy statutes, there was no real world precedent for this practice until recently. Only Andalusia has acted in this regard, via the passage of Law 6/2010, of 11 June, which regulates the sharing of local governments in the autonomous community's revenues.

This brief account of the regulatory framework of local government financing in Spain has afforded a glance at the situation on the ground, which has deteriorated in the wake of the 2008 economic crisis. One of the long-standing demands that Spanish municipal governments have made has been for the reform of the model of financing for local authorities that was instituted under Law 39/1988, which regulates local treasuries and remained largely intact when updated in 2004. At the core of the grievances aired by local governments are the "unreserved powers" (*competencias impropias*) and the question of how they are financed. A report on this topic by the local government association, the Spanish Federation of Municipalities and Provinces (Federación Española de Municipios y Provincias -FEMP), estimated that over 30% of the powers exercised by municipalities fall into this category. This means that they are activities and services that should, in theory, be covered by other parts of the public administration, but that in reality are addressed on a local level, even though localities do not receive clear or sufficient financing to carry out these tasks.

The economic crisis has encouraged a new debate regarding the desirability of maintaining the current number of municipalities. The provincial government model has also been called into question, with critics questioning the role of provinces as governmental and administrative bodies, charging that they contribute to the economic deficit.

Notes

1. This report was drafted by Enrique Orduña Prada.
2. See Spanish Constitutional Court decision 111/2016, of 9 June 2016, available at www.boe.es/boe/dias/2016/07/15/pdfs/BOE-A-2016-6839.pdf.
3. www.boe.es/diario_boe/txt.php?id=BOE-A-1991-9704.
4. www.boe.es/diario_boe/txt.php?id=BOA-d-2006-90038.
5. www.boe.es/diario_boe/txt.php?id=DOGC-f-2003-90015.
6. www.boe.es/buscar/act.php?id=BOE-A-2010-14562.
7. www.boe.es/diario_boe/txt.php?id=BOE-A-2001-11816.
8. Local Governments 'Portal, Ministry of the Finance and Civil Service Government of Spain, http://ssweb.seap.minhap.es/REL/.
9. See the document entitled *Nota Explicativa de la reforma local. Ministerio de la Presidencia y para las Administraciones Territoriales, 24 de enero de 2017*, pp. 22-23, www.seat.mpr.gob.es/dms/es/portal/areas/politica_local/regimen_juridico/NOTA-EXPLICATIVA-MODIFICADA-29-04-2016/NOTA%20REFORMA%20LOCAL-27-10-2016.pdf.
10. The Registry of Local Entities. Ministry of the Presidency and Territorial Administration, http://ssweb.seap.minhap.es/REL/.
11. www.dipuleon.es/frontdipuleon/frontDipuleonAction.do?action=view Category&categoryName=Presentaci%F3n&id=13944.
12. www.dipgra.es/contenidos/organigrama-asistencia-municipios/.
13. www.dival.es/es/content/asesoramiento-y-asistencia-de-municipios.
14. STC 237/1992 SSTC 109/1998 y 48/2004. Available at the Constitutional Court website, www.tribunalconstitucional.es/es/jurisprudencia/Paginas/default.aspx.

ORGANISATION FOR ECONOMIC CO-OPERATION AND DEVELOPMENT

The OECD is a unique forum where governments work together to address the economic, social and environmental challenges of globalisation. The OECD is also at the forefront of efforts to understand and to help governments respond to new developments and concerns, such as corporate governance, the information economy and the challenges of an ageing population. The Organisation provides a setting where governments can compare policy experiences, seek answers to common problems, identify good practice and work to co-ordinate domestic and international policies.

The OECD member countries are: Australia, Austria, Belgium, Canada, Chile, the Czech Republic, Denmark, Estonia, Finland, France, Germany, Greece, Hungary, Iceland, Ireland, Israel, Italy, Japan, Korea, Latvia, Luxembourg, Mexico, the Netherlands, New Zealand, Norway, Poland, Portugal, the Slovak Republic, Slovenia, Spain, Sweden, Switzerland, Turkey, the United Kingdom and the United States. The European Union takes part in the work of the OECD.

OECD Publishing disseminates widely the results of the Organisation's statistics gathering and research on economic, social and environmental issues, as well as the conventions, guidelines and standards agreed by its members.

OECD PUBLISHING, 2, rue André-Pascal, 75775 PARIS CEDEX 16
(42 2017 26 1 P) ISBN 978-92-64-27545-4 – 2017

www.ingramcontent.com/pod-product-compliance
Lightning Source LLC
Chambersburg PA
CBHW061207240926
51846CB00006B/1142
* 9 7 8 9 2 6 4 2 7 5 4 5 4 *